Energy Management in Africa

J. Baguant
M. Teferra
L. Mohapeloa
P. M. Nyoike
B. A. Okech

Edited and Introduced by

M. R. Bhagavan and S. Karekezi

Zed Books Ltd
London and New Jersey

in association with
African Energy Policy Research Network – AFREPREN
Gaborone

Energy Management in Africa was first published by Zed Books Ltd, 57 Caledonian Road, London N1 9BU, UK and 165 First Avenue, Atlantic Highlands, New Jersey 07716, USA, in association with the African Energy Policy Research Network, NIR, University of Botswana, Private Bag 0022, Gaborone, Botswana in 1992.

Cover designed by Sophie Buchet.
Typeset by Opus 43, Cumbria, UK.
Printed and bound in the United Kingdom
by Biddles Ltd, Guildford and King's Lynn.

A catalogue record for this book is available from the British Library.
US CIP is available from the Library of Congress.

ISBN 1 85649 051 3

Published with the support of the Swedish Agency for Research Cooperation with Developing Countries (SAREC), Stockholm.

Contents

List of Tables

List of Figures

Acknowledgements

A large number of individuals and institutions, both official and private, have assisted the authors in many ways. They are too numerous to be mentioned here by name. The authors gratefully acknowledge this invaluable help and extend their sincere thanks.

The staff of the National Institute of Development Research and Documentation (NIR) of the University of Botswana deserve warm thanks for the administrative support given to the authors during the course of their research.

Generous financial and professional support by the Swedish Agency for Research Cooperation with Developing Countries (SAREC) is gratefully acknowledged. Thanks are also due to SAREC for financing the publication of this volume.

A Short Note on AFREPREN

The African Energy Policy Research Network or AFREPREN was created in 1989 in Gaborone, Botswana, under the auspices of the National Institute of Development Research and Documentation (NIR), University of Botswana. Funded by the Swedish Agency for Research Cooperation with Developing Countries (SAREC), the Network is aimed at promoting research relating to the formulation and implementation of appropriate policy in the field of energy in countries of East, Central and Southern Africa. It also seeks to strengthen research capability within the region. Currently, under its sponsorship, more than 25 African energy professionals from 16 countries are engaged in research on six themes – biomass; coal; electricity; oil; renewable energy technologies; and institutions and planning relevant to the generation, distribution and use of energy.

Notes on Contributors

Jawaharlall Baguant is a chemical engineer. He is Professor and Head of Department in the School of Engineering, University of Mauritius, Reduit, Mauritius.

M. R. Bhagavan is a physicist and an economist. He works in the Swedish Agency for Research Cooperation with Developing Countries (SAREC), Stockholm, Sweden, where he heads the Natural Sciences, Technology and Industrialization Section.

Ansu Datta is a sociologist and political scientist. He is the Director of the National Institute of Development Research and Documentation (NIR), University of Botswana, Gaborone, Botswana, and is the Principal Co-ordinator of AFREPREN.

Stephen Karekezi is a mechanical and industrial engineer, with post-graduate specialization in industrial management. He is the Executive Secretary of the International Foundation for Woodenergy and Development, Nairobi, Kenya. He is the AFREPREN Network Facilitator and also edits the AFREPREN Newsletter.

Mengistu Teferra is an electrical engineer, with postgraduate specialization in energy studies. He is the Senior Energy Expert and Energy Team Leader in the Office of the National Committee for Central Planning, Addis Ababa, Ethiopia.

Lietsiso Mohapeloa is an economist. He was the Deputy Principal Secretary in the Ministry of Water, Energy and Mining, Maseru, Lesotho. He is now a Managing Director in the parastatal Lesotho Telecommunication Corporation.

Patrick Mwaura Nyoike is a mathematician and economist, with post-graduate specialization in energy management and planning. He is a Chief Economist and a Director in the Ministry of Finance, Nairobi, Kenya.

Benjamin Aggrey Okech is a mining engineer and an economist. He is a Research Fellow and Lecturer at the Institute of Development Studies, University of Nairobi, Nairobi, Kenya.

Preface

M. R. Bhagavan and A. Datta

The need for the network

Over the last two decades, the countries of sub-Saharan Africa have been subjected to several extremely grave crises, caused by factors both internal and external, both man-made and natural. Among these are the crises in both the modern and traditional energy sectors. Since energy cuts across the whole of the economy, its crisis has caused severe disruptions in virtually every section of society. Prime indicators of the energy crisis are the drastic reduction in the import of crude and refined petroleum products; deterioration in equipment for generating and distributing electricity due to cuts in the imports of spare parts, new equipment, and repair and maintenance know-how; and soil erosion or desertification in the savannahs and dry forests.

By the very nature of their responsibilities and tasks, African policy-makers have had to resort to short-term crisis management measures. While they are aware in a general sense that research on a broad front in the technical, economic and social fields may make a significant contribution to the formulation and implementation of sound and practical policies, they may still need to be convinced that research is essential for solving problems in the longer term. On the other side of the coin, researchers inside and outside Africa may not have appreciated fully the indispensability of close contact with policy-makers for identifying research topics that would help to overcome the problems posed by the crisis.

It would therefore be valuable to bring together researchers and policy-makers in a network so as to deepen mutual awareness of problems, perspectives and priorities. Since energy is of immediate practical interest, the approach to the energy establishment has to be different from the conventionl one of 'academic research'. The themes and topics that would interest the energy establishment depend on whom one is talking to. Non-establishment figures – a description that would fit most researchers today – have very limited influence at present.

But research ideology has its limits: research cannot be expected to provide practical solutions to every problem that crops up. Further, policy-makers have to be made aware that it may not be possible to handle immediate problems requiring short-term solutions without simultaneous attention to long-term perspectives and solutions. It may well be that solutions to major problems can come from 'fringe' research. New types of thinking have to be opened up and one has to find out what topics and approaches would capture the attention of the policy-makers.

The countries of sub-Saharan Africa display several common features which are integral to the origin and evolution of the crisis: a fragile economic, social and higher-educational infrastructure; shortcomings in the quantity, quality and diversity of skilled people; extreme dependence on a few export crops and minerals for earning hard convertible currencies, etc. They have similar ecological zones, natural resources, population distribution and agricultural practices. Given these similarities, certain energy research topics of relevance to energy policy-making and energy planning are tackled in the most resource-effective way on a sub-regional basis, while others will necessarily be country-specific. A network would be ideal for identifying, classifying and discussing research problems specific to sub-regions, and how best to organize work on them.

There is some research going on in the region, and some research skills have been created, but the emphasis is mainly on the 'hardware' aspect of Renewable Energy Technologies (RETs). Only rarely does current research help policy-makers in their work. The focus on economic, social and cultural aspects is weak. There are substantial gaps in knowledge that prevent policy-makers intervening in a positive and constructive way.

There is now a growing awareness that the energy crisis is not amenable to purely technical (hardware) solutions, nor to solutions which are entirely supply-oriented. Economic, social and cultural factors play an equally decisive role in an approach that considers need, demand and end-use orientation. The network would deliberate on the relative balance of these various factors in specific problem areas and, wherever possible, identify the best path to a solution.

Policy-makers are understandably looking for quick ways of obtaining research results that they can use in crisis management. This more often than not means, firstly, a recourse to expatriate researchers based in the industrially and technologically developed countries, and, secondly, funding by foreign agencies to pay for the services of the expatriate researchers. While this is a perfectly reasonable and legitimate method to adopt in the short term, it is untenable in the longer term. The solutions to local, national and sub-regional problems cannot be sustained unless national research capacity is built up. Further, it is by no means certain that foreign researchers would be able to produce research results applicable to problems requiring an intimate non-technical understanding of the local environment. It is therefore a matter of urgent priority that African policy-makers and researchers should deliberate together on how best to allocate the limited resources available to them. They must decide when to obtain quick research results and when to build up national and sub-regional research capacity in terms of research personnel, infrastructure and institutions. One does not, of course, exclude the other.

While it is important *firstly* to pursue alternative institutional structures for getting research done, and *secondly* to promote research *about* institutions, it would be wise to build on, and support, existing structures and institutions.

The number of energy researchers in Africa is very small at present. To attract more researchers into the energy area and to broaden its base, one has to involve and support researchers from adjacent, relevant areas which are not strictly 'energy topics' in the narrow sense; this is particularly so for the non-technological (i.e., economic, social and cultural) dimensions.

In deciding 'what to do research on' and 'how to research', it is as important to be guided by research practitioners and existing research structures and institutions as well as by policy-makers and the establishment.

It is also important to create 'demand' for research among policy-makers, and to make them aware of the existence of ongoing research in their countries.

The process of setting up a network

In May 1987 a small preparatory meeting in Gaborone, Botswana was hosted by the National Institute of Development Research and Documentation (NIR) of the University of Botswana, with support from the Canadian International Development Research Centre (IDRC) and the Swedish Agency for Research Cooperation with Developing Countries (SAREC). Six African researchers and policy-makers of high standing took part. The meeting identified a number of topics of central importance for energy policy and energy planning research in Africa in the following six sectors: (1) RETs, (2) bio-energy, (3) electricity, (4) oil and natural gas, (5) coal and gasification and (6) institutions and planning. It was decided to convene a two-week workshop in November–December 1987 in Gaborone on 'Energy Policy and Energy Planning Research in East Africa and Southern Africa'.

The workshop was organized by NIR, with assistance from IDRC and SAREC. The 30 African researchers and policy-makers who attended came from Botswana, Burundi, Ethiopia, Kenya, Lesotho, Mozambique, Rwanda, the Seychelles, Somalia, the Sudan, Swaziland, Tanzania, Uganda, Zambia and Zimbabwe. Eight resource persons of international repute from Canada, China, Ethiopia, Ghana, Sweden, the UK and the USA, chosen for their expertise in the six sectors mentioned above, were invited to assist the sector groups. The workshop discussed in considerable detail and depth the topics put forward by the May 1987 preparatory meeting and decided to undertake 26 short research studies as the next stage in setting up the network.

Twenty-two of the planned 26 studies were completed during 1988, and presented at a second workshop held by NIR in Gaborone in March 1989. Their findings where published in 1990 by Zed Books, London, in a volume entitled *African Energy: Issues in Planning and Practice*. The research studies, as well as the March 1989 workshop, were funded by IDRC and SAREC.

The 30 African energy researchers and policy-makers attending the March 1989 workshop decided to launch the African Energy Policy Research Network (AFREPREN) with research programmes in the six areas mentioned above. The AFREPREN Programme for the 1989–93 period is funded by SAREC.

Coordination and administration of the network

The University of Botswana was called upon to coordinate and administer the network, a task which was entrusted by the University to its National Institute of Development Research and Documentation (NIR). The philosophy and basic direction of NIR, as well as its structure and functioning, have understandably shaped the quality and style of the coordination that the Institute has been able to provide.

The work of administering the activities of AFREPREN entails five main functions: (1) liaising with researchers, theme coordinators, resource persons and sponsors; (2) disbursement of funds to the researchers, and other financial activities integral to the running of the network; (3) organizing periodic regional workshops; (4) preparation of technical and financial reports; and (5) reproducing and distributing the network's research output. As the existing administrative capacity of the NIR was required to service the Institute's ongoing work, it became necessary to appoint a part-time professional administrator to deal with the network.

Besides an administrator, the network clearly required the services of an energy professional who could deal with the technical aspects of coordinating the work in the six AFREPREN research programmes mentioned above. To fulfil this function, a Nairobi-based member of AFREPREN was appointed to act as a part-time network facilitator. He combines this role with his other roles in the network as a researcher and theme coordinator. While the division of coordination between Gaborone and Nairobi has its obvious problems, it has also manifest advantages for a network as widely spread as AFREPREN's.

Botswana enjoys certain advantages such as relatively smooth foreign exchange transactions when disbursing research funds to various countries in the network, good air connections and telecommunications with East Africa and Southern Africa, and an ethos of relatively efficient administration. Further, the country has accumulated a certain amount of experience in conducting environmental research which is useful in the context of administering the network. Similarly, Nairobi has certain advantages, in particular its air connections and telecommunications, and an infrastructure created for the functioning of regional and international activities.

Researchers are proverbially individualistic, being accustomed to their own particular styles of functioning. But they have to operate within frameworks which are progressively being 'bureaucratized'. Within the confines of the same society, certain expectations and norms are taken for granted. But in the present case, with network participants hailing from diverse societies, cultures and traditions – stretching from the Sudan in the north to Lesotho in the south, from Angola on the Atlantic to the Seychelles in the Indian Ocean – the constraints are liable to be experienced as even more complex and compelling. If one adds to this the problems of the physical means of transportation and communication within the African continent, the allegiance to different cognitive specializations, and the unpredictable chemistry of human relations, it would have been surprising if very delicate and sensitive issues had not cropped up. But happily such contingencies have been rare in the life of the network so far. In responding to these various challenges AFREPREN has contributed to the wider pattern of regional coordination and administration.

Coordination in the research process takes place at different levels. In describing the role of NIR as a coordinating agency we have dealt with the official levels, linking policy-makers in government institutions and researchers in universities. However, other important levels need to be brought into the network, in particular the non-governmental organizations active in energy research in the region. This will help to avoid duplication, facilitate a wider exchange of ideas and experiences, and provide resources for research to other relevant individuals and bodies. Another significant component in the network would consist of 'reference groups', drawn from producers and consumers of energy across the region, to advise each of the six theme groups now comprising AFREPREN. This would help, among other things, to integrate the findings of the research teams into policy-making and policy implementation on a much wider scale throughout the region. Contacts with networks dealing with subjects other than energy will also contribute to AFREPREN's learning of the network process.

1 Introduction

M. R. Bhagavan and S. Karekezi

Why energy management?

There are several important reasons why management is now at the centre of the debate over energy development in sub-Saharan Africa. One is the growing disenchantment over the recurrent need to rehabilitate national energy infrastructures, in particular in the electric power and petroleum sectors. Capital shortage is another reason. With Eastern Europe and the now sovereign republics of the ex-Soviet Union joining the fierce global competition for hard convertible currency capital, the chances of sub-Saharan Africa attracting substantial volumes of fresh capital, or credit, for investment in energy are minimal. Perhaps the strongest reason is that energy efficiency provides the opportunity of using energy savings to increase energy supply at a fraction of the cost required for new energy production, while simultaneously reducing the negative impacts on the environment that current energy practices incur.

The introduction and use of energy-efficient methods and technologies are critically dependent on good management, which is itself a product of organizational skills. Without appropriate management strategies, sub-Saharan Africa will be unable to learn and benefit from the energy efficiency practices that were innovated by, and are now integrated into, the leading economies of Western Europe and East Asia.

It is against this background that the policy research reported in this volume was carried out. The authors analyse the current situation and make policy recommendations on how to improve the use of energy in the transport and industry sectors, as well as in the generation of electric power. Mengistu Teferra and Lietsiso Mohapeloa look at the transport sectors in Ethiopia and Lesotho respectively, Patrick Nyoike and Benjamin Okech deal with manufacturing industry in Kenya, and Jawaharlal Baguant examines electricity generation in Mauritius. These four countries between them display some of the major features which are common to the energy scene in sub-Saharan Africa.

Energy in the transport sector

Of the four main traffic systems – road, rail, air and sea – only road traffic accounts at present for non-negligible volumes of passenger and freight traffic in sub-Saharan Africa. The other three are still very poorly developed. Petrol (gasoline) and diesel (gas oil) between them account for almost all the energy used in the road transport sector. However, in comparison with the industrialized countries, the volume of road traffic and its consumption of petroleum fuels in sub-Saharan African countries is pathetically small. For instance, while the world petroleum consumption is at present about 4.4 barrels per capita per year, the figure for Ethiopia is 0.15 barrels, a mere three per cent of the world average. If and when sub-Saharan Africa begins to pull itself out of its present very deep economic and social crises and restarts its journey on the road to development, its traffic fuel consumption would have to rise by quick stages to the world average levels, which means by factors of several tens. Thus, one of the primary tasks of energy management will be the crafting of strategies to enhance the supply of transport fuels massively and efficiently. That being said, one must simultaneously implement strategies that will substantially improve efficiency in the use of fuels.

The mean age of buses, lorries and trucks plying the roads in East Africa and Southern Africa lies between seven and fifteen years, while it can be as high as twenty years for private automobiles and collective taxis. These fleets are therefore much less fuel-efficient than the recent models available on the world market. Maintenance of the ageing fleet is extremely poor, which further increases its inefficiency. Reduction in the levels of fuel consumption per vehicle per unit of distance travelled is not a goal that is at present built into the vehicle maintenance schedules. Nor is the specific fuel consumption of vehicles monitored during test runs after maintenance.

There is no effective system of penalties and rewards that would encourage fleet owners, drivers and mechanics, whether in the public or private sectors, to handle and maintain vehicles properly.

Fuel price subsidies are common. They accrue equally to both private and public transport operators. Governments tend to favour the public sector as against the private sector in the expansion of commercial freight traffic and passenger bus traffic.

If they heed the studies by Mengistu Teferra and Lietsiso Mohapeloa, governments will encourage private investors to take over more of the road transport services. Firstly, these services are already too much of a drain on the public exchequer; secondly, this move may succeed in introducing the efficiencies without which private enterprise cannot survive in a climate of competition.

Concurrently, governments should liberalize the import of highly fuel-efficient buses, lorries and trucks now available on the world market, and the spare parts which are essential for keeping the imported fleets on the road. Incentives and training schemes for mechanics and drivers should be instituted for proper preventive maintenance and repair.

Drastic cuts are called for in price subsidies on motor fuels wherever they are now operative. Simultaneously, incentives should be provided for switching from petrol-driven to the relatively more energy-conserving diesel-driven vehicles, and from higher-capacity to lower-capacity engines.

Technical efficiency improvements, the expansion of bus transport for passenger traffic, the blending of indigenously produced ethanol (a renewable resource) with imported petroleum, and reduction in retail price subsidies would result – and quickly, too – in gross savings of up to twenty per cent in the petroleum consumption of the road transport sector.

The partial substitution of petrol by ethanol, produced locally by medium-sized plants using locally grown sugar cane or other appropriate renewable raw material, would be technically feasible and economically viable if the import price of petroleum were to rise substantially above twenty dollars a barrel. Substitution of both petrol and diesel by ethanol and other natural gas derivatives should be taken more seriously. Before launching projects in these areas, however, one ought to study carefully the experience of countries in other parts of the world which have gone some way along this road. To obtain a better comparative understanding of the use of petroleum fuels, and to formulate policies for relatively optimal uses in various sectors of the economy, a reliable system of reporting should be set up.

Countries like Botswana, Lesotho and Swaziland (BLS) which belong to the South African Customs Union, face special problems. The free flow of goods and services between BLS and the Republic of South Africa (RSA) makes it pointless to try and impose constraints on BLS vehicle owners, such as selective import of vehicles and much higher fuel prices than in the RSA, when such constraints can be circumvented very easily by registering the vehicles and filling up the tanks across the border.

In the BLS countries, the only viable strategy besides positive incentives seems to be to mount an information campaign to persuade vehicle owners and fleet operators that it is in their own economic interest to adopt fuel-efficient practices.

Energy in manufacturing industry

With very few exceptions, most countries in sub-Saharan Africa still have very little in the way of manufacturing industry. The little there is consumes both modern and traditional forms of energy, the latter largely in the form of fuelwood. Manufacturing industry comes next to transport in its level of consumption of electricity, petroleum and coal. Although this consumption is very low in absolute terms at present, it is important to pay attention to it now because these levels are bound to rise substantially with economic recovery, when efficiency will become a critical factor. The study by Patrick Nyoike and Benjamin Okech of energy consumption in the Kenyan manufacturing sector brings out many of the main features that apply to industrial sectors across the continent.

They see cooperation and coordination between the main institutional actors as indispensable to the promotion of higher efficiency. They analyse, in the Kenyan context, the roles played by the oil multinationals (who have in practice, though not in theory, an effective say on the import and sale of petroleum products), the international financial and bilateral aid agencies (who control access to hard currency capital and thus access to the latest energy-efficient technology), the Kenyan Ministry of Energy, the local Manufacturers' Association, the local electricity utility, the local owners of energy-intensive plants (e.g. cement), the local universities and the industrial research establishments. Their study shows that while the various actors find it not too difficult to agree on the main lines of policy, the implementation of policy gets derailed by hidden vested interests which surface at the stage of implementation.

The initial steps usually consist of energy auditing of industrial establishments and training courses for technical and managerial personnel. These are embarked on enthusiastically. That is the first, easy stage. The next one, getting the industrial owners to put the energy-efficiency measures into effect, has so far proved very difficult to realize. It depends on several factors: the local industrialists' perception of whether there is anything substantial to be gained in the short and medium terms by taking energy efficiency on board, the related issue of energy price structures and subsidies, financial incentives for retro-fitting and re-equipping, the status and influence of energy-conscious factory managers, etc. The public and private sectors have to address themselves jointly to these specific questions if energy saving and energy efficiency are to make any real headway in the industrial sector.

Energy for electricity generation

The electrical energy elasticity of the GDP in sub-Saharan Africa is high. For instance, under present-day conditions in Mauritius, to achieve an increase of one unit in the GDP would require an increase in electricity consumption of 1.3. Such a situation is incompatible with sustainable long-term economic development. Major effort will be required to increase the efficiency of electricity use, so that the rise in electricity consumption does not outstrip the rise in the GDP. This problem is now being addressed in the AFREPREN Research Programme and the findings will be reported in a later volume.

It is clear that in the short and medium terms the supply of electricity has to increase sharply to fuel economic growth in the more dynamic and successful African economies, of which Mauritius is currently the prime example. This raises the question of cost-effectiveness and other criteria of technical and economic efficiency in the production of electricity, in particular in thermal generation based on imported petroleum. J. Baguant has tackled this problem and advocates an approach whose major thrust is the partial replacement of petroleum firing by a combination of coal and bagasse (a by-product of the sugar industry). The Southern African region has abundant coal reserves and active coal-mining industries. It would be cheaper to use this coal than to rely on intercontinental imports of petroleum. Further, bagasse is also an abundant renewable resource in many sugar-producing African countries, which today is going to waste. Baguant demonstrates that more than sixty per cent of future electricity demand can be met by taking the coal-cum-bagasse route, while simultaneously ensuring greater cost-effectiveness and energy efficiency. He also shows that by installing pump-hydro generation, about a third of unused base-power can be converted to peak-power.

Concluding remarks

The economic and social development of sub-Saharan Africa requires sharp increases in the supply of modern energy inputs, as well as great improvements in the present abysmally low levels of efficiency in the use of energy. Such a situation calls for both supply and demand management. Measures such as better management of existing energy systems through improved technical maintenance, planned and non-disrupted supply of inputs, dismantling of price and other subsidies to consumers, and effective collection of energy bills can lead, within a short time, to marked improvements in the performance of the continent's energy sector. Management is a knowledge-intensive activity, requiring both formal and on-the-job training, with ready access to the latest systematized information. Training of personnel in various sections of energy institutions in the skills of better technical, economic and organizational management should result in handsome dividends, even in the short and medium terms.

PART I

Energy Management in the Transport Sector

2 The Case of Lesotho

L. Mohapeloa

Economic background

The Kingdom of Lesotho is a country in Southern Africa with a population of
1.5 million people (1986 census) and a surface area of 30,350 square kilometres.
The country is a former British colony, having been under colonial rule for the
century between 1865 and the advent of independence in 1966. The country
is completely surrounded by the Republic of South Africa (RSA).

Lesotho's mountains cover large areas, and numerous hills and rock outcrops
dot the lowlands: as a result, cultivable land amounts to less than 297,000
hectares or 13 per cent of the total area. The mountain areas are suitable for
grazing, though most of this land is deteriorating as soil erosion is accelerated
by overstocking and the resultant overgrazing, and by the general depletion of
vegetative cover due to the gathering of fuelwood or other forms of biomass.

The whole country is drained by the Senqu (Orange) River system, the main
streams of which flow in a south-westerly direction and are separated by
mountain ridges. The country is divided into four major regions: the lowlands
along the western plateau, the Senqu Valley, the foothills and the mountains.

Lesotho is highly dependent on the RSA's economy for employment, trade
and monetary arrangements. About half of the country's male labour force
depends directly on the RSA for employment and income; labour force
remittances constitute over 40 per cent of GNP.

Over 70 per cent of the government's income is derived from the Customs
Union formed in 1910 by the colonial governments of Basotholand, the
Bechuanaland protectorate, Swaziland and the Union of South Africa. The
agreement continues under the independent governments of Botswana,
Lesotho, Swaziland and the RSA, which is the dominant partner. The existence
of the Customs Union has had both positive and negative effects on the Lesotho
economy. On the one hand the union has had a price-escalating effect estimated
at fully 14 per cent of Lesotho's CIF import bill; on the other hand, Lesotho's
share of the revenues is vital to its survival.

While in principle the Customs Union opens up a potentially larger market
to Lesotho-based industry, in practice industrial growth has been restricted
given the difficulty in competing with the more developed RSA industries
which are dominant in the area. Also, the Customs Union agreement has some
limited instruments for restricting trade in selected agreed areas. In the case

9

of industry, for example, a clause was inserted that dealt with protection of infant industries. Attempts to use the provisions of the clause, however, met many obstacles in implementation. The end result was that infant industries had to compete with mature counterparts in the RSA.

As might be expected, the RSA is Lesotho's chief trading partner, accounting for over 95 per cent of Lesotho's imports, including nearly all its energy requirements. Almost 80 per cent of Lesotho's exports either end up in the RSA or go to the rest of the world through the RSA's ports. Lesotho is also a member of the Rand Monetary Area (RMA), a RSA monetary arrangement extended to cover Lesotho and Swaziland. Botswana was formerly part of this agreement but withdrew in 1976 to establish its own currency, the Pula. As a result of this membership, the Rand, RSA's currency, is at par and circulates side by side with the Maluti, Lesotho's currency. Under this monetary arrangement, the Reserve Bank of South Africa provides guarantees for Lesotho's external financial commitments.

The access that the Customs Union and RMA agreements gives the neighbouring countries to RSA goods and services markets, and vice-versa, is very important. These agreements limit the influence of fiscal measures (e.g. duties or taxes) on consumption patterns within individual countries because of the easy access to the alternative markets of the neighbouring countries.

Lesotho faces a number of constraints in achieving her development goals given her limited natural resources and unique geographical position. The long-term effects of the current changing political situation in South Africa also provide an added variable in the country's uncertain economic future, especially with respect to future migrant remittances, while continued soil erosion impedes growth in agricultural productivity.

Lesotho's only known and exploitable natural resource, now that the diamond mines have closed down, is water. The government is presently investing in the Lesotho Highland Water Project (LHWP) which will export water to the RSA. Hydro-electric power will also be generated by the project, reducing Lesotho's dependence on the RSA for electricity by approximately 80 per cent. Although the LHWP should contribute significantly to economic growth, it will not be a panacea of development in terms of its impact upon diversification of the economy and employment creation.

After more than a decade of financial stability and relatively high growth in real GDP and GNP, which averaged 7 to 8 per cent per annum in the 1970s, the performance of Lesotho's economy in the early 1980s was characterized by low growth, rapidly rising fiscal deficits and a substantial deterioration in the external current account and the balance of payments.

To counter this setback, the Lesotho government embarked in early 1988 on an economic adjustment and restructuring programme backed by the International Monetary Fund and World Bank and aimed at remedying the emergent macro-economic imbalances and setting the economy on a sound footing for long-term economic development. This programme included policies to increase agricultural and manufacturing productivity and output, reducing the fiscal deficit and strengthening the balance of payments position.

In the first year of the programme (1988/9) there was little improvement in the external position. The external current account fell slightly to 6.6 per cent of GNP while the overall balance of payments also remained substantially in deficit. Real GDP growth rate is estimated to have grown by 9.2 per cent due mainly to good harvests arising from favourable weather conditions and the implementation of the preparatory phase of the LHWP. Real GNP per capita grew at 3.2 per cent, despite lower growth in the real value of migrant workers' remittances, while gross investment, also assisted by the LHWP's related construction activity, rose to 31.4 per cent of GNP. The fiscal deficit reached 9.7 per cent of GNP compared with the programme target of 5.9 per cent, and the rate of inflation (which is essentially imported from the RSA) was 12.3 per cent, compared with the programme target of 5.9 per cent.

Performance in the second year of the programme (1989/90) was encouraging. Real GDP and GNP are estimated to have grown by 9.3 per cent and 7 per cent respectively (Table 2.1), compared with programme targets of 6.3 per cent and 2.6 per cent, reflecting primarily increased activities associated with the LHWP and, in the case of GNP, larger-than-envisaged growth of migrants' remittances as a result of significant increases in wages for Basotho mine workers in South Africa. The rate of inflation is estimated to have been slightly less than 15 per cent, compared with the programme target of 16 per cent (Ministry of Planning). There was also a significant improvement in the balance of payments in that the external current account deficit fell from 6.5 per cent of GNP in 1988/9 to the programme target of 3.7 per cent. Although the overall fiscal deficit of 4.4 per cent of GNP in 1989/90 exceeded the programme target of 4.0 per cent, it represented a significant improvement over the previous year's level of 9.5 per cent of GNP (Table 2. 2).

The preliminary data for the third year of the programme (1990/1) indicate that growth in real GNP and GDP, though lower than in the previous year, continues to be encouraging (8.2 per cent and 7 per cent respectively, compared with the programme target of 9.3 per cent and 6 per cent). The rate of inflation is also expected to decline further than the previous year's level of 15 per cent. The overall fiscal deficit is expected to fall from 4.4 per cent of GNP in 1989/90 to 1.7 per cent of GNP in 1990/1.

However, this positive outlook does not take into account the impact of the recent oil price increases, the uncertainties regarding political developments in the region, particularly with regard to the prospects of Basotho miners in South Africa, and the impact of the recent drought on the economy. Over the years employment in the mines was shunned by urban black South Africans because of the harsh conditions. The jobs were reserved for labourers from rural South Africa and neighbouring countries. In recent years, however, fewer places have been available for labourers from Lesotho and other neighbouring territories.

In the light of the current Gulf crisis, assuming no significant increase in oil consumption, there would probably be an adverse effect on the external current account and the overall balance of payments, resulting in some large losses of foreign exchange. The rate of inflation is expected to rise significantly as the higher prices of oil products take hold on the economy.

Table 2.1 Lesotho: macro-economic indicators (in millions of maluti)

Macro-economic framework	1986/7	1987/8	1988/9	1989/90	1990/1	1991/2	1992/3	1993/4	1994/5	1995/6
Gross national product	1276.2	1522.4	1905.1	2347.1	2843.9	3418.1	4044.7	4719.5	5525.1	6519.8
Net factor income from abroad	630.2	731.7	858.0	1025.9	1216.5	1392.9	1500.7	1717.0	1988.3	2286.3
Gross domestic product	646.0	790.7	1046.4	1322.0	1627.4	2025.2	2456.1	2947.7	3536.8	4233.5
Consumption	1125.7	1403.3	1643.1	1805.0	2231.7	2484.7	2837.0	3357.0	3872.0	4600.7
Government consumption	162.1	180.8	228.8	309.0	362.7	439.7	530.1	633.6	757.0	903.0
Private consumption	964.6	1222.5	1414.3	1496.6	1868.9	2045.5	2307.0	2723.7	3115.1	3597.7
Investment	326.9	412.1	618.1	1060.2	1428.7	2040.3	2599.7	3090.0	3741.0	4063.0
Gross fixed capital:										
Formation	323.3	412.2	615.7	1057.4	1279.8	2036.7	2595.6	3085.3	3735.6	4059.9
Government	89.1	107.3	134.3	345.0	401.5	404.1	492.1	590.4	710.3	860.6
Private	234.2	304.9	428.9	502.1	601.3	1007.3	1226.7	1471.8	1770.4	2145.2
LHWP	–	–	62.5	210.3	277.0	625.3	876.8	1023.0	1254.9	1051.1
Change in stocks	3.6	–0.1	2.4	2.7	3.1	3.5	4.2	4.7	5.4	6.2
Net exports	–802.6	–1024.7	–1214.7	–1543.2	–2033.0	–2425.7	–2881.3	–3407.7	–3852.3	–3864.7
Exports of merchandise	75.4	101.0	165.4	152.3	175.0	220.0	272.7	334.6	409.9	502.1
Imports of merchandise and non factor services (net)	880.0	1125.7	1380.1	1695.5	2208.0	2645.8	3154.0	3742.3	4262.2	4466.8
Memorandum items :										
Gross national savings 1/	324.9	304.4	494.3	973.3	1335.5	1856.7	2369.8	2727.4	3331.1	3583.8
Private savings	265.1	245.3	350.8	521.7	705.8	864.1	1082.3	1157.2	1341.5	1528.2
Public savings 2/	59.8	59.1	81.0	241.3	352.8	374.6	566.8	704.0	844.5	955.7
LHWP transfers	–	–	52.5	210.3	277.0	818.0	720.5	886.2	1145.1	1099.9
Gross domestic investment	326.9	412.1	618.1	1060.2	1428.7	2040.3	2599.7	3090.0	3741.0	4063.0
Private investment	237.8	304.8	431.3	504.9	581.3	1010.9	1230.0	1476.6	1775.9	2151.4
Public investment	89.1	107.3	134.3	345.0	401.5	404.1	492.1	592.4	710.3	860.6

LHWP investment	–	–	52.5	210.3	277.0	625.3	876.8	1023.0	1254.9	1051.1
Resource balance (= foreign savings)	–2.0	–107.7	–123.7	–85.9	–93.2	–183.6	–230.0	–352.5	–410.0	–479.2
Per capita consumption index	94.9	104.6	105.0	94.2	102.8	97.2	95.2	97.7	97.7	100.7
Consumer price index (% change)	16.5	12.1	12.3	14.9	14.4	14.8	13.6	12.4	12.4	12.4

(In % of GNP, unless otherwise indicated)

Gross national savings 1/	25.5	20.0	25.9	41.5	47.0	54.3	58.6	57.8	50.3	55.0
Private savings	20.8	16.1	18.9	22.2	24.8	25.3	26.8	24.5	24.3	23.4
Public savings 2/	4.7	3.9	4.3	10.3	12.4	11.0	14.0	14.9	15.3	14.7
LHWP transfers	–	–	2.8	9.0	9.7	18.1	17.8	18.4	20.7	16.9
Stocks	0.3	-0.0	0.1	0.1	0.1	0.1	0.1	0.1	0.1	0.1
Resource balance (= foreign savings)	–0.2	–7.1	–6.5	–3.7	–3.3	–5.5	–5.7	–7.3	–7.4	–7.3
Real GDP growth	2.3	8.3	10.7	9.3	8.2	7.0	5.0	5.0	5.1	5.0
Real GNP growth	1.5	5.3	6.6	7.0	4.1	3.6	3.2	3.6	4.5	
Real growth of non-imported consumer goods	0.6	5.4	–6.9	4.6	30.4	–2.3	2.5	13.7	3.0	4.0
GDP deflator (% change)	15.7	13.3	17.4	15.2	13.3	15.5	14.3	13.1	13.6	12.0

1. including unrequited transfers
2. including grants
3. assumes all stocks held privately
4. relates to private consumption only

Table 2.2 Lesotho: central government's budgetary operations (in millions of Maluti)

For fiscal years beginning 1 April

	1987/8	1988/9	1989/90	1990/1*	1990/1	1991/2	1992/3	1993/4	1994/5	1995/6
Revenue and grants	362.0	465.0	677.2	821.1	821.1	989.7	1167.9	1369.0	1674.1	1995.3
Revenue	299.0	368.4	525.3	620.4	623.6	754.0	865.3	1012.0	1201.3	1445.3
Customs receipts	157.4	193.2	263.6	354.7	354.7	424.0	459.0	506.0	550.0	600.0
Grants	62.6	96.6	151.9	197.5	197.5	235.7	302.6	357.0	472.8	550.0
Expenditure & net lending	522.5	646.1	780.4	866.6	868.0	1039.8	1206.6	1383.5	1617.3	1904.2
Current	302.9	381.0	435.9	465.2	468.6	560.5	638.9	722.2	839.7	984.2
Wage & salaries	117.2	170.0	174.4	170.0	178.8	252.3	296.4	345.0	403.6	476.3
Interest payments	29.9	43.4	97.5	96.5	96.5	80.0	70.0	60.0	65.0	70.0
Other goods & services	155.8	170.6	164.0	189.9	191.3	230.1	272.5	317.2	371.1	437.9
Development outlays	219.6	262.1	344.5	401.4	401.4	479.4	557.7	661.4	777.6	920.0
Overall deficit (including grants)	(160.5)	(181.1)	(130.2)	(48.7)	(46.9)	(50.2)	(38.7)	(14.5)	(56.7)	(91.2)
Overall deficit (excluding grants)	(223.1)	(277.7)	(255.1)	(246.2)	(244.4)	(285.9)	(341.3)	(371.5)	(416.1)	(458)
Government savings	(3.5)	(15.6)	(89.4)	(155.2)	(157.0)	(193.5)	(226.4)	(289.9)	(361.5)	(461.2)
Total financing	160.5	181.1	103.2	48.7	46.9	50.2	36.7	14.5	(56.7)	(91.2)
Foreign	70.3	71.2	111.8	105.2	105.2	140.0	162.2	189.1	213.3	256.5
Borrowing	92.7	106.2	160.2	144.6	144.6	180.0	200.9	224.1	250.6	285.8
Amortization	22.4	35.0	48.4	33.4	39.4	40.0	38.7	34.7	37.3	39.3
Domestic	90.2	109.9	(8.6)	(56.5)	(58.3)	(89.8)	(123.5)	(175.2)	(270.0)	(347.7)
Bank	70.8	91.9	(4.4)	(58.3)	(60.1)	(94.8)	(129.5)	(182.2)	(278.1)	(357.7)
Non-bank	19.4	18.0	(4.2)	1.8	1.8	5.0	6.0	7.0	6.1	10.0

Memorandum (percentage ratio to GNP)

	1987/8	1988/9	1989/90	1990/1*	1990/1	1991/2	1992/3	1993/4	1994/5	1995/6
Revenue and grants	23.8	24.4	28.9	28.9	28.9	28.8	28.0	30.3	30.6	30.6
Revenue	19.7	19.3	22.4	21.8	21.9	22.0	21.3	21.4	21.7	22.2
Customs receipts	10.3	10.1	11.2	12.5	12.5	12.4	11.3	10.7	10.0	9.2
Other receipts	9.3	9.2	11.1	9.3	9.5	9.6	10.0	10.7	11.8	10.0

Total expenditure	34.3	33.9	33.2	30.5	30.5	30.4	29.8	29.3	29.3	29.3
Current expenditure	19.9	20.2	18.6	16.4	16.4	16.4	15.8	15.3	15.2	15.1
Wages and salaries	7.7	8.9	7.4	6.3	6.3	7.3	7.3	7.3	7.3	7.3
Other goods & services	10.2	9.0	7.0	–	6.7	6.7	6.7	6.7	6.7	6.7
Capital expenditure	14.4	13.8	14.7	14.1	14.1	14.0	14.0	14.0	14.1	14.1
Overall deficit (incl. grants)	(10.5)	(9.5)	(4.4)	(1.7)	(1.6)	(1.5)	(1.0)	(0.3)	1.0	1.4
Overall deficit (excl. grants)	(14.7)	(14.6)	(10.9)	(8.7)	(8.6)	(8.4)	(8.4)	(7.9)	(7.5)	(7.0)
Foreign financing	4.6	3.7	4.8	3.7	3.7	4.1	4.0	4.0	3.9	3.9
Domestic financing	4.7	4.8	(0.2)	(2.1)	(2.1)	(2.8)	(3.2)	(3.9)	(5.0)	(5.5)
Government savings	(0.2)	(0.8)	3.8	5.6	5.5	5.7	5.6	6.1	6.5	7.1
GNP at current market price	1522.4	1905.1	2347.1	2843.9	2843.9	3423.9	4054.9	4724.4	5525.7	6519.1

* reflects the impact of petroleum price increase effective November 5, 1990

Source: Ministry of Planning, Economic and Manpower Development

Lesotho's future prospects will depend largely on economic and financial developments in the region (especially in the RSA), the implementation of the LHWP, and the government's continued pursuit of the appropriate economic policies and structural reforms. Assuming no adverse external developments, favourable weather conditions and appropriate economic policies, real GDP is projected to grow by 7 per cent in 1991/2 and at an annual average rate of 5 per cent thereafter, reflecting the pattern of investment under the LHWP (see Table 2.1). Real GNP is projected to increase more slowly due to the absence of growth in real terms in migrant remittances. The balance of payments is expected to show a reduction in the current account deficit in 1991/2 and a widening thereafter, largely as a result of the imports associated with the hydro-electric component of the LHWP. A further contributing factor could be the expected decline in migrant remittances. The fiscal situation is expected to improve. The budgetary deficit should decline steadily to 0.4 per cent of GNP in 1993/4 before becoming a surplus in 1994/5 (Table 2.2). Customs receipts are expected to remain the single largest source of government revenue.

In summary, then, to achieve its medium-term development objectives, Lesotho will have to pursue sound macro-economic policies and structural reforms aimed at promoting domestic savings and investment, diversifying production and exports, strengthening the balance of payments, and thus laying the ground for sustained economic growth. The question we can now pose is: how should the energy sector contribute to this development drive?

Energy supply and demand

A recent Department of Energy (DOE) survey shows Lesotho's total energy consumption at 26,000 TJ, which represents 18,000 MJ or an equivalent of 430 kg of oil per capita per annum. An examination of the structure of this consumption shows that the traditional fuels still play a dominant role in the provision of fuel, representing about 77 per cent of total consumption. These traditional fuels are fuelwood, shrubs, cow dung and crop residues. Demand by sector is dominated by the residential sector (90 per cent); transportation accounts for 7 per cent and productive services for 3 per cent.

Lesotho depends for its lighting, cooking, industry and transportation on the following energy resources: electricity, petroleum, coal, firewood and various new and renewable resources. The major forms of so-called non-traditional energy – petroleum, electricity and coal – are all imported from the RSA. The 'traditional' energy sources are cow dung, residues, shrubs and firewood. These forms are gradually becoming significant to the energy base due to the high rate of depletion of biomass. Already, firewood is largely imported from the RSA, and increasingly paraffin is the fuel used for cooking. Indeed, the depletion of the woody biomass resources, and the increased dependence on imported wood, brings into question the categorization of wood as a traditional fuel: today, it is mainly a commercial fuel.

Electricity

The Lesotho Electricity Corporation (LEC), a government-owned parastatal, is responsible for the supply of all electrical power through the national grid and from the mini-hydro generation plants, some of which are not connected to the national grid.

Apart from the mini-hydro plants which supply about 7 per cent of the country's electricity needs, the LEC imports about 93 per cent of its electricity from the RSA's Electricity Supply Commission (ESCOM) through three electricity intake points at Maseru, Maputsoe and Hendrick's Drift. An additional power intake is currently under construction at Hololo which is aimed primarily at serving the LHWP construction sites. At present the Maseru intake accounts for 99 per cent of the imports, a figure likely to change with increased importation to support the LHWP construction. Electricity consumption is estimated at about 110 GWh, with a growth rate of about 20 per cent. Both the growth figure and the consumption rate will be distorted by construction work at LHWP.

Hydro-power is clearly the most important potential energy source. Water resources are plentiful in areas where they can be dammed with relative ease while achieving maximum results. A number of areas have been identified for the development of generating plants (Table 2.3). These plants are all very small, with the obvious exception of Muella.

Table 2.3 Hydro-power plants in development

Project	Capacity (MW)	Annual generation (GWH)	Status
Mantsonyane	2.0	6.6	Complete
Semonkong	0.34	1.3	Complete
Tlokoeng	0.67	3.3	Under construction
Qacha's Nek	0.4	2.1	Complete
Muella	54.0	154.0	To start 1992
Total	57.41	167.3	

Coal and firewood

There are no known deposits of coal in the country, though attempts to follow seams that looked like coal deposits have led to fatalities when shafts collapsed during mining operations. Nothing of any commercial interest has been found.

As we have seen, deforestation has meant that wood is no longer a freely available resource and has to be imported. Attempts are being made to remedy this situation by planting fuelwood through the Woodlot Project. Some 7000 hectares have been planted and about 1000 hectares are being harvested during the 1990/1 season (Woodlot Project, Ministry of Agriculture). Indiscriminate grazing and pasture fires have greatly reduced the area ready for harvesting.

Petroleum

Supply

There are no known deposits of petroleum in Lesotho. There were some explorations for petroleum in the 1970s in the Mahobong area of Leribe district. In 1974/5 a single borehole was sunk to the depth of 2000 metres, without success (Department of Mines and Geology). No further exploration has been undertaken to date.

All petroleum products are imported through the RSA as finished products. Five oil companies have distributorships in the country: Shell, BP, Total, Caltex and Mobil. None of these companies operates a refinery in Lesotho, as they have facilities in the RSA with adequate capacity to supply Lesotho.

The peculiarities and problems of sourcing oil through the RSA are addressed below. Each of the oil companies has its own depot for supplying the retailer service stations; there are 102 private retailers and about 20 government stations. In 1989, Lesotho's total fuel consumption was 139.3 million litres, of which the government's share was 8 million litres or 6 per cent.

Storage

For the most part, petroleum is supplied by railway and road tankers to the Maseru depot, and redistributed from there. Some of the outlying and remote areas are supplied directly by road tankers from depots in the RSA. There are two major depots in Maseru, with the capacities shown in Table 2.4 (Dothunts'ane, 1989). In addition, there are two storage tanks at Mejametalana and Moshoeshoe airports with capacities of 80,000 litres and 160,000 litres respectively. Another storage facility exists at the defunct Letseng la Terai diamond mine, but its capacity is either unknown or a closely guarded secret.

Table 2.4 Petroleum storage capacity, Maseru

Product	Caltex-BP-Shell (litres)	Mobil (litres)	Total
Petrol	240,000	274,000	514,000
Diesel	160,000	178,000	338,000
Paraffin	240,000	236,000	476,000
Aviation gas	80,000	–	80,000
Total	720,000	688,000	1,408,000

In January 1986, when amid serious political tensions the RSA imposed sanctions against Lesotho by closing the border posts, the inadequacy of the storage facility became apparent. Supplies quickly ran low and rationing was introduced. Though the impact of the petroleum shortage was never measured, there was a state of general chaos within seven days of the border closure.

Retailing

Petroleum is retailed by the private service stations, which supply the full range of products with the exception of aviation gas. The licensing of petroleum retailing is carried out by a service station rationalization committee. In examining the applications, the committee ensures that the required standards are maintained and that the number of service stations is restricted to a viable maximum. Thus the committee ensures that government has a complete list of dealers for control purposes. We should mention here that, on a daily basis, control refers to monitoring prices, which are gazetted. In special circumstances this could include rationing, as mentioned earlier. The retail prices are uniform throughout the country except for selected remote areas, where a surcharge is made to cover additional transport costs. Prices are generally agreed at the level of the Southern African Customs Union Inter-state Committee. Each member state, however, can still introduce its own surcharge, which would affect the price. It is, however, important to note that in the case of Lesotho, because of the proximity of RSA dealers and easy access to RSA petroleum, a high price differential could cause cross-border trading. Lesotho cannot sell at prices that differ substantially from those of its neighbour. This constraint on deciding prices independently of the RSA takes away an important tool for influencing petroleum demand, as will become apparent in our discussions on institutional mechanisms. The pricing mechanism used by the Customs Union member states has ten components: in-bond landed cost, industry margin, duty, impost, SFF (Synthetic Fuel Fund) levy, road delivery, depot storage and handling, dealer's margin, sales tax, and transport differential.

In-bond landed cost

This is the cost of fuel when it arrives at the depots in Maseru. At this point fuel cost is determined by factors such as average crude oil/refined products prices in the world market, seafreight, and railage to Maseru. There are other factors but these are usually constant. The crude oil price, and hence the refined product price, affects the overall price of fuel most because it also depends on the prevailing exchange rate. In fact, it is the exchange rate which is the key factor in price fluctuation.

Duty, impost, sales tax

These components of the fuel price are basically taxes charged by the government.

SFF levy

This is the levy which member states of the Inter-state Committee contribute to a fund. This fund incorporates many constituent levies. Lesotho contributes to three of these constituents.

- *Equalization on Fund – Basic*. This fund finances increased purchasing cost of crude oil and petroleum products. It is also used to stabilize the short-term fluctuations of the crude oil price in the world market.
- *Indigenous Raw Material Incentive*. This is the incentive for the production of fuel from indigenous raw materials and also helps to finance synthetic fuel projects such as the blending of alcohol from sugar plants.

- *Fire and Security*. This fund is meant for the upgrading of fire-fighting and security facilities at the depots in the RSA. The balance obtained after the upgrading is completed is returned to each country upon that country's request.

Table 2.5 Petroleum product consumption (in millions of litres), 1982–9

	Petrol	Diesel	Paraffin	Liquid gas	Aviation	Total
1982	31	26	22	0.44	1.5	81
1983	32	26	25	0.66	1.5	85
1984	36	26	27	0.67	1.6	92
1985	36	27	25	0.55	1.7	90
1986	34	28	21	0.48	1.6	84
1987	38	32	26	0.27	1.7	98
1988	41	38	37	0.29	3.7	120
1989	44	42	44	2.40	2.3	130

Industry and dealer's margins, road delivery, depot storage handling, transport differential

These are components which cater for the oil industry and the local dealers/ retailers and are meant to cover their costs (storage, transport and overheads). The transport differential is levied on sales in the mountain districts only.

The relation between world market prices, RSA prices and Lesotho prices is on the whole limited to the in-bond landed cost. Beyond in-bond landed cost, Lesotho acts independently according to its socio-political and economic conditions. When the in-bond landed cost drops, a surplus is created in the price structure. This surplus, which is known as 'overrecovery', can be used to tide the consumer over when the in-bond landed cost rises unexpectedly and an 'underrecovery' results. The over- and underrecovery circumstances of Lesotho and the RSA are different because of the different price components of the two countries' price structures. The fuel price components may be increased or reduced when government deems it necessary. In Lesotho the prices are in general at par or less than the RSA's (Department of Energy).

Consumption

The primary source of consumption data is the Bureau of Statistics. The import data, however, are unsatisfactory in that the time series present irregularities that point to errors in data compilation. There are, for example, differences in consumption growth rates that suggest horizontal or vertical skips in data compilation.

Horizontal skips can occur when quantities of one product are recorded as quantities of another product. Vertical skips occur when the cut-off point in data collection is not clear and as a result figures for one year are treated as those of another year.

Petroleum consumption figures were never recorded properly in the period before 1982. As a result only the post-1982 period data are shown in Table 2.5. It might have been expected that the oil companies would have figures for the earlier period based on their wholesale purchases, but they too only have data from 1982. The staff at the local oil company offices are not able to explain why they do not have records before 1982. It is possible that such data are in the archives with their main offices in the RSA (Shell Lesotho).

Other data sources are records kept by the petroleum retailers and the government garages. However, record-keeping practices are unreliable and fear of exposing themselves to the tax agencies is not a negligible factor (Service Station Rationalization Committee). The retailer outlets are grouped as follows:

BP	27
Shell	21
Government	23
Caltex	14
Mobil	13
Total	4
Total number	102

It has been suggested that a method of arriving at an accurate estimate would contain the following components for cross-checking:

- Oil imports
- Oil dealer sales
- Service station survey
- Reconstruction of the fleet
- Industry and commerce survey
- Any new hypothesis to combine these elements in a suitable manner.

However, such a method has yet to be established.

The transport sector

The transport sector of Lesotho consists of air and road traffic only. The latter consists of passengers and haulage transport.

Air

Air transport is used for external traffic linking Lesotho with other countries, regionally and internationally, and to connect remote areas within the country where road access is difficult and time-consuming. Basically, the use of air transport to destinations within the country is declining, mainly because of improvements in the road network.

There are several airfields throughout the country, some of which were rated regional mainly because they were equipped with air traffic control facilities, all-weather runways, terminal buildings, emergency equipment and vehicles. Recently, some of these have been downgraded to ordinary airfields because of a reduction in air traffic. Between 1977 and 1987 there was a drop in the number of flights from 9336 to 6719, due to the improved road network. The road network increased by 54.7 per cent from 2775 km (1986) to about 4294 km (1987) as shown in Table 2.6 (Ministry of Works). Other factors besides the improved road network have contributed to the shift to road transport. Firstly, ground travel allows for more baggage (almost unrestricted) as compared to air travel, and with a reduced ground travel time (because of improved roads) it becomes easier to trade off savings on travel time for increased baggage capacity. A second factor, one which has been overlooked, is the positioning of the new airport – about 23 km from town with no public transport between it and Maseru or any of the other centres. This can mean long hours of waiting at the airport for an irregular airport bus service, a situation that can be aggravated by the changing of air schedules due to frequently adverse weather conditions in the mountain areas during the rainy season, or other causes.

Table 2.6 Length of road network (km), 1978–87

Year	Bitumen	Gravel	Earth	Total
1978	215	410	945	1570
1979	223	640	943	1806
1980	232	894	914	2040
1981	234	1058	632	1924
1982	268	1278	472	2018
1983	302	1474	344	2120
1984	342	1690	266	2298
1985	458	1808	232	2498
1986	475	2078	222	2775
1987	628	1697	1969	4294

Source: Ministry of Works

This drop in local air travel contrasts with an increase in international passenger loads from 37,773 in 1977 to 47,268 in 1987 (Bureau of Stastistics). This increase is seen by Lesotho Airways Corporation (LAC) as in line with their projections. LAC is the single largest air transport operator in the country. It accounts for more than 90 per cent of air transport traffic. It is also the biggest consumer of aviation fuel.

There are two other operators, which operate very small fleets for scheduled passenger flights and for charter operations. One of these operators, Senqu

Air, operates from the RSA and flies mainly to areas that LAC does not service, due to the size of the airstrips and the volume of passenger travel, which are below the capacity of LAC planes. Highland Air is principally a charter operation. Occasionally Lesotho Airways leases it to fill in for its scheduled operations. LAC and Highland Air draw their fuel from the LAC depot at Moshoeshoe airport, while Senqu Air draws its fuel from Matatiele in the RSA.

Other aircraft operators are the army and the Lesotho Flying Doctor Service, which both draw from the Majametalana Airport where they are supplied by the government.

It is estimated that LAC's monthly fuel bill is of the order of M100,000 (US$40,000). Aviation fuel costs about M1.50 per litre (US$0.6 /litre): LAC consumes on average 70,000 litres in a month or 840,000 litres a year, an annual expense of M1.26 million.

When addressing the question of conservation or efficiency in utilization, a few points can be made: First, for aviation fuel (jet A1) there is no substitute, as there can be for petrol in motor vehicles. This leaves the task of ensuring that energy-efficient airplanes are used. At the moment, however, the planes used by the local carriers can be considered reasonably efficient in fuel consumption. LAC uses the Fokker Friendship F27–600 (a fairly up-to-date aircraft) and De Havilland DHI 400 Twin Otters. Other carriers operating to the country (Air Botswana and Royal Swazi, for example) also utilize efficient equipment, though there would be no means of persuading them to change if they were not. A third factor, optimization in terms of improving passenger loads, could be looked into.

The airline management says in an interview that fuel consumption represents one of the most important running costs and therefore they cannot help but give it close attention. Considering that over the past ten years most airlines have been operating on the margins, and have had to cope with a squeeze in credit facilities due to the economic downturn, it seems that the quest for profitability is in itself an incentive for improved efficiency in operation. Prescriptions therefore seem beside the point. One should also remember that air transport represents only about 3 per cent of all transport in Lesotho. The impact of marginally improved efficiency would thus be negligible.

Road

Road transportation in Lesotho is undertaken by private operators, with very limited parastatal and government participation. Road transport claims fully 77 per cent of all passenger and freight movements in Lesotho. Data are very scanty. Our main sources have been the service station survey conducted by the DOE in 1986 and the *Statistical Yearbook 1988* of the Bureau of Statistics.

Road network

Table 2.6 above shows the increase in the road network within the country. This table only shows the roads for which the Ministry of Works is responsible. There are, in addition, strips of road that are maintained by churches, business people and NGOs. This increase in road network further supports the point made earlier that there has been a shift from air to road transport for local commuting.

Most of the traffic is by public transport, which in the local context means passenger and freight transportation on a commercial basis. According to figures from the Bureau of Statistics, the public transport fleet consists of about 2000 buses and minibuses and 10,500 trucks and vans. Of the vans, about 60 per cent are not in commercial service but are used as family vehicles. The vans range from 700 kg to 2000 kg, while the trucks range from 2000 kg to 11,000 kg. It is therefore important that measures aimed at rationalizing the use of petroleum should focus on the public transport sector.

Fuel consumption by type of vehicle

Tables 2.7a and 2.7b (Department of Energy) show consumption ratios and number of vehicles ratios. Consumption ratios outline the percentages of fuel consumed by categories of vehicle. To illustrate, we can say that 26.88 per cent of petrol is consumed by private cars, while vans account for 33.33 per cent of petrol and 4.23 per cent of diesel, etc.

Similarly, the number of vehicles ratios show the percentages of vehicle categories using either petrol or diesel. The table reveals that all private cars (100 per cent) that were covered in the survey consumed petrol, while 92.63 per cent of minibuses consumed petrol and 7.37 per cent consumed diesel. It should be noted that the category of minibus includes larger vehicles seating up to 25 people. It is these vehicles that comprise the 7.37 per cent utilizing diesel. The 92.63 per cent consists of 11–15 seaters.

Table 2.8 shows the total fleet by type of vehicle in Lesotho. Using the results of the service station survey and additional information available at the Traffic Department and the Bureau of Statistics, the vehicles have been classified by type of fuel consumption – Tables 2.9 and 2.10. The reliability of the data is questionable; it is hoped that the Bureau of Statistics, in conjunction with the Traffic Department, will soon develop a more comprehensive and reliable data base.

A striking but not unusual features of Table 2.9 is that there are no buses, tractors or construction machines that use petrol. Conversely, Table 2.10 shows no motor cycles or motor cars that use diesel. Looking at both tables, it can be seen that more than 60 per cent of the total fleet uses petrol and less than 40 per cent consumes diesel.

Figure 2.1 (Caltex Oil SA) shows the consumption of petroleum products during the years 1982 to 1989. For all products, the table shows a sharp increase in consumption. The figure for aviation fuel soars between 1987 and 1988. This could be due to the increase in international flights as the result of the purchase and use of a Boeing 707 jet in 1988. The drastic drop in aviation fuel in 1989 could to some extent be attributed to the reduced use of the jet, as it stayed idle for a good part of that year until it was disposed of a year later in 1990.

It is extremely difficult to assemble data on the transportation sector and the fleet structure presented here is based on estimates. At present the

Table 2.7a Service station survey – 1986

Type of vehicle	Fuel consumption (%)	
	Petrol	Diesel
Private car	26.88	0
Van	33.33	4.23
Land Rover	17.00	2.09
Tractor	0	17.86
Minibus	18.79	4.92
Bus	0	34.73
Truck	2.15	33.07
Construction machines	0	1.15
Other	1.85	1.95
Total (%)	100.00	100.00

Table 2.7b Service stations survey – 1986

Type of vehicle	Vehicle (%)		
	Petrol	Diesel	Total
Private car	100.00	0	100.00
Van	64.60	35.4	100.00
Land Rover	NA	NA	NA
Tractor	100.00	0	100.00
Minibus	92.63	7.37	100.00
Bus	0	100.00	100.00
Truck	32.18	67.82	100.00
Construction machines	0	100.00	100.00

Department of Transport makes decisions affecting public transport operators without knowing fully the size and other characteristics of the national fleet. The department needs to carry out data collection, validation and compilation as a matter of priority.

Energy institutions and policy interventions

The supply and distribution of petroleum and other oil-based fuels was not controlled by the government until the establishment of the Ministry of Water, Energy and Mining (WEMIN) in 1978. Before that, the oil companies operated as they saw fit and government was not involved. Other responsibilities of the new ministry had rested previously with the Ministry of Works.

WEMIN was made up of three departments: the Department of Water and Sewerage Works, the Department of Mines and Geology, and the Department of Hydrology. There were also plans to establish a Department of Energy. All of these departments had been functional under the Ministry of Works, as

Table 2.8 Number of vehicles by type

Year	Motor-cycles	Motor cars	Vans	Land Rovers	Mini-buses	Buses	Trucks	Tractor	Cons. mach.	Total fleet
1975	221	2413	1835	850	553	192	1322	982	72	8440
1976	249	2607	2029	941	665	206	1457	1004	95	9253
1977	281	2824	2244	1040	787	222	1605	1089	119	10211
1978	315	3064	2481	1150	920	240	1769	1183	146	11268
1979	353	3330	2742	1271	1066	260	1951	1287	175	12435
1980	395	3624	3030	1404	1227	282	2150	1401	207	13720
1981	441	3947	3348	1552	1405	305	2371	1528	243	15140
1982	492	4303	3699	1714	1602	332	2614	1667	283	16706
1983	548	4695	4086	1894	1821	361	2883	1820	327	18435
1984	610	5186	4515	2092	2064	392	3179	1989	376	20403
1985	679	5600	4986	2311	2334	427	3506	2174	431	22448
1986	756	6121	5507	2552	2633	466	3866	2378	491	24770

Table 2.9 Number of vehicles by type consuming petrol

Year	Motor-cycles	Motor cars	Vans	Land Rovers	Mini-buses	Buses	Trucks	Tractor	Cons. mach.	Total fleet
1975	221	2413	1734	782	512	0	425	0	0	6087
1976	249	2607	1918	865	616	0	469	0	0	6724
1977	281	2824	2121	956	729	0	517	0	0	7428
1978	315	3064	2345	1057	852	0	569	0	0	8202
1979	353	3330	2592	1168	987	0	628	0	0	9058
1980	395	3624	2864	1291	1136	0	692	0	0	10002
1981	441	3947	3165	1426	1301	0	763	0	0	11043
1982	492	4303	3497	1576	1484	0	841	0	0	12193
1983	548	4695	3863	1741	1687	0	928	0	0	13462
1984	610	5126	4267	1923	1912	0	1023	0	0	14861
1985	679	5600	4713	2124	2162	0	1128	0	0	16406
1986	756	6121	5206	2346	2439	0	1244	0	0	18112

Table 2.10 Number of vehicle by types consuming diesel

Year	Motor-cycles	Motor cars	Vans	Land Rovers	Mini-buses	Buses	Trucks	Tractor	Cons. mach.	Total fleet
1975	0	0	100	69	41	192	897	982	72	2353
1976	0	0	111	86	49	204	988	1004	95	2537
1977	0	0	125	88	58	282	1089	1089	119	2850
1978	0	0	136	98	68	240	1200	1183	146	3071
1979	0	0	180	103	79	260	1383	1287	175	3467
1980	0	0	166	114	90	282	1458	1401	207	3718
1981	0	0	183	118	104	205	1608	1528	243	3989
1982	0	0	208	139	118	332	1773	1667	283	4520
1983	0	0	224	153	134	361	1855	1820	327	4874
1984	0	0	247	89	152	392	2186	1989	376	5431
1985	0	0	273	87	172	427	2376	2147	431	6913
1986	0	0	301	296	194	466	2672	2578	491	6998

Source for tables 2.8, 2.9, 2.10: Department of Energy

Figure 2·1 Petroleum product consumption

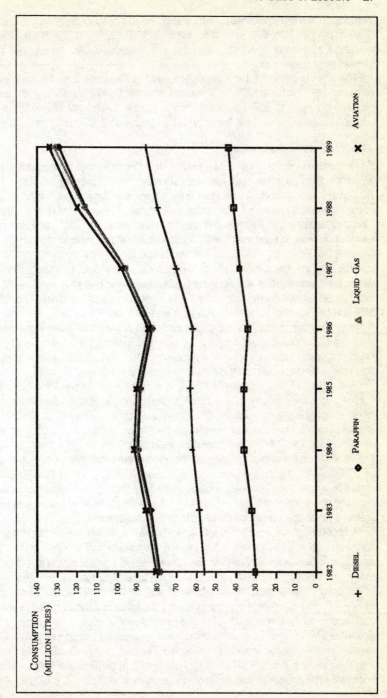

branches if not as departments, with the exception of Energy. A search through the Ministry of Works does not reveal even a single file that was specifically assigned to energy matters – an absence echoed in the records of other government ministries.

The energy crisis of 1973 brought a sudden awakening to the seriousness of the energy problem. The government now initiated a number of measures, perhaps the most significant of which was the establishment of a Cabinet sub-committee on oil, pointing the way to the creation of an energy portfolio.

The Inter-state Committee

At the time of the 1973 oil crisis, there existed an informal arrangement under which the BLS countries had access to oil products purchased by the RSA. These BLS states were involved in neither the sourcing nor the pricing for the retailing of the petroleum resources. The understanding ultimately rested on the Customs Union agreement which they had entered into with the RSA. The Southern African Customs Union Agreement (SACUA) dates back to pre-independence days and has been revised on a continuing basis to accommodate changing economic and commercial circumstances. The principal features of SACUA are a free flow of goods, commodities and services (excluding those that may be classified by agreement) within the member states, and a common external tariff. The RSA is effectively a senior partner in this agreement by virtue of its being the principal economy in the region. Having greater exposure to the world petroleum markets than the BLS countries, the RSA was a natural leader of the SACUA group in instituting petroleum conservation measures. The BLS countries took their cue from there, and introduced their own and similar measures.

With the 1973 oil crisis, the SACUA members recognized the need for a body to focus specifically on control of the sourcing, pricing and distribution of the oil product. Accordingly, the Inter-state Committee was established with a mandate to coordinate the policies and activities of SACUA member states in the oil sector. This sub-committee held meetings twice a year, at which information on the current oil market situation was exchanged. A rationalization of institutional policies was also undertaken, with the aim of bringing about stability in the local oil distribution network, taking into consideration the position of the international oil markets. An example of this function is the oil slate, or petroleum retail price stabilization mechanism.

A theoretical stable retail price, x, is agreed on, which roughly averages the international market prices, allowing for fluctuations. The slate price x may be at a point lower or higher than the actual market price, e.g. $x = m + 2$ (where m = market price). The stabilization fund has an account into which the surplus is deposited when there is an over-recovery at the retail point (at price $x = m+2$). Likewise, when the price is below the current market price ($x = m-2$) and there is an under-recovery, the difference is met from the stabilization fund account. The aim of the slate stabilization system is to keep prices relatively stable even when the market is unstable. The Inter-state Committee ensures that this position holds in all member states, with minimum disruptions in other sectors of the economy due to frequent changes in the oil price.

Cabinet oil sub-committee

As the intricacies of the situation unfolded, the government of Lesotho established, for purposes of addressing the petroleum crisis, a Cabinet sub-committee on oil. The sub-committee had rather vague terms of reference which compromised its usefulness. It was supposed to assess the petroleum situation and report on developments to Cabinet, but without having to meet set deadlines in carrying out this urgent task. While it could give the impression of being some kind of crisis committee, studying the present crisis and making recommendations as appropriate, it also had the potential to be permanent.

As the practicalities of work emerged, it became necessary to reduce this committee to an operational level with the appointment of a permanent sub-committee partly staffed by civil servants attached to various ministries, which would have enough time to give thorough attention to the issues raised. This committee was to be coordinated from the Cabinet Office through the Office of the Senior Permanent Secretary (SPS), the head of the civil service, with the Deputy Senior Permanent Secretary (DSPS) specifically designated to this task. His other responsibilities in the Cabinet Office, however, were too pressing to permit him to develop the permanent sub-commitee into an effectively functioning body, while the constant turnover of civil servants appointed to the sub-committee by various ministries made his task all the more difficult. The government continued to address issues in an ad-hoc manner. Despite this background, however, in 1973 Lesotho introduced its first legislation to regulate conservation, the Fuel and Services Control Act.

The Fuel and Services Control Act was necessitated by a series of conservation measures proposed by the RSA which required legal enforcement to be effective. The point to be borne in mind here is that Lesotho (and the other BLS countries) were following the lead of the dominant SACUA member at a time when their own awareness of the problem was inadequate. The conservation measures proposed at this point had two features: to restrict the sale of petroleum to 66 hours a week and to restrict the speed limit to 90 kilometres per hour, while at the same time forbidding the possession of portable fuel supplies.

It would appear that it was around the time of the formalization of the Interstate Committee, and with it the coordination of petroleum distribution and retailing, that the need for greater control of the petroleum industry was recognized – along with the inappropriateness of the Cabinet Office for the task. The new Ministry of Water, Energy and Mining (WEMIN), which we have mentioned, was to assume this task. The Cabinet sub-committee was subsequently dissolved, as is explained below.

Creation of the Ministry of Water, Energy and Mining

WEMIN was formed, as we have seen, from three former branches now separated from the Ministry of Works. The mines and geology branch became the Department of Mines and Geology, the hydrology branch became the Department of Water Affairs, and the Department of Water and Sewerage was formed from the old branch of the same name. These departments were headed by directors who reported to the office of the Principal Secretary as shown in Figure 2.2.

Each department consists of different sections. At the time, however, the structure for the DOE was not fully developed. The new structure shown in Figure 2.2 only came into being with the energy institution building project in 1985.

The mandate on control and monitoring of petroleum distribution and retailing, and on implementing the Legal Notice Number 34 of 1974 (which was to give effect to the Fuel and Services Control Act 1973) was not entrusted to a department, a division, or even a special desk for petroleum in WEMIN. Instead it was handed to an individual who, by coincidence, was Deputy Permanent Secretary in WEMIN. We can conclude that this was by coincidence because, when the designated officer left the Ministry, the responsibility was taken over by a civil servant who held a different office. Thus, even at this stage, government had not seen the need to firm-up the mandate on petroleum. Even with the creation of the DOE, the petroleum mandate remained with an officer on the headquarters staff of WEMIN. The mandate was only transferred to the DOE in 1986.

To the extent that petroleum was imported, and so represented a foreign exchange cost to the economy, it would seem that government should have taken measures to strengthen the institutional approach to its management, aiming to involve government and private institutions that control or are primary users of the resource. In this connection, the Ministries of Transport and Commerce, for example, should have been involved in the planning exercises. Equally, as the purchase of the resource represented a measure of financial expenditure, the Ministries of Economic Planning and of Finance should have been consulted. In the period immediately after the establishment of WEMIN, the Cabinet sub-committee continued to function. It might have complemented the functions of the Ministry by giving wider recognition to the importance of the petroleum issue to development. The structural weaknesses mentioned earlier prevented the sub-committee from playing this role, however.

Petroleum supply emergencies

In the end, the function of the sub-committee came to be split between routine work and fire-fighting in times of emergencies, with little attention paid to planning for the development and the strengthening of its mandate. The routine activities included attending inter-state committee meetings, often with minimal pre-meeting briefings.

Among the emergency activities that were a function of the sub-committee one can cite discussions on alternatives for sourcing petroleum at a time when relations with the RSA became strained. Along with the problem of sourcing petroleum, the sub-committee discussed the question of the establishment of strategic oil reserves to provide a buffer in the event of sanctions by the RSA as a reaction to Lesotho's strong criticism of the RSA's internal policies at the time. This contingency was always a real possibility for the pre-1986 government, which had acrimonious relations with the RSA due to the latter's internal policies. When the threat of an emergency seemed to be averted, considerations such as the above received no further attention.

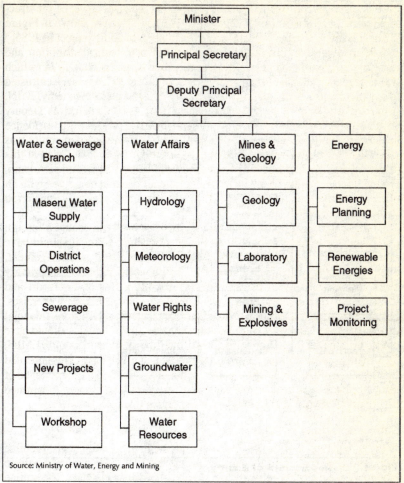

Source: Ministry of Water, Energy and Mining

Figure 2.2   Ministry of Water, Energy and Mining

Multi-sectoral considerations

When the Cabinet Office retained its dominance over the sub-committee and, therefore, the leading role in energy matters, it was at the expense of the role of the newly created WEMIN, and of efficient and continuous planning in this sector. In a memorandum on the matter, the Deputy Principal Secretary of WEMIN commented on the frustration of having decisions taken by officers who had very little grasp of the issues being decided on, while those with a grasp had a peripheral role: 'You will appreciate that ours is a ministry in an awkward position, whereby it has maximum accountability but minimum control' (Ministry of Water, Energy and Mining).

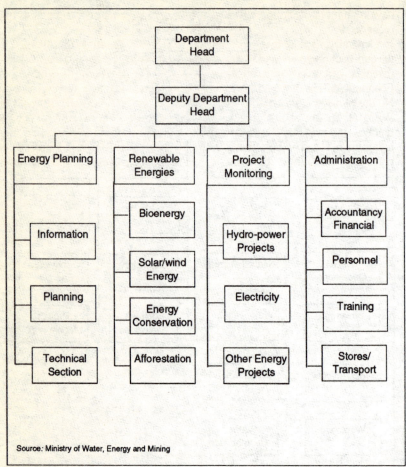

Source: Ministry of Water, Energy and Mining

Figure 2.3   Department of Energy

From the point of view of a well coordinated plan, there are, as mentioned earlier, a number of institutions which should be involved in all preparations. If Figure 2.4 is to be followed, at least all ministries tasked with developing and maintaining the economic infrastructure area should have been involved. It is striking, however, that during the period of the oil sub-committee's dominance, very few institutions played an active part in energy matters. With the establishment of the sub-committee, the following ministries became members: Works, Economic Planning, Finance, Foreign, with Cabinet Office chairing. One would hope that the identification was accurately made, consisting of ministries with a likely influence in the development of economic infrastructure. It is, however, worth noting that the Ministry of Transport and Communications was excluded from this list of participants. In this respect, one is led to conclude that the importance of the transport sector in the development of economic infrastructure and as an energy consumer was not recognized.

Generally, an examination of the performance of the ministries involved in the sub-committee, including discussions with officials from these ministries, reveals a very scanty regard for energy issues. The Ministry of Planning and Economic Affairs only participated in the sub-committee in an ad hoc manner. No desk was given a specific mandate for energy until the establishment of WEMIN. There was thus no section of the Ministry that focused on energy matters, and indeed this was reflected in its participation in the Cabinet sub-committee. The only time that the Ministry of Planning played a prominent part was when Lesotho refused to recognize the independence of the Transkei

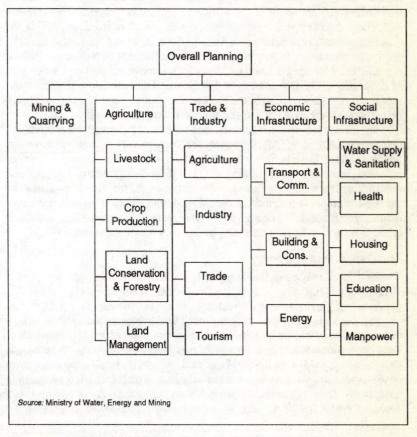

Source: Ministry of Water, Energy and Mining

Figure2.4 National planning

bantustan in 1976, and the RSA reacted by sealing off part of the border which ran through Transkei. The Ministry of Planning participated in discussions that were held at the time on establishing a strategic oil reserve under the UN Special Assistance Programme (SEAP). Apart from this, the Ministry of Planning's role appears to have been a peripheral one, notwithstanding its mandate to coordinate development efforts in the economy.

The Ministry of Finance, despite its involvement in the sub-committee, seems to have had no distinct role in energy issues. A more forceful presence might have been expected in the light of expenditures on fuel and, particularly, the foreign exchange cost. The Ministry of Transport and Communications, excluded from the sub-committee as we have seen, perhaps did not seek a role for itself. A 1980 'Lesotho Transportation Study' by Dorsch Consult GmbH, was undertaken on behalf of the Ministry. The study included fleet analysis and reflected on petroleum consumption patterns and means of improving the efficient utilization of petroleum. Though the issues were well presented, the proposals were never followed up and it is possible that nobody ever read the report. Part of the reason could be a very high turnover of staff and hence lack of continuity in the Department of Traffic and Transportation. Copies of the report are still stacked high in the Department, but because it was never used, no parts of it were ever revised and it is now totally out of date.

The Cabinet sub-committee continued functioning even after the establishment of the DOE in WEMIN. Its meetings became very infrequent, however, and in 1985 the Deputy Senior Permanent Secretary was assigned to another post, thus removing the remaining hinge of the sub-committee. The post was not filled and soon after abolished, and with it went the function of coordinating the sub-committee – and, indeed, the sub-committee itself, though it was never officially disbanded. The change in government in 1986 ensured that, at Cabinet level, there was to be no continuing tradition of the oil sub-committee.

The Department of Energy

The DOE itself only came into being in 1985. As an institution building project with a limited staff component, it started to draw up an energy masterplan aimed at bringing out the inter-sectoral linkages of the energy equation, and to carry out a dissemination programme. The department suffered from lack of staff and was not able to achieve the progress it had hoped for. This lack of local professional staff has been a problem of most energy projects and needs to be addressed (Mohapeloa and Lebesa, 1990). In particular, the manpower development programme was behind schedule, which restricted progress in other fields. The situation has improved, however, to the point of having a staff component of about 80 per cent, with the manpower development programme well under way.

The DOE was given a mandate to undertake the following tasks:
- Establish medium- and long-term national energy plans by forecasting future demand for commercial and non-commercial energy and by optimizing the alternative supply options.
- Determine feasible energy strategies aimed at extensive use of local

energy resources and at import substitution of commercial energy.
- Promote the institutionalization of new and renewable resources of energy.
- Monitor all projects studied and carried out in the energy sector.

To carry out the responsibilities that are part of this wide coordinating role, the Department must, for example, ensure that building standards accommodate energy efficiency, and that technical standards in industry include energy efficiency. Thus the department has to obtain representation on various building and industry licensing committees. In addition, the department has, under its Energy Planning Division, an information section. This section has, among other responsibilities, the function of disseminating information on various aspects of the energy strategies adopted. It also has the capacity to run campaigns on energy conservation.

Up to the present only one demand management measure has been adopted in the country – Legal Notice No. 34 of 1974, which, as we have seen, gave effect to the Fuel and Services Control Act of the previous year. The effectiveness of these measures has never been known as government was not monitoring implementation. The control measure used in Lesotho during the blockade by the RSA in 1986 took the form of permits issued for petrol and diesel purchase upon application to WEMIN. The system was set up on the spur of the moment and was not designed to meet any objectives other than the immediate one of reducing the rate of petroleum utilization to stretch the supply until the border problem with the RSA had been resolved. It is worth noting that, even though the DOE had been established in 1985, this permit system was operated by WEMIN in January 1986. Again, the effectiveness of this measure was not known as there had been no targets against which the government was operating. The blockade, in any event, was soon lifted, thus obviating the need to control access to petroleum.

The other demand management mechanism is dissemination campaigns to educate people on the importance of practising conservation and thus appealing for self-restraint. This method was not used, however.

At this point the DOE would seem to have the potential to be effective in influencing the pattern of utilization of energy resources and, in particular, petroleum use in the transportation sector through focusing on educating the consumer and not acting as a policeman. The only requirement is that the department should not relent in awareness campaigns and should continue with surveys to bring a close understanding of the full extent of the problem being addressed, as well as monitor the effectiveness of the measures adopted.

Policy options for petroleum conservation

General

The need for petroleum conservation is now well documented, with an abundance of evidence of the adverse effects when conservation is neglected. Initially, we had the crisis of 1973 followed by that of 1979, which shocked the whole world. Many developing countries are now experiencing a strain on foreign exchange reserves, without a corresponding increase in productivity to compensate for the foreign exchange shortfall. In many cases this has disrupted the pace of development. And yet, the question of cash flow is not the only consideration. Injudicious or excessive use of energy resources also has serious environmental consequences.

The researcher who has recognized these problems and is seeking to make concrete recommendations is confronted by the question: what policy instruments should be singled out for use? The instruments available to any regulatory body range from fiscal (using price to influence demand) to physical (placing restrictions on the quantities available to the public). Among the less conventional methods suggested are a massive conservation awareness campaign to encourage self-restraint, and incentives for people who opt for energy-efficient motor vehicles. A more conventional measure, which on the surface appears likely to be the most effective, would be to levy a higher duty on petroleum and thus push the price higher. To this measure could be added restricting petrol sales hours and perhaps, going further, restricting the quantity that an individual may purchase at any one time. These various measures address the question of access to the product, whether the approach is fiscal (the former) or physical (the latter).

The strength of these measures lies in being able to control the supply of the product in absolute terms. In the case of Lesotho, the following issues should be taken into consideration:

1. Because of its location, Lesotho has easy physical access to RSA markets.
2. Because of the SACUA arrangement, access to these markets is not quantity-restricted generally; and
3. Because of the Rand Monetary Agreement, Lesotho residents also have financial access to these markets.

All these factors lead to a significant volume of cross-border trade. If a high price differential is introduced in retail petrol prices between the two markets, this trade will be accelerated. Vehicle owners can fill up their tanks across the border, and nobody can control that kind of import.

As a conservation measure, it has been suggested that an effort should be made to influence the buying of motor vehicles, so that the national fleet would comprise conservative consumers in the form of diesel-powered vehicles or those below a certain engine displacement capacity (e.g. 2 litres in petrol-driven vehicles). A discriminatory or incentive tax could be levied against vehicles that do not meet these criteria. The reasoning here is that private motor vehicles under, say, a 2-litre engine displacement would consume considerably less than makes with a capacity of over 2 litres. For example, figures from one manufacturer show a 10 per cent petrol consumption differential between their own 1.8 litre and 2.0 litre motor vehicles at a steady 120 k.p.h. Assuming a 10 per cent saving in petrol consumption, and a consumption of 43 million litres in 1989, the saving would equal 4.3 million litres or M5.2 million at retail, which is 0.3 per cent of GNP. Similarly, a diesel-powered vehicle achieves more kilometres per litre than the petrol-driven version. In both these instances, the net result is lower fuel consumption than the present level. Upon reflection, however, doubts appear as to the ease of implementing a discriminatory levy which would mean a higher purchase price, duty or sales tax. The Department of Traffic and Transportation, which is responsible for the registration of motor vehicles, say they would have difficulty in enforcing such a measure, as vehicle owners could register their vehicles in one of the neighbouring states to by-pass the levy, in spite of the fact that there is national legislation obliging resident car owners to register imported cars locally after a certain length of time.

Constraints, control and action

Free cross-border trade

During the 1989/90 fiscal year, as part of the Structural Adjustment Programme of the IMF, a discriminatory levy was imposed on motor vehicles classified as luxury motor vehicles in an effort to curb national expenditure. A 25 per cent sales tax was levied on motor vehicles costing more than M30,000. Following this, there was a marked increase in the number of restricted motor vehicles with foreign registration, while the sales tax department was registering a drop in revenue. The Department of Traffic and Transportation, meanwhile, recorded a marked drop in vehicle registrations. It was quite clear what was happening. Motor vehicle owners continued to buy vehicles of their choice in excess of M30,000 and simply registered in the neighbouring countries. The government subsequently abandoned the high sales tax rates. In a sense, this underlines the constraints on independent government action.

Because of the free flow of goods and services within the customs area, the vehicles that deliver these goods and services are not subjected to thorough daily checks at border crossings, unless it is suspected that a criminal offence is being committed by the occupants of such a vehicle. In other words, a vehicle is not declared upon arrival and, hence, it is difficult to establish when it first entered the country and at what point the driver/owner may be called upon to declare whether he is re-exporting or registering the car. The system at present does not treat vehicles from the neighbouring countries as imports and, therefore, monitoring of the length of stay is difficult.

Declaring vehicles upon crossing international boundaries is the usual practice and was, therefore, considered as the obvious means of enforcing local registration. The Department of Transport explains that this practice was not pursued because their investigations revealed that:

1. Given the volume of cross-border trade, it would cause inconvenience by slowing down traffic flows.
2. The slowing down of traffic flows could be construed as a violation of the principle of free flow of goods and services embodied in the SACUA agreement.
3. Similar action by neighbouring countries could be very disruptive to Lesotho's daily economic activities.

It seems, for the time being, that this method of discrimination against owners of less fuel-efficient vehicles cannot be implemented. However, commercially registered vehicles – licensed passenger carriers, hauliers, etc. – could still be given a special incentive, as they have to register locally to be licensed. This incentive is lost to private vehicle owners who do not use their vehicles commercially, are not licensed as such, and, therefore, do not need local registration to operate their vehicles on a daily basis.

If we take 1986 figures as an example, which show that out of 20,322 registered vehicles, 13,244 were commercial – trucks, buses and vans – it would seem likely that this number can be converted fairly readily to diesel engines using adequate incentives to owners. Diesel engines are already more common in commercial vehicles, and it seems that giving incentives to owners of commercial fleets to opt for diesel would be an appropriate strategy providing clear-cut results. An incentive package could be introduced in the form, perhaps, of reduced sales tax on purchasing a new vehicle. The effectiveness of this approach, however, would be undermined by the non-availability of diesel powered vehicles in a major sector of the market. The minibus taxis – carrying 15 passengers and less – which account for over 90 per cent of urban public transport, are models that do not have diesel-driven engines.

Vehicle market

The minibus makes that are used as taxis in the South African market are Toyota, Nissan, Isuzu and, to a lesser extent, Volkswagen. None of these makes fits diesel engines in its South African production line, and Lesotho accounts for such a small slice of the market that it would not be cost-effective for the producer to meet its specific needs. For example, the South African Black Taxi Association buys 500 Toyota Hi-Aces per month, while one of Lesotho's two dealers, Pioneer Motors, sells 18 per annum (Pioneer Motors). When we have added to this an equal number assumed sold by the other dealer, and some purchases from RSA dealers, Lesotho's share of the market remains insignificant. Even fewer family cars are fitted with diesel engines, as mentioned earlier. Volkswagen used to produce diesel engines for the Golf, but has since discontinued production for the South African market. This leaves only Mercedes Benz in this sector of the market and the high price restricts the number of people who can avail themselves of the technology.

Some new prospects

An option that remains, and does not carry the traditional punitive connotations, is that of calling for voluntary conservation. This means mounting a vigorous dissemination campaign, stressing the importance of petroleum conservation and how it can be achieved. The benefits would be shown as savings on the national scale, with improvement of individual or company cash flows.

The dissemination programme would include such areas as driving and traffic control practices, and thus urge the public and traffic authorities to support the following measures:

- Reduce petrol consumption by curbing driving habits such as fast take-offs, sudden stops, and staying in low gears for too long.
- Avoid peak periods and save petrol (consumption is increased by bumper-to-bumper driving during traffic jams).
- Design roads to permit a free flow of traffic.
- Synchronize traffic lights; introduce yield signs where stop signs are not strictly necessary; and provide adequate parking spaces to prevent double parking and the congestion caused by motorists hunting for parking.
- Stagger working hours and plan delivery schedules to avoid peak-hour congestion.
- Pool transport and opt for public transport where suitable.

It will be vital to the success of such a programme to win the support, cooperation and participation of all employers and fleet owners. The point to build on here is that there is probably more goodwill in the public than we commonly believe: the right approach will gain their backing.

The peculiar geopolitical situation of Lesotho means that all conservation codes and regulations should be checked closely for feasibility of implementation. Easy financial and physical access to RSA markets is a constraint on independent action in this field. Lesotho must identify means uniquely suited to its situation. It is clear that, until now, the DOE has not focused on energy use in transportation. This is because, in its few years of existence, it has targeted industry, households and related areas as priorities. It is clear that improved utilization of petroleum should be the main objective, since there seems to be rather limited scope for reducing consumption by other means. An effort should be made to maximize the value generated per unit of petroleum consumed. Further, the DOE should study the methods used by Lesotho's neighbours.

Finally, it should be underlined that, because of Lesotho's unusual setting, its most accessible instruments are those that citizens will support voluntarily. The key, therefore, is an effective energy conservation dissemination campaign. The function of the DOE in this regard should be seen as catalytic, focusing more on information than on regulatory functions. The overall aim should be to make the consumer a part of the energy demand management drive and not an object of it. This more dynamic approach also seems best suited to Lesotho's conditions.

Note

The economic data from this chapter is from the Ministry of Planning, Economic and Manpower Development.

Appendix: Petroleum Pricing Components and Formulae

1. FOB: based on BP, Shell, Mobil and Caltex posted price at Singapore.
2. Freight.
3. Insurance: 0.1009 per cent of the FOB plus freight (1 + 2).
4. CIF (1 + 2 + 3).
5. Ocean leakage: 0.3 per cent of CIF.
6. Landing/Wharfage: 1.8 per cent of FOB.
7. Coastal storage.
8. Railage Durban/Maseru.
9. In-bond landed cost (4 + 5 + 6 + 7 + 8).
10. Margin: 12 per cent of IBLC (9).
11. Levy (Lesotho impost).
12. Rounding.
13. Basic price (9 + 10 + 11 + 12).
14. Duty.
15. Depot Storage/Handling.
16. Road delivery.
17. Price ex-Maseru Depot (13 + 14 + 15 + 16).
18. Dealer margin.
19. Road delivery to sales zones.
20. Retail price (17 + 18 + 19).

Data Sources

Bureau of Statistics. (1988). *Annual Statistical Bulletin*.
Caltex Oil (SA) (Pty) Ltd.
Department of Energy.
Department of Mines and Geology.
Dothunts'ane, L. (1989). 'Strategic oil supply and storage', paper delivered at STCC Petroleum and Transportation Seminar. Ministry of Agriculture. Woodlot Project.
Ministry of Planning, Economic and Manpower Development.
Ministry of Water, Energy and Mining.
Ministry of Works – Planning Section.
Lebesa, M. and Mohapeloa, L. (1990). 'The efficiency of foreign technical assistance in manpower development in Lesotho', in AFREPREN, *African Energy Policies – Issues, Planning and Practice*, AFREPREN/Zed Books, pp. 127–131.
Pioneer Motors (Toyota dealer).
SEAP.
Service Station Rationalization Committee.
Shell Lesotho.

Abbreviations

BOS	Bureau of Statistics
CIF	Cost, Insurance, Freight
DOE	Department of Energy
DSPS	Deputy Senior Permanent Secretary
ESCOM	Electricity Supply Commission
FOB	Free on Board

GDP	Gross Domestic Product
GNP	Gross National Product
GOL	Government of Lesotho
IBLC	In-Bond Landed Cost
IMF	International Monetary Fund
LAC	Lesotho Airways Corporation
LEC	Lesotho Electricity Commission
LHWP	Lesotho Highlands Water Project
M	Maluti
OPEC	Organization of Petroleum Exporting Countries
RMA	Rand Monetary Area
RSA	Republic of South Africa
SACU	Southern African Customs Union
SAP	Structural Adjustment Programme
SEAP	UN Special Assistance Programme
SFF	Synthetic Fuel Fund
SPS	Senior Permanent Secretary
UN	United Nations
WEMIN	Ministry of Water, Energy and Mining

3 The Case of Ethiopia

M. Teferra

Ethiopia is endowed with vast energy resources, including biomass, coal, geothermal sources, natural gas and solar energy. The gross hydro-energy potential of the country is estimated at 650 TWh per year (CESEN, 1985) of which 25 per cent could be exploited for power. Between 30 and 50 billion cubic meters of natural gas, more than 1000 MW of geothermal power, several hundred million tons of coal, and oil shale constitute the energy potential so far discovered. The total solar radiation reaching the territory is 2.3 million TWh / year, while annual wind energy is estimated to be 4,800,000 Tcal/ year (CESEN ,1985). The country's woody biomass energy resource is 14 million Tcal in standing stock and 930,000 Tcal in terms of annual yield. The yearly agricultural waste available for energy is about 176,000 Tcal / year. Traces of uranium and other radioactive minerals have been found in several regions. Ninety-five per cent of the total energy consumed is derived from traditional energy resources such as fuelwood, dung, crop residues, and human and animal power. The 5 per cent balance is supplied by electricity and oil products. Electricity supply is wholly from local generating stations, with hydro-electricity accounting for about 82 per cent of supply. Oil supplies, on the other hand, are imported, whether in the form of crude or refined products.

The major consumer of energy is the household sector, which takes 82 per cent of the total energy supplied. The transport sector utilizes more than 70 per cent of imported oil while agriculture uses only 3 per cent. The prime objective of the energy policy is to enhance the reliance on indigenous sources of energy wherever such measures prove economically sound, technically feasible and environmentally sustainable.

Ethiopia's transport system includes approximately 3,700 km of asphalt roads, 8,700 km of gravel roads, 5,000 km of rural roads and 20,000 km of dry weather roads, two ports at the Red sea, 780 km of railway line linking Addis Ababa and the port of Djibouti, four international airports and about 30 scattered airfields and airstrips (1988/9). The contribution of the transport sector to GDP is only about 7 per cent despite its great potential. It has, in fact, been inadequate to support an effective production and distribution system. It is particularly poorly developed in the agriculturally rich west, south and south-eastern regions of the country. A serious lack of links between adjacent regions hinders the development of a strong integrated national economy.

The road transport sector handles over 90 per cent of passenger and freight traffic in the country. However, the provision of an efficient road transport system has been made difficult and expensive by the country's large geographical area, rugged topography, severe climatic conditions and widely dispersed population. The country has a road density of only about 0.9 km per 1000 people, virtually the lowest in Africa where the weighted mean is 2.6 km. Density per 1000 square km is only 39 km, also well below the continental mean which is 58 km.

The Ministry of Transport and Communications, which oversees the development of the road sector, is currently structured into four major sub-sectors: Surface transport, sea transport, air transport and communications. According to the 1987/8 figures, a total of 62,540 vehicles were registered in the country (excluding military vehicles), out of which 46 per cent were private automobiles, 29 per cent commercial passenger and freight vehicles, and the rest government-owned non-commercial vehicles. This study deals with both commercial and non-commercial road transport vehicles.

The commercial road transport service is closely regulated and controlled by the government. The Road Transport Authority, a regulatory organ of the Ministry of Transport and Communications, sets and enforces tariffs, determines routes, licenses vehicles and generally regulates the road transport operations. Actual freight and passenger transport are conducted by Freight Transport Corporation (FTC) and Public Transport Corporation (PTC) respectively. Both of these corporations are autonomous entities under the Ministry of Transport and Communications.

Commercial road transport sub-sector

Operational aspects

Passenger transport

The passenger transport service comprises urban and regional services. The urban service is provided by government-owned buses and privately owned taxis, while the regional service is provided by small, medium and big buses owned by government and private associates.

In Addis Ababa there are currently a total of 247 buses with a standard capacity of 100 persons. City bus service is provided in three other cities, namely Asmara, Jima and Matsawa. There are only 32 buses in Asmara, 5 in Jima, and 3 in Matsawa. With regard to Addis Ababa's city bus service, a survey conducted in 1985 revealed that only 12 per cent of daily trips were handled by buses, while walking accounts for the lion's share of 70 per cent (CESEN, 1985). In Addis Ababa the number of buses per 1000 persons is only 0.15. The average for other African cities of similar population size like Abidjan (1.7 million), Accra (1.4 million) and Nairobi (1.2 million) has been calculated to be 0.7 per 1000 inhabitants (Jorgenson, 1983).

The city bus service was operated by private shareholders until it was nationalized in 1974. Since then, the government has attempted to improve the service by increasing the fleet size and strengthening the maintenance section. The most dominant models are Fiat, Mercedes and Volvo (Public Transport Corporation). Although these vehicles are well known for their sturdiness, most of them could not effectively service their economic life due to overloading and poor road conditions. It is customary for these buses to carry 150–200 per cent of their specified capacities.

The existing tariff (15 Ethiopian cents per trip) has not been changed since its introduction in 1956, except for the elimination of the 25 cents round-trip

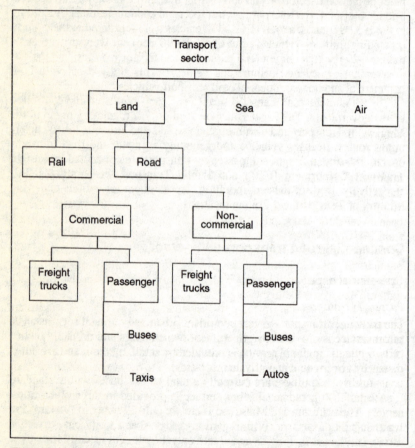

Figure 3.1 Structure of road transport in Ethiopia

ticket and the shortening of a few of the longer routes by half. The cost of buses, spare parts and fuel increased considerably in these years. The ex-refinery price of diesel (gas oil) has also increased from 8.75 cents/litre in 1971 to 52.75 cents/litre in 1990 (EPC). The government has opted to subsidize the service rather than introducing cost-based tariff. Accordingly, buses are

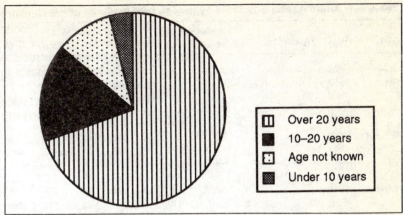

Figure 3.2 Age of Addis Ababa city taxis – % of total of city population

imported free of duties, and diesel – which currently costs 76 cents per litre in Addis Ababa – is purchased at 69 cents by the PTC.

The focus of the service effort has mainly been on purchasing new and improved model buses and strengthening the maintenance branch. Accordingly, the existing garages have been updated and one modern garage costing over 15 million birr is nearing completion. In total, a sum of 87 million birr has been invested for construction of garages and purchase of buses and spare parts from 1980 to 1988. Attempts were also made to introduce a trolley bus service in the city but this alternative has not progressed beyond the study stage. The municipality of Addis Ababa, the probable future administrator of the city buses, is also closely following a study which looks into the possibilities of a light rail transit service to the city.

Taxis are owned and operated by private citizens. A total of 17 cities are currently providing taxi services for their inhabitants. Five cities for which information could be obtained have a total of about 5200 taxis. These taxis are of two types: the short-distance taxis, with 4 seats capacity, and the long-distance taxis, with capacities ranging from 5 to 12 seats. The small taxis constitute over 70 per cent of the total fleet.

Availability of data on taxis in Addis Ababa permits a better analysis of the service. There are a total of 4400 short- and long-distance taxis (1985 figures) which handle about 10 per cent of all daily trips performed in the city (CESEN, 1985). The service is currently organized in a zonal system of operation whereby taxis are required to operate only on assigned routes and at a fixed tariff. The long-distance taxis serve on distances of about 7 km while the short distance taxis shuttle within 5 km limits. There are about 18 different models of taxis, and 59 per cent of all taxis are Fiats. The age structure of the existing fleet is an area of real concern. As Table 3.1 and Figure 3.2 show, about 80 per cent of the Addis Ababa taxis are over 20 years old while only 4 per cent of them are less than 10 years old.

Table 3.1: Addis Ababa city taxis by model, type and age group

Model	Type	\	\	\	Age group	\	\	\	\	\	\
		0–5	6–10	11–15	16–20	21–25	26–30	30+	NA	Total	%
	Big	–	–	–	–	17	101	–	1	119	
Fiat	Small	–	–	–	–	9	892	1038	224	2163	
	Total	–	–	–	–	26	993	1038	225	2282	51.8
	Big	–	168	–	–	334	–	–	–	502	
Peugeot	Small	–	–	.	–	37	–	162	1	200	
	Total	–	168	–	–	371	–	162	1	702	15.9
	Big	5	12	266	–	–	1	–	5	289	
Toyota	Small	–	–	–	–	8	13	179	77	277	
	Total	5	12	266	–	8	14	179	82	566	12.9
	Big	–	–	33	39	–	63	–	19	154	
Datsun	Small	–	–	–	10	–	19	–	19	48	
	Total	–	–	33	49	–	82	–	38	202	4.6
	Big	–	–	105	–	–	–	–	–	105	
Mazda	Small	–	–	1	–	5	–	–	–	6	
	Total	–	–	106	–	5	–	–	–	111	2.5
	Big	–	–	–	–	–	–	5	–	5	
Opel	Small	–	–	–	–	–	–	70	3	73	
	Total	–	–	–	–	–	–	75	3	78	1.8
	Big	–	–	12	–	–	–	–	–	12	
Ford	Small	–	–	–	–	–	–	53	–	53	
	Total	–..	–	12	–	–	–	53	–	65	1.5
	Big	–	–	–	–	–	–	–	–	–	
Lada	Small	–	–	–	–	–	112	47	–	159	
	Total	–	–	–	–	–	112	47	–	159	3.6
	Big	–	–	–	–	–	–	170	–	170	
VW	Small	–	–	–	–	–	–	–	–	–	
	Total	–	–	–	–	–	–	170	–	170	3.9
	Big	–	–	1	11	1	5	–	3	21	
Others	Small	–	–	–	5	28	7	4	2	46	
	Total	–	–	1	16	29	12	4	5	67	1.5
	Big	5	180	417	50	352	170	175	28	1,377	31.3
Total	Small	–	–	1	15	87	1,043	1,553	326	3,025	68.7
	Total	5	180	418	65	439	1,213	1,728	354	4,402	–
%		0.1	4.1	9.5	1.5	10.0	27.0	39.0	8.0	–	100

Source: Public Transport Corporation, 1989

There exists a dire need to replace these old taxis if the service is to continue unabated. Taxi riding now is becoming dangerous as many taxis operate below an acceptable level of safety. Many taxis have faulty indicators, horns and brakes. As most doors don't close tight, it is not uncommon to see them opening wide as taxis take sharp turns. Most of these taxis are still operating thanks to the high creative capacity of the private maintenance sector. Although there is an obvious shortage of foreign currency for spare parts, most of the taxis are obsolete models for which spare parts could not be found in any case. The 1985 liquidation of Fiat Sacafet, a major spare parts importing company for Fiat model vehicles in Ethiopia, has further aggravated the situation. The company was closed down mainly for reasons of insufficient foreign currency allocation for the importation of spare parts .

Leonchinas are privately owned medium and big buses which supplement public buses and taxis during rush hours. About 110 such buses are daily assigned on major traffic routes of the city. Otherwise, they serve the suburb towns of Addis Ababa. These buses are much preferred to the normal public buses and taxis for both lower fares and comfort.

Regional passenger transport service is rendered by government and private fleets in accordance with a zonal system of operation. For this purpose, the Public Transport Corporation has divided the country into seven transport zones where buses are assigned on a rotation basis. There is also one cross-country transport service which radiates from the capital. The corporation deploys 316 government buses and about 3200 privately owned small, medium and big buses. The government fleet predominantly comprises Fiat, Mercedes and Daf models while there are over 18 models in the private sector. Currently the private fleet handles over 80 per cent of the national commercial passenger transport service while the rest is handled by the government fleet.

Reliable information regarding the age structure of vehicles is not usually easy to obtain. Of the seven transport zones, only the central zone (covering a radius of about 150 km from Addis Ababa) provided data on ages of vehicles and fuel consumption patterns (PTC, 1990). This region administers over 40 per cent of the total regional transport vehicles and is therefore a good sample for the total vehicle population. All vehicles in the central zone are privately owned and their capacity ranges from 5 to 50 seats. There are over 15 different models in this zone with Fiats making up 61 per cent of all vehicles. The mean age of this vehicle group is around 20 years.

Freight Transport Corporation

Freight transport service was exclusively run by private truck owners until the 1974 revolution when the government entered into the service by deploying its own fleets. Since then, private truckers (associates) have been required to operate within assigned zones of operation and at a fixed tariff.

According to 1986/7 figures, there were a total of 1177 government-owned dry and liquid cargo trucks, while the private sector, which handles about 70 per cent of all freight traffic, owned about 6630 dry and liquid cargo vehicles of various capacities (FTC, 1988). A survey of the dry cargo fleet carried out in 1987/8, indicated that the government fleet was on average 7 years old, whereas the mean age for private trucks was 13 years (FTC, 1988).

Government has been investing heavily to increase its share in the service, to strengthen the maintenance facilities and to modernize the operation. From 1979/80 a total of 176 million birr has been expended in the freight sector for the purchase of vehicles and spare parts, the construction of garages and workshops, and other development measures. This figure represents over 10 per cent of all investments undertaken in the transport and communications sector during the same period.

A plan has been mooted to construct a railway line to connect the port of Assab with Addis Ababa. This route presently handles over 67 per cent of the total annual ton kilometres of freight in the country. The estimated cost of constructing the railway was over 2.8 billion birr. The traditional financiers, like the World Bank, were not interested in the project mainly because of the envisaged heavy investment and suggested postponement until the route's traffic makes implementation a necessity.

The maintenance branch of the government fleet is headquartered in a modern garage in Nefas Silk at the south end of the capital, constructed at a cost of more than 30 million birr. This garage with its well-equipped workshop is expected to meet the maintenance needs of government-owned trucks. The private associates are, on the other hand, facing serious problems of maintenance. With old age, the spare part requirements of private trucks are increasing. Although foreign exchange is annually allocated for these vehicles, the amount, ironically, is decreasing (Table 3.2 and Figure 3.3).

Table 3.2 Foreign currency allocated for spare parts for private and government-owned buses and trucks (000s Birr)

Years	Private	Government	Total
1986/7	22512	12491	35003
1987/8	13521	7000	20521
1988/9	9724	7040	16764

Source : ONNCP documents

The existing freight transport tariff goes back to 1980 and its fairness has been challenged. The economic analysis of the adequacy of fares carried out in 1985 under the Road Transport Study (RTS) concluded that fares were not sufficient to cover costs except under the most favourable road conditions and that they did not permit enough capital recovery (World Bank,1988).

The freight transport operation, which is highly centralized and closely controlled, has not proved to be the most efficient way of organizing the service. Studies have indicated that decentralization, elimination of bureaucratic procedures and revision of tariffs, coupled with sufficient allocation of foreign exchange both for replacement of vehicle and purchase of spare parts, could lead to a reduction of the total number of vehicles required in the service.

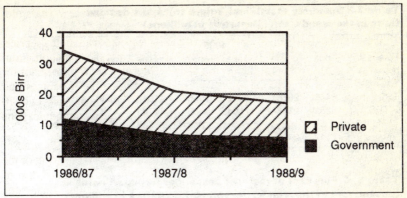

Figure 3.3 Foreign currency allocation

Estimation of future freight and passenger transport demand

Available estimates of future demand for freight and passenger transport are based on the business-as-usual scenario prevailing prior to 1990. Future freight transport demand has been forecast by different bodies at different times. The four important estimates are discussed below.

A 1983/4 Louis Berger transport sector study (*TSS*) forecast the national freight transport demand in terms of tonnage. The average distance one ton travelled for the years 1979/80 to 1987/8 (400 km) was used as a multiplier to arrive at the total ton kilometre forecasts for 1990 to 2005.

The Rail India Technical and Economic Services (RITES) study forecast the total import and export traffic on the Addis Ababa–Assab corridor (RITES,1986). The corridor, which connects the capital with the important port of Assab, currently handles 32 per cent of the national freight traffic in terms of tonnage. The corridor traffic forecast was converted to the national traffic and the result was multiplied by the average distance covered by one ton.

The World Bank (World Bank, 1986) estimated the Addis Ababa–Assab corridor traffic for the years 1990–2000. The result was converted to the national traffic in terms of tonnage and ton kilometres. in the same way as described earlier. The national estimate for 2005 was forecast by using the growth rates applied for 1995–2000.

Based on the 1979/88 to 1987/8 figures, a regression model was constructed to estimate the national traffic for the years 1990–2005, both in tons and tons/km. The results of the different forecasts are presented in Table 3.3.

The World Bank and RITES estimates are rather low because the actual accomplishment of 1986/7 for dry cargo transport alone has already surpassed forecasts for 1990. The regression result is also difficult to accept because of its in-built assumption of a similar growth rate throughout the forecast period. It is therefore more acceptable to work with the estimates of the Transport Sector Study (TSS), which is optimistic about the future of the economy: it is expected to leap ahead once the drought is over and peace has returned.

Table 3.3 Summary of national freight transport demand (tons in thousands, ton kilometres in millions)

Forecast by	1990		1995		2000		2005	
	Tons	Ton km	Tons	Ton km	Tons	Ton km	Tons	Ton km
TSS	6446	2636	8792	3596	11218	4589	4222	5818
RITES	5252	2148	7504	3069	10743	4394	4589	5967
World Bank	3554	1421	4601	1840	5706	2282	7282	2753
Regression	7117	2906	8364	3460	9612	4053	10859	4567

Table 3. 4   Forecast of regional passenger transport demand (passengers in thousands, passenger kilometres in millions)

Forecast	1990		1995		2000		2005	
	pass	pass. km	pass	pass. km	pass	pass. km	pass	pass. km
TSS	52672	3693	58949	4126	66573	4660	75223	5265
Regression	57600	4932	69100	4837	80500	5635	91900	6433

The TSS forecast regional passenger transport demand. In the present analysis regression was run based on the data for the last nine years (1979–87). Comparison of the two forecasts indicated the TSS estimate to be rather on the low side as the actual accomplishment for 1987/8 was already higher than forecast figures for 1990 (Table 3.4).

So far, there has not been any forecast with regard to bus and taxi services in Addis Ababa. Regression analysis was used to forecast the number of passengers to be transported by buses and taxis. The present average distance travelled by a bus passenger (7 km) was assumed to increase to 10 km by 2005 owing to the expansion of the city boundary and increases in personal income. The available information regarding the number of passengers and average distances travelled by taxis today should be treated with caution. Currently the data is collected for taxis which depart from or reach the origin/destination points in the respective zones. There are however a considerable number of taxis which do not depart from or reach such points but rather shuttle in between. Furthermore, the enumerators located at the terminal points do not work in the evenings when taxis are still operating. The number of passengers transported during these hours is estimated as a certain percentage of the daily traffic. Consequently, the data on taxi passengers and average distance covered by passengers could not be taken as anything more than indicative figures. With this in mind the forecast for taxi transport demand was estimated by regressing the past trends and by assuming the current average distance covered by a passenger per trip (0.85 km) to increase to 1.5 km by the end of the forecast period, mainly due to expected increases in the number of taxis and the expansion of city limits. The summary is given in Table 3.5 and Figure 3.4.

Table 3. 5 Addis Ababa city passenger transport demand forecast

Mode	1990		1995		2000		2005	
	pass	pass. km	pass	pass. km	pass	pass. km	pass	pass. km
Bus	103	723	130	1041	157	1414	184	1839
Taxi	169	143	290	261	412	41	533	800
Total	272	866	420	1302	569	1826	717	2639

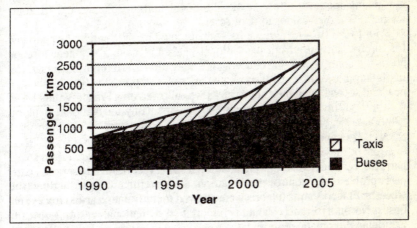

Figure 3.4
Passenger transport demand forecast: Addis Ababa, 1990–2005

Government policy in the sector

The policy of the government regarding the commercial road transport service could be generalized as having been one of strengthening the state sector and regulating the service by means of tariff setting and route allocation. The Ten-year Plan (1984/5–1994/5) envisaged an increase in the share of the government by 75 per cent and 50 per cent in freight and passenger transport services respectively. To realize this objective, a total of 265 million birr was invested in the sector during 1979/80 to 1987/88. This was about a third of total investment in the transport sector (excluding telecommunications and Ethiopian Airlines, which rely heavily on foreign loans).

Some studies have indicated that the government sector operates inefficiently compared to the private sector. For instance, the average annual distance covered by a private truck is 42,000 km, while a government-owned truck accomplishes only 35,000 km (Swedish Development Corporation, 1987). On the other hand, cost per km for government-owned trucks is 105 cents, while for private trucks it is only 95 cents (Swedish Development Corporation,1987). These variations are explained by delays in the maintenance section, bureaucratic procedures, the high rate of accidents, a lack of incentives and the huge overhead costs observable in the government sector. The strategy of expanding the share of the government has therefore meant expanding the inefficient sector at the cost of the efficient private sector.

The need to decentralize some elements of trucking and taxi operations has been established in different studies. With decentralization, low capacity vehicles could be assigned for short-haul operation with a revised tariff system, and average vehicle capacity would gradually increase, resulting in a reduction of the total number of vehicles required (World Bank, 1988). Zonal allocation of taxis has also been criticized as inflexible and strong recommendations are now being made to allow small old-model taxis to operate out of zone restrictions and give door-to-door service.

Prior to the 1974 revolution, individuals could import vehicles by applying for foreign currency from the national bank. Later on, a stringent foreign currency control was introduced and allocation of foreign currency for importation of vehicles by the private sector was stopped. In 1984, imports of new and second-hand buses and trucks was allowed on a Franco Valuta basis (i.e. without involving foreign currency payments by the National Bank of Ethiopia). Accordingly, between 1984 and 1987/8 a total of 717 buses and trucks were imported (FTC, 1988; PTC, 1988).

Most of these vehicles were later found to be old and thus required spare parts the very next year, putting additional strain on the already serious spare parts problem. To control this situation, the government issued a directive whereby Franco Valuta imports were allowed for only one-year-old trucks and buses. Normally Franco Valuta is importation by nationals residing abroad, Ethiopian diplomatic representatives and scholars returning home. The level of imports then decreased markedly owing to the substantial financial requirements imposed on the importation of one-year-old vehicles. The series of import regulations have, until recently, totally excluded the importation of automobiles either for commercial or non-commercial activities. Even foreign loans and assistance for the purchase of vehicles were restricted to station wagons and pick-ups. Government agencies were therefore forced to use such vehicles for routine transport requirements which otherwise could have been satisfied by automobiles.

The restriction on the importation of automobiles by individuals has also affected the taxi service, as it is the private automobiles that are eventually transformed into taxis. The impossibility of replacing old taxis and thus improving the service is one main outcome of this restriction.

Thus the vehicle importation policy of the government has resulted in the weakening of the commercial transport sector and led to the uneconomic use of vehicles in the non-commercial transport sphere. Consideration of the total vehicle import requirements (pick-ups, station wagons, trucks, buses, etc) by government organizations from 1984/5 to 1989/90 indicated another problem area. In those seven years it was possible to satisfy only 34 per cent of the requests made by government institutions and the commercial transport sector (ONCCP/TCD). The cumulative unsatisfied demand appears large but the import policy is being revised presently and this could go a long way to ease the strain.

We have seen that the existing tariff for the city bus service has not been improved since its introduction in 1956. Although cost per km of this service is difficult to obtain (there is no independent cost accounting for city and regional services) it is clear that change in the city service tariff is well overdue. Consideration of recent figures alone indicates that a Mercedes bus which cost 193,000 birr in 1987, cost 248,000 birr in 1989 (PTC,1989). Tariff for regional passenger services was last revised in 1980 following increases in the diesel price.The total wage bill of the corporation, on the other hand, has shown average annual increases of 7 per cent from 1980 to 1988 (PTC,1989). Despite such obvious increases, the government has opted to subsidize the operation rather than adjusting tariffs.

The freight tariff, which was last revised in 1980, is now insufficient to cover costs except under favourable road conditions. It has also been shown that the existing tariff subsidizes the low-capacity vehicles (World Bank,1988). For instance, the tariff for dry cargo trucks with trailers is 0.125 birr/ton kilometre and 0.02049 birr/ton kilometre for a single truck on asphalt roads, while it ranges from 0.5 to 0.8 birr/ton kilometre on the gravel roads usually used by low-capacity vehicles. This is probably one of the explanations for the fact that 75 per cent of the trucks imported by the private sector were of smaller capacities (FTC, 1988; PTC, 1988).

Tariff revision has now become a condition for obtaining loans from donor agencies like the World Bank. The latest loan from IDA to the transport and communications sector has recommended that a new freight tariff should be drafted prior to the loan negotiations (World Bank,1988) and the government is expected to give its decision in the near future.

The tax policy of the government regarding the commercial road transport sector is mainly designed to 'limit imports and increase government revenues'. The tax policies introduced thus far complement the import restriction policies. The tax structures in force to date have been based on the C&F values with depreciation allowance of 1 per cent per month.

According to the earlier tax policy (1980–9) a sedan automobile was taxed at between 99 per cent and 209 per cent of its C&F value (depending on the value of the vehicle once the depreciation is deducted). If the vehicle had been brought in for use in a taxi business it was taxed at only 74 per cent. All other vehicles, including buses and trucks, were charged at 44 per cent of their C&F values. If these imports were on the Franco Valuta basis, an additional 50 per cent was charged as surtax. Surtax for sedan automobiles was 100 per cent .

A revised tax structure (October 1989) is more refined and to some extent encourages the commercial transport sector. Accordingly, imports for taxi business purposes of vehicles with 15 seats and 15 quintals capacity are exempted from the 75 per cent surtax charge which is levied on vehicles imported for other uses. Furthermore, trucks and buses with capacities of more than 30 seats and 50 quintals are required to pay only 25 per cent surtax over the 44 per cent fixed tax rate. This policy has therefore a tendency to encourage higher-capacity vehicles which was lacking in the previous tax structure. Like import policy discussed above, the tax policy, too, is being constantly revised and is changing for the better.

Technical energy efficiency in the commercial road transport sector

The fuel consumption of motor vehicles is dependent on its design and technical state, on climatic conditions, on road conditions, and on the skill and experience of the driver and maintenance personnel. Operational organization can also play a significant role in the fuel efficiency of the fleet as a whole. The technical and physical deterioration of a vehicle tends to increase its fuel consumption, as does wrong adjustment of the fuel distribution and ignition systems of the engine. Over-cooling of the engine usually impairs the proper combustion of the fuel and results in higher fuel consumption. The condition of the chassis and wrong adjustment of the drive gears, bearings, brakes and steering system cause additional resistance to motion, thereby increasing the fuel consumption. Proper and timely maintenance of all these components is important.

The following paragraphs describe the findings from the visits we made to garages run by public corporations and the discussions we had with the technical personnel at various levels. Handling and upkeep of vehicles was the focus of the investigations.

National Freight Transport Corporation (NFTC)

Most trucks of the National Freight Transport Corporation (NFTC) operate on the Addis Ababa–Assab route. All inbound trucks are subjected to routine inspection and service at Nefas Silk garage in Addis Ababa. Defective parts are sent for maintenance at one of the corporation's three garages in Addis Ababa. All maintenance except engine overhaul and fuel injection system maintenance is carried out at Nefas Silk garage. The Nefas Silk garage is still under construction and is expected to house full maintenance facilities when completed. Outside Addis, the corporation runs one garage at Awash Town.

Engine overhaul is seldom initiated purely on grounds of high fuel consumption. To start with, test pit checks on fuel consumption of trucks consist of visual observation of the exhaust gas and thermometric tell-tale of engine overheat. Moreover, no test measurements of fuel consumption or torque output are made on engines at the end of the overhaul process. It is also noteworthy that fuel injection pumps and injectors are tested and maintained only in the course of engine overhaul. During actual operation of the trucks, too, there is a lack of thorough procedures to monitor the state of fuel consumption. It doesn't appear that there is a conscious effort to tackle the problems of fuel efficiency directly. A major problem both in the maintenance and the operation is the high labour turnover. This is due to lower salary rates in the corporation, especially with regard to technical personnel. A considerable number of experienced technicians have left the corporation in the past few years.

About 95 per cent of all spare parts are acquired through imports. Engine parts, brake parts and suspension elements are some of the most frequently demanded major components. The demand for brake and suspension parts is believed to arise from poor road conditions. All in all about 3.8 million birr per year is presently spent on the purchase of spare parts. Locally made spare parts consist of such items as bushings, bolts and nuts. However, modifications of used parts such as shafts, gears, axles, brackets and housings are common. Industrial spare parts establishments are expected to play a larger role in vehicle spare parts manufacture in future, if due effort is made.

The fleet operation of the NFTC on the Addis–Assab route is on a relay basis and demands frequent changes of drivers. The present system of reward and penalty does not effectively encourage drivers in better handling and upkeep of their trucks or in making optimum use of fuel. In fact, the driver's sole mission is to get the trucks to the next driver on the relay line in the stipulated time. Most of the trucks are said to have no kilometre gauges and therefore it is difficult to know the exact fuel consumption for each truck. The fuel consumption is based on the amount of fuel taken from the depot and the estimated distance between destinations.

The benefits of turbocharging and the advantages of using radial tyres are well understood by the corporation. Out of the total fleet in operation, about 300 trucks have turbocharged engines. In fact, one of the conditions set in the specifications at purchase is that trucks have turbocharging units. With respect to tyres, it is estimated that 50 per cent of the corporation's fleet are fitted with radial tyres.

National Public Transport Corporation (NPTC)

NPTC presently operates four types of buses. These are Fiat, Volvo, DAF and Mercedes buses. The corporation does not seem to have maintenance problems related to the large variety of buses. NPTC actually believes in maintaining different brands of buses in order to avoid the dictation of terms, conditions and prices by any one supplier.

NPTC presently runs four garages in Addis Ababa, namely, Yeka, Lidetta, Shegole and Diabaco garages. Lidetta garage caters for heavy maintenance of all models of buses. The rest of the garages specialize in either Fiat, Mercedes or Volvo models. The maintenance facility at Lideta includes fuel pump calibration and injector nozzle test stands. Spare injector pumps and injector nozzles are maintained and kept in stock. Records are maintained for individual units of pumps and nozzles. Tests are carried out on each unit that comes for maintenance. There is a routine test programme largely based on manufacturers' recommendations for all bus models. This ensures satisfactory maintenance on the fuel delivery system. Here, too, overhauled engines are not tested for torque output or fuel consumption before being put into operation.

Most (about 90 per cent) of the vehicles under the NPTC utilize diesel fuel and paper air filters. Whenever the paper filters get dirty, dust is blown in with compressed air. This is one of the areas where close attention should be paid as fuel economy is directly related to the air intake. The problem is most serious for inter-city buses operating on dusty roads. On city buses, injection pumps and injectors are said to be areas of most trouble. The direct in-line type of fuel injection pump, with individual pipe lines to injectors, is widely used on all the buses.

The NPTC, though it has a very high labour turnover, has qualified maintenance personnel, most of whom are technical school graduates. The technicians have specialized skills for specialized maintenance. A technical school graduate on recruitment starts as an apprentice, learning skills on the job as well as being sent to the training centre for additional tuition. Promotions are also effected through practical and theoretical examinations. This creates a sense of competition which has a positive effect on the maintenance activity within the corporation.

Most NPTC buses (335) use radial tyres and a saving of about 50 litres per week per bus has been observed since they were fitted. Radial tyres are not produced locally and have to be imported from abroad. The basis of tyre change within the corporation is the measurement of thread depth or failure through puncture. The worn-out tyres are usually used after recapping.

The major source of spare parts is the foreign market. The scarcity of spare parts sometimes forces the agency to resort to modifications, undertaken both in the corporation's workshops and in external garages. These modifications are mostly (95 per cent) made to the older models and only occasionally (5 per cent) to the new models. Some local workshops produce spare parts such as bushing U bolts for the corporation, and NPTC personnel believe that the Akaki spare parts industry could play a significant role in alleviating their spare parts problems. The amount of budget utilized for spare parts purchase in 1989 was about 3.8 million birr, of which about 0.78 million birr was allocated for private buses (spare parts for private operators are ordered through NPTC). The availability of funds and especially bank permits for foreign currency is the major problem. Otherwise, spare parts from foreign suppliers are readily available.

In almost all cases, the buses bought by NPTC meet the specifications laid for gradients, specific fuel and lubricating oil consumption. Supercharging improves the fuel economy at higher altitudes as it increases the air–fuel ratio. For this reason all recently purchased buses have supercharged engines.

Non-commercial road transport sub-sector

Non-commercial government vehicles

This category of vehicles includes all government-owned automobiles, and passenger and freight fleets which render non-commercial transport services. The number of these vehicles has shown a remarkable increase particularly during the last decade. They increased from 8,224 in 1980 to 14,755 in 1988 (ONCCP/RTA). This increase is mainly due to the creation of numerous economic and non-economic government institutions, increased government and party representations in the rural areas and the favourable foreign exchange allocation for purchase of vehicles by the government sector.

In 1984, the Government Vehicles Control Department was established within the Road Transport Authority with the objective of ensuring an efficient utilization of fuel by vehicles in the government sector. This department introduced a system whereby all government vehicles were required to have a travel permit for every trip made. Private use of government vehicles was also prohibited and government vehicles could be used by assigned drivers and for approved government transport services only. Although no reliable figures are available, it was claimed that these steps initially led to a noticeable decline in the fuel bill for the government. More than the control aspect, the department had taken very important steps towards compiling data on various aspects of government vehicles.

For the present study, a sample of 300 vehicles were randomly picked by considering every 50th vehicle data card from a total population of 15,000 data cards that had been filled in by various government organizations as requested by the Road Transport Authority. The data pertain to the year 1989 and the results of the analysis of data so obtained are discussed below. Over 12 different makes of vehicles were identified, with Toyota models comprising 26 per cent of the sample followed by the Fiat models (15 per cent), Mercedes (6 per cent) and Volkswagen (5 per cent). Regarding the age structure of the vehicles, out of the total sample for which age information was available, over 90 per cent were found to be less than 16 years old.

Disaggregation of the sample vehicles by type of fuel used indicated that 172 of them (57 per cent) consume petrol and the rest (43 per cent) used diesel. With regard to specific fuel consumption, the average for petrol vehicles was reported to be 5.5 km/litre. The age versus fuel consumption profile of the petrol vehicles showed a somewhat inconsistent correlation between the two indices. The average fuel consumption for 1–5-year-old vehicles was only 5.25 km/litre while that for vehicles 6–7 years old was 6.25 km/litre. Furthermore, vehicles in the 11–15-year category were reported to have a higher fuel consumption ratio (4.94 km/litre) than the vehicles that were 16 years old and upwards (5.75 km/litre). Although the type and model of vehicles in each age category have bearings on the level of specific fuel consumption, the degree of accuracy of the base data for fuel consumption is itself too limited to allow an age-level analysis. Regarding diesel vehicles, out of the total of 128 vehicles, 94 were freight vehicles with a capacity range of 10 to more than 100 tons and the rest were passenger vehicles with seat capacities of up to 70. From the diesel group, the most numerous (31 per cent) were Fiat models, followed by Toyota (20 per cent) and Nissan/Datsun models (12 per cent). Out of the total number of diesel vehicles for which age information was available, over 96 per cent were reported to be less than 16 years old. Their specific fuel consumption average was calculated to be 3.8 km/litre. This figure was 3.4 km/litre for the freight and 4.9 km/litre for the passenger diesel vehicles.

Private automobiles

The total number of private automobiles registered in the country is about 35,000 and over 90 per cent of these are in Addis Ababa. Reliable and complete data are hard to obtain about the characteristics of these vehicles. However, the Road Transport Authority has recently started to compile vehicle data with the aid of computers. Currently, information on make and age structure of only

12,660 private automobiles is available in the Authority. About 75 per cent of the private automobiles for which computer information could be obtained were over 16 years old. Over 13 different makes of vehicles were observed and the predominant ones were Volkswagen (25 per cent), Fiat (17 per cent) and Peugeot (13 per cent).

A field survey was undertaken to get complete vehicle data. Accordingly, a sample of 300 private automobiles in Addis Ababa was randomly picked when they appeared for the annual inspection and registration. Caution was taken in the selection of the most appropriate time, when both old and new vehicles were expected to come up for annual inspection. The registration and inspection season for all cars in the country extends from September to March. Experience showed that the newer vehicles go for inspection during the beginning of the inspection period and the old ones show up at the end of the season. This is mainly due to the fact that the newer vehicles will face no problem in passing the inspection while the older ones need time to correct their defects. December was found to be an ideal month, when both new and old vehicles show up for inspection. Accordingly, the survey was conducted in the first week of December 1990.

Out of the 300 completed questionnaires, 224 were analysed and the results are discussed below. Out of those vehicles for which age information was available, 52 per cent were over 16 years old and only 10 per cent were less than 5 years old. With regard to the composition of vehicle types, it was found that 23 per cent were Volkswagen, 15 per cent Fiat, 13 per cent Toyota and 12.5 per cent Peugeot cars. This result is in line with the computer information.

With regard to specific fuel consumption, the sample average was found to be 8.8 km/litre. The most fuel-efficient vehicles (Renault) showed a 28 per cent higher fuel efficiency than the average. The age versus fuel consumption profile of the sample vehicles showed that age and fuel consumption were inversely related, ranging from 9.8 km/litre for age group 1-5 years to 8.6 km/litre for the age group of 16 years and above.

Growth rates for transport services in the non-commercial road transport sub-sector

Attempting to forecast demand and supply for the non-commercial road transport services in a rapidly changing socio-economic and political environment, such as that prevailing in Ethiopia today, is by all measures a difficult exercise. One can, nevertheless, sketch a possible future by following a cause/effect approach for key variables.

Public non-commercial sub-sector

The past decade has witnessed a proliferation of public institutions, public enterprises and mass organizations. This trend has given rise to perceptible growth in the population of public non-commercial (government) vehicles. Vehicle population growth was on average 8.8 per cent per year for this category (ONCCP/RTA). This trend is not expected to continue under the present economic policy which is based on the express objective of enhancing private participation and initiative as opposed to the hitherto condoned system of a strongly centralized control of economic and social activities. With the anticipated decline in the activities of some huge state enterprises – the Ethiopian Domestic Distribution Corporation (EDDC), and the Agricultural Products Marketing Corporation (AMC), for example – and even state farms, it is fair to assume that the growth rate for transport services in this category will fall and eventually stabilize at about 2 per cent per year.

Private automobile transport service

The past decade was for the most part marked by an almost complete ban on the import of private vehicles. The population of such vehicles actually fell from about 29,000 to about 25,000 between 1979 and 1988. Since May 1990, however, the import restriction has been substantially relaxed, with the tax rate none the less remaining at about 200 per cent of CIF value. Moreover, importation is only possible on a Franco-Valuta basis, with no foreign currency disbursements allowed from the National Bank for the purchase of private automobiles.

Whatever the importation constraints, there has been a sustained inflow of about 300 private automobiles per month for the nine months since May 1990. Students and diplomatic personnel returning from abroad, Ethiopians residing abroad and businessmen in the import/ export trade constitute the bulk of the group sustaining the inflow. One of its effects has been a fall in the price of used cars in Ethiopia. It is expected that at some stage in the future potential importers will be less inclined to put up with the difficulty of importing vehicles and opt instead for buying used cars from the local market, which will restore their value. In the final analysis, the size of the local demand for imported automobiles will also depend on the absorption capacity of that segment of the Ethiopian population which can afford a car and the subsequent running costs in spare parts and fuel. That economic base is quite narrow and the market could reach saturation point at an import rate of about 100 cars per month. This amounts to a net growth rate of 3 per cent per year over the present population of functional private automobiles, which stands at about 30,000.

Import and tax policy for non-commercial transport vehicles

The essentials of import and tax policy for such vehicles have been covered in the discussion of commercial transport vehicles. Here we shall touch lightly on the chequered history of the importation of private automobiles to Ethiopia in the 1980s.

The importation of private automobiles was allowed for short periods of time in the 1980s. All these imports had to be made on a Franco Valuta basis. Imports continued until March 1985, when the proclamation banning the import of private automobiles came into force. Imports for the period 1977–March 1985 were governed by a maximum cylinder capacity limit of 1.6 litres. The import tax for the period 1977–83 followed a scheme whereby the charge ranged from 99 per cent to 209 per cent of the vehicle's C&F value. This was a significant increase over the earlier tax rate of a maximum 120 per cent of

C&F values prevailing in the period prior to 1977. Imports for the period July 1983 to March 1985 were, in addition, subject to a surtax charge minimum of 100 per cent.

The period March 1985 to October 1989 saw a total ban on the import of private automobiles. The ban was lifted in October 1989, but with a further restriction besides the cylinder capacity limit: the maximum age limit of the imported vehicles was put at three years. May of 1990 saw a relaxation of the import regulations:vehicles of all ages, makes, cylinder capacities and fuel types can now be imported, with the tax rate depending on the cylinder capacity and favouring lower capacity vehicles. The revisions of import and tax policies were largely prompted by the rising price of oil and were, until recently, restrictive of imports.

Technical energy efficiency improvements in the non-commercial road transport sector

The following paragraphs describe the findings from visits made to five private and two government garages in Addis Ababa selected as random samples from an inventory of 640 garages of various grades as compiled by the Road Transport Authority. Discussions were held with technical personnel at various levels. In addition to these, findings from a field survey carried out on 300 private automobiles have been included. The investigations focused on the handling, upkeep and fuel consumption aspects of vehicles.

Ethiopian Electric Light and Power Authority (EELPA)

EELPA operates about 752 vehicles of 26 manufactures and 95 different models. EELPA has two garages, one of which caters for the construction department of the authority. A modern garage is being built and is expected to alleviate the deficiency that currently exists in terms of equipment.

Generally, maintenance is initiated by drivers' reports. Most maintenance is done at the two garages while some is contracted to external garages. The reasons for sending vehicles to external garages are the high volume of work and maintenance facilities which require specialized equipment. Due to a lack of calibrating equipment, fuel injection pumps are maintained at external garages such as ORPI. Cylinders, crankshafts and other parts which require machining work are usually sent to Tana and Morisque garages.

About 95 per cent of all spare parts are acquired either through local suppliers or imported during the purchase of vehicles. Engine parts, fuel supply system parts and some electrical parts are most frequently demanded. Bushings, bolts and nuts are part of the local supplies; modifications are also made on some old-model vehicles for which spare parts are not available. Many vehicles are also reported out of service due to lack of spare parts.

Frequent change of drivers is believed to be a major reason for the frequent breakdown of vehicles. No log book is provided to the operators to register remarks on the vehicles. Most of the kilometre counters of the vehicles are inoperative. They are either deliberately detached or damaged to evade fuel consumption controls. Sometimes these parts are worn out during operation and no replacement is available. Hence fuel consumptions are often mere estimates.

The usefulness of radial tyres has also been realized by the authority and most of the heavy trucks are fitted with radial tyres and turbocharger engines. However, the shortage of tyres seems to be a very acute problem and some vehicles are said to be out of service for lack of tyres.

Batu Construction Agency

Batu operates more than five types of vehicles and some construction equipment. The majority of the trucks and vehicles are Volvo, Mercedes, Nissan, Fiat and Kamazu models, while most of the construction equipment is made by Caterpillar. Vehicle maintenance is programmed on regular routines at intervals of 2 months, 6 months and 12 months which cover inspection and light and heavy maintenance.

Batu gets most of its spare parts (90 per cent) from the local truck and vehicle dealers, while it utilizes a small proportion of locally manufactured parts. The spares obtained locally are used in outdated and older vehicles and equipment. The spares made locally are parts such as bushings, leaf springs, pulleys, etc. The Akaki spare parts factory, in spite of its slow response, is said to alleviate the spare parts problem. Spares which contribute to fuel economy such as injectors, carburettors, pistons, piston rings, oil rings, injector nozzles and tyres are the major constraints.

Currently, 50 per cent of Batu's fleet is fitted with turbocharged engines and these have been found to be more efficient as regards fuel consumption. The trend in the agency is to extend the use of turbochargers. At present, only 15 per cent of the fleet is equipped with radial tyres, which have demonstrated an advantage in terms of fuel economy.

Private garages

Visits were also paid to private garages, randomly selected from the inventory of garages in Addis Ababa. Discussions were held with the garage owners and the findings are described below.

V. Williams, M. Gurmu and D. Desta garages specialize in vehicle body work, and in the servicing and maintenance of Volkswagen and Peugeot models. In each case, only the minimum set of garage equipment necessary for basic services is installed. Specialized maintenance of parts is left to workshops like Tana and Morisque which possess the requisite equipment and offer *de facto* centralized service. The single most acute problem of these garages is a lack of spare parts or the exorbitant prices charged by the retail shops which are bent on making the most of their meagre stock. Government distribution shops seem to have been of no help, as their stocks are siphoned off to retailers in illegal dealings with the employees.

A specialized service is offered by Mengesha Carburettor Repair Workshop. Carburettor malfunction results in high fuel consumption and starting difficulties. Reasons for this phenomenon are clogging of idling nozzles and wear of nozzles and butterfly valves. Parts are either cleaned or modified to remedy the situation. A carburettor so maintained would run for a minimum of one year without further maintenance. The *raison d'être* for the workshop appears to be the unavailability or high cost of carburettors on the market.

ORPI Garage (Injection Pump Repair Shop) is a workshop where fuel pumps and accessories are maintained. The workshop is well equipped for the maintenance and calibration of the fuel supply system of diesel engines. Injection nozzles are said to wear out within one to three years depending on the quality of the fuel. No modification is possible on injection nozzles (injectors) since they are sensitive and precision-made. Injection pump spare parts are said to be mostly unavailable and sometimes operators are forced to run on defective parts, paying for it in excessive fuel consumption. Tractors which have been lying idle for two years in the workshop's premises for lack of spare parts demonstrate the extent of the problem.

Private vehicles

Questions related to problems of spare parts and fuel consumption were included in the field survey of 300 private automobiles in Addis Ababa. Various respondents referred to the components listed in Table 3.6 as problem areas or hard-to-find-on-market items. References to other components were considerably fewer. The same survey indicated that 30 per cent of the respondents were satisfied with the fuel efficiency of their cars. The rest believed their cars were not fuel-efficient and cited lack of proper maintenance (35 per cent) or old age (35 per cent) as a reason.

Table 3.6 Reported shortages of spare parts for motor vehicles

Item no.	Problem item	% respondents referring to the item
1	Electrical parts – generators, HV distribution, spark plugs, contact points, lamps, etc.	72
2	Motor parts – cylinders, pistons, piston rings, etc.	59
3	Wheel parts – tyres, brakes, brake shoes	54
4	Clutch parts – pressure plates, clutch plates, cables, etc.	13

Problems of the transport sector and their energy implications

Fleet size

In the foregoing sections we have established that there will be a perceptible increase in dry cargo freight and passenger transport demand in the years ahead. The TSS forecast envisages an annual growth in freight transport demand of about 5.5 per cent (see ton kilometres entries in Table 3.3) up to the year 2005. If one assumes that the additional freight transport demand will not be met by rail or air transport, it is imperative that the present fleet of 6818 commercial transport sector trucks be augmented by about 375 trucks every year. Moreover, about 30 per cent of the present truck fleet is over 15 years of age and will soon require replacement.

The forecast for commercial buses envisages a demand growth of about 3.2 per cent for inter-city passenger transport and about 6.5 for urban transport up to year 2005. This in turn calls for an infusion of about 112 new regional buses and 16 urban transport buses into the existing bus fleet every year. Likewise, about 623 new vehicles have to join the existing taxi fleet every year up to 2005 to satisfy the demand, especially at peak hours , if no alternative measures are taken. The foregoing analysis assumes that the present fleet of trucks, buses and taxis will survive all accidents, aging and other hazards, and will continue to be roadworthy up to year 2005. Even with this optimism, the requirement for new vehicles is quite heavy in terms of financial outlay, with the probable exception of urban transport buses. Under the circumstances, one would consider the purchase of more city buses than indicated by the forecast to reduce the immense demand envisaged for taxi services.

Rising petroleum fuel demand

Ethiopia is not a great consumer of petroleum fuels by any measure. For example, the world oil consumption presently stands at about 4.4 barrels per capita per year. Ethiopia's per capita oil consumption for the year 1989 was about 0.15 barrels or 3.4 per cent of the world average. Ethiopia's gross annual consumption of oil, which stands at about 1 million tons, is only a minuscule component of annual world consumption (about 3 billion tons). Yet the continued supply of oil is important in Ethiopia because the modern transport sector is wholly dependent on oil and absorbs about 70 per cent of total petroleum imports. More important still, the importation of this minuscule quantity of oil presently gobbles up about 30 per cent of total export earnings. Obviously, changes in petroleum fuels demand in the transport sector would have a profound impact on the magnitude of the oil import bill.

The fuel consumption by the commercial road transport sector can be estimated roughly from available statistics for each vehicle category . We shall consider 1985/6 as a sample year.

Freight transport – dry cargo
Total distance covered by all trucks = 277.3 x 10^6 km
(CSA,1989)
Average distance covered per litre of diesel oil consumed = 1.5 km
Total fuel consumed by trucks =184.9 x 10^3 m^3

Freight transport–wet cargo (fuel)
Total annual m^3 km performed by fuel trucks = 573 x 10^6
(CSA,1989)
Average fuel consumption per m^3 km = 0.1 litre (estimate)
Total fuel consumption by fuel trucks = 57.3 x 10^3 m^3

Passenger transport – public buses
Total distance covered by all buses =112.7 x 10^6 km
(CSA, 1989)
Average distance covered per litre of diesel oil = 4 km
(Public Transport Corporation, 1990)
Total fuel consumption by all buses = 28 .2 x 10^3 m^3

Passenger transport – small taxis
Total no. of small taxis = 2900
Average no. days in service = 200 per year (estimate)
Average distance covered per day = 100 km
Average fuel consumption = 5 km / litre
Total petrol consumption for 1985/6 by small taxis =11.6 x 10^3 m^3

Passenger transport – large taxis
Total no. of large taxis = 1300
Average no. of days in service = 300 (estimate)
Average distance covered each day = 175 km
Average fuel consumption = 5 km/litre
Total petrol consumption for 1985/6 = 13.6 x 10^3 m^3
Total petrol consumption for 1985/6 by all taxis = 25.2 x 10^3 m^3

Other categories
These consist of light commercial service pick-ups and commercial personnel transport. Estimated annual petrol consumption for this category is about 20,000 cubic metres.

Thus we can conclude that the commercial road transport sector consumed 270.4 x 10^3 m^3 of diesel oil and 45.2 x 10^3 m^3 of petrol in 1985 / 86. Available statistics indicate that the national consumption of diesel oil was about 405 x 103 m^3 and that of petrol was about 169 x 10^3 m^3 (ONCCP/RTA, 1982–9). Hence it can be assumed that the commercial road transport sector is responsible for 67 per cent of the total diesel oil consumption and 27 per cent of the national petrol consumption.

In the interests of brevity we have excluded details on fuel import expenditure. However, it is worth noting that the import value of the commercial road transport sector's diesel oil and petrol consumption was about 31 per cent and 5 per cent, respectively, of the net fuel import expenditure for 1985/6 in Ethiopia. We observe here that freight transport accounts for about 90 per cent of the diesel oil consumption in the commercial road transport sector and the envisaged growth of 5.4 per cent per year in freight transport activities (see TSS forecast) is expected to give rise to perceptible growth in diesel oil consumption. Petrol demand by taxis was a relatively small portion of the national petrol demand in 1985/6, but if taxi services grow at the envisaged rate of 12 per cent per year (see Table 3.5) then the commercial road transport sector will soon be a significant consumer of petrol. The situation could be improved by expanding bus services in preference to taxis.

Fuel consumption by the non-commercial RTS is likewise treated below. The base data is obtained largely from sample surveys of vehicles and 1985/6 is again used as a sample year:

Government fleet
Total no. of vehicles = 13867 (ONCCP/RTA)

Government fleet – petrol vehicles
Per cent of petrol vehicles = 7904
Average distance travelled per vehicle per year = 16,145 km
Specific fuel consumption = 5.58 km /litre
Thus, total petrol consumption by government vehicles = 22.9 x $10^3 m^3$

Government fleet – diesel vehicles
Per cent diesel vehicles = 43 (sample survey)
No. of diesel vehicles = 5963
Average distance travelled per vehicle per year = 24,000 km
Specific fuel consumption = 3.75 km /litre
Thus, total diesel consumption by government vehicles = 38.2 x $10^3 m^3$

Private autos – all vehicles assumed petrol vehicles
Total no. of vehicles = 31,000 (ONCCP/RTA)
Average distance travelled per vehicle per year = 15,060 km
Specific fuel consumption = 8.8 km /litre
Thus, total petrol consumption by private autos = 53.4 x $10^3 m^3$

Other categories
Included here are diplomatic, UN and relief aid vehicles. Fuel consumption figures are based purely on estimates.
Other categories – petrol vehicles
Total no. of vehicles inspected = 4509 (CSA ,1989)
No. of petrol vehicles = 2170
Average distance travelled per vehicle per year =10,000 km

Specific fuel consumption for petrol vehicles = 8 km/litre
Thus, total petrol consumption for this category = $2.7 \times 10^3 m^3$
Other categories – diesel vehicles
No. of diesel vehicles = 2339
Average distance travelled per vehicle per year = 20,000 km
Specific fuel consumption = 1.5 km /litre
Thus, total diesel consumption for this category = $31.2 \times 10^3 m^3$

Therefore fuel consumption by fuel types for the non-commercial RTS can be calculated as shown below:
Total petrol consumption = $79.0 \times 10^3 m^3$
Total diesel consumption = $69.4 \times 10^3 m^3$

Efficiency of fuel utilization

Fuel costs constitute only one component of the overall cost of supply of transport services. Therefore, it would be most rewarding to approach the problem from a benefit/cost analysis point of view and understand improving the efficiency of petroleum fuels to mean 'maximizing the overall benefit/cost ratio for the transport sector'.

We shall first look at some country figures pertaining to the utilization of petroleum fuels. A compilation of various World Bank figures indicates that petroleum consumption per unit of GDP places Ethiopia in a mid-table position among the countries (synthesis of World Bank reports). No action-oriented statement can be made from this finding.

Average fuel consumption per vehicle in Ethiopia is abnormally high in comparison to figures for other countries, indicated in Table 3.7 and Figure 3.5. One can hypothesize that either the utilization factor for the vehicles in Ethiopia is high or fuel efficiency of vehicles is low, or both. In practice , if the utilization factor of vehicles is unusually high, then the fuel efficiency is

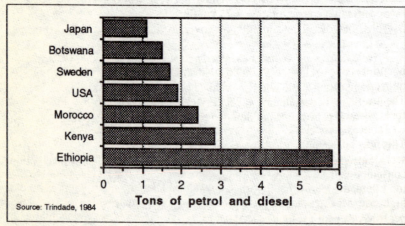

Figure 3.5 Annual fuel consumption per vehicle, 1983

Table 3.7 Annual fuel consumption per vehicle for selected countries, 1983

Country	Petrol consumption 000 tons	Diesel consumption 000 tons	Total fleet (000s)	Average fuel consumption per vehicle
Japan	26876	19620	42939	1.08
Botswana	41	9	32	1.56
Sweden	4834	1312	3584	1.74
USA	272716	39238	159509	1.96
Morocco	358	1326	712	2.37
Kenya*	269	180	154	2.92
Ethiopia	88	243	57	5.81

Source : Trindade , 1984
* Kenya's total vehicle fleet is about 258,000 according to a World Bank report (see WB,1984). The corresponding
  figure for fuel consumption per vehicle then becomes 1.74

Table 3.8 Specific fuel consumption (energy intensiveness) for some transport sector modes in some countries*

	Vehicle energy intensiveness		
	City buses (litres per passenger km)	Private autos (litres per passenger km)	Inter-city freight trucks (litres per ton km)
India	6.6×10^{-3}	7.4×10^{-2}	$5.7 \quad 10^{-2}$
Sweden	41.0×10^{-3}	7.5×10^{-2}	$2.7 \quad 10^{-2}$
France	28.9×10^{-3}	11.6×10^{-2}	$6.4 \quad 10^{-2}$
Ethiopia**	5.3×10^{-3}	5.9×10^{-2}	$9.1 \quad 10^{-2}$

Source: Based on Geltner ,1985
* Figures for India, Sweden and France are for mid 1970's. Figures for Ethiopia are current estimates.
** Estimates for Ethiopia are on the basis of 92 passengers per bus and 7.4 tons per truck average loads. These load
   ranges are based on reports by the Ethiopian Public Transport Corporation and CSA.

bound to be low. Therefore a more plausible hypothesis would be that the utilization factor for vehicles in Ethiopia is high and the fuel efficiency is low. The low fuel efficiency is likely to be attributable to the truck fleet since diesel fuel consumption is by far the largest component.

Table 3.8 indicates a rather low fuel consumption for city buses in Ethiopia. This may be accounted for by the high load factor of these buses. Quality of service aside, the operation appears to be fuel-efficient. Likewise, specific fuel consumption is rather low for private autos in Ethiopia. Fuel consumption per ton kilometres performed by trucks in Ethiopia, on the other hand, is on the high side. Most trucks are of 16 ton capacity or higher. But the average load per truck is about 7.4 tons. This must be a contributing factor to the relatively high fuel consumption per ton kilometres. As shall be shown later, however, the fuel consumption in litres/km is also high for commercial transport trucks.

Available data on inter-city buses and taxis in Ethiopia does not permit a parallel analysis. This could be the subject matter of a subsequent study. Whatever its relative position *vis à vis* performances on the international scene with regard to petroleum utilization efficiency, Ethiopia should continue to seek better ways of meeting transport demand at the lowest overall cost. Improved upkeep of vehicles would simultaneously extend the lives of vehicles, thereby making it possible to defer new fleet investments, and also improve the fuel efficiency of vehicles. Improved maintenance facilities and provision of spare parts are *sine qua non* conditions for efforts along these lines. These conditions are not lacking in the government-run passenger and freight transport corporations. Private sector maintenance garages, however, do not enjoy the same privileges.

Improved handling of vehicles by drivers is also akin to improved upkeep of vehicles. Drivers must be trained, financially remunerated or otherwise psychologically prepared to care for the longevity of vehicles and be guided by an attitude of fuel consciousness. Regular maintenance of city streets and roads along important corridors would admittedly contribute to the overall cost efficiency of the transport sector. The challenge lies in the proper balancing of resource allocation for road maintenance extensions, especially in the planning phase.

Price revisions, a ban on Sunday driving, and physical rationing of fuel were some of the measures taken by the government to curb the demand on petroleum fuels. The regulations banning Sunday driving and enforcing fuel rationing were lifted as of 24 September 1989. Concomitantly, pump prices of petrol and taxi fares were revised upwards in apparent recognition of the potency of proper pricing mechanisms for the rational use of petroleum .

There are as yet unsettled issues in the realm of petroleum products pricing and subsidy policy. In principle, money spent on fuel imports must be retrieved fully in a realistically shadow-priced local currency equivalent. Subsidies must be kept to the minimum, serve a transitional purpose towards an alternative long-term solution, and reach an intended beneficiary group. The practice of this principle remains a challenge.

The use of alternative indigenous fuels and alternative modes of transport may also open up a fresh avenue in making the utilization of petroleum fuels more efficient (see a later section of this chapter).

In a nutshell, the key challenges facing Ethiopia's road transport sub-sector are:

1. Expanding the fleet size to meet the growing passenger and freight transport services demand.
2. Meeting the demand for petroleum fuels generated by the expanding fleet size.
3. Making the utilization of petroleum fuels more efficient to curb the overall cost to the transport sector.

Subsequent sections of this chapter will investigate various policy and technical options for addressing the above three challenges.

Policy options for alleviating transport sector problems

In this section we shall first address the regulatory, administrative and managerial dimensions of the strategies that would enhance the efficient utilization of petroleum in the transport sector of Ethiopia. We shall then turn to technological interventions which are inextricably linked to most policy options and are therefore briefly reviewed within the context of setting priorities for their implementation.

Expanding fleet size

With respect to expanding the size of the truck fleet it would be rational to look for ways and means of taking the burden off the government and redistributing it among other financial backers – local freight transport operators, foreign loan agencies and donor agencies, or even a joint-venture scheme between foreign and local partners. Import regulations and duties have been relatively more attractive for freight trucks, but the requirements for their import and operation by private investors may be improved upon according to circumstances.

Possibilities for the improvement of load factors must be looked into, as present indications are that poor load factors are unfavourably affecting the efficient utilization of fuel. Due recognition must be given to the fact that freight transport capacity affects export activities whose earnings are needed for the import of petroleum. The envisaged growth in freight transport services demand should not give cause for alarm: the demand would arise primarily from increased economic activities which would generate the resources for meeting the demand.

With respect to passenger transport, it would be most rational to look into ways and means of inducing passengers to make greater use of mass transport, especially buses. Considering both the need to expand the fleet size and the need to meet the resulting fuel demand, it is fairly obvious that the bus service in urban areas has to be expanded in preference to taxi services. The findings of this report have strengthened this point. The effort to expand bus services must include expansion of the fleet size and improvement in the quality of service. This would demand a substantial amount of investment but it would still be economical to finance this scheme from government sources, external loans and assistance.

If the quality of service is improved, an upward revision of bus fares would not result in loss of demand. Though we have not made a formal opinion survey, it is fairly obvious that passengers who presently take taxis do not do so for the luxury of it but mostly because buses

- are immensely overcrowded;
- are infrequently available;
- have practically no fixed time of arrival at any bus stop;
- are a hazard to the unwary traveller who takes his mind off his pockets;
- are prone to grave accidents and characterized by rough driving.

Otherwise, city buses provide the longest straight-through means of transport to a given destination for the smallest amount of money. This contrasts sharply with the taxi option, whereby passengers must make up to three connections, at several times the bus fare, to reach the same destination. Unlike the demand for freight services, growth in passenger transport demand can come about not necessarily as a result of increased economic activity but as a result of increased urbanization, growth in population or even increases in school attendance, none of which generates financial resources as such. In this respect passenger transport demand is a more serious and urgent problem than the demand for freight transport services. Government must take every opportunity to encourage the influx of passenger vehicles, even if it be individuals importing small cars for family use.

It is worth mentioning here the success of at least one measure taken by government in curbing the demand for passenger transport: office hours were rearranged so that the lunch break was reduced to one hour and the lunchtime journey to and from home was avoided. In extreme cases one could likewise consider shift attendance in government offices, or declaring Saturday as a holiday for some offices.

Enhanced management and administration

One of the major problems in the transport sector is the lack of incentives. High accident rates, most of which are attributable to drivers, could be improved by injecting well designed and thought-out incentive mechanisms. In 1989, there were 811 bus accidents in Addis Ababa, 67 per cent of which were caused by drivers, 19 per cent by other parties 3 per cent by mechanical failure, and 11 per cent by various other factors like bad road conditions, heavy traffic and car overload.

Better maintenance services, more careful handling of vehicles by drivers and effective managerial and administrative support could all be attained through performance-oriented incentives aimed at eliciting desired employee behaviour at all levels of responsibility, thereby ensuring safer services and increased output.

Basically, two types of incentives could be considered here, depending on the nature of the problems encountered. The first type of incentive is a reward given to an employee for desired performance, in the form of a salary increase, fringe benefits, a better job or working environment, or other opportunities like training to expand personal horizons. The second type of incentive is penalties to force workers to adjust and modify their behaviour towards better performance. Such negative incentives include all punishments and disciplinary measures, with outright dismissal as the final sanction.

The existing national labour policy was drafted under a strict socialist labour and management relationship. This policy tends to overprotect the workers and immobilize the management. One of the explanations given for the high number of accidents caused by drivers stems from the incapacity of the management to take strict disciplinary actions to stop such misbehaviour. Management should therefore be given the power and autonomy to apply both the positive and the negative forms of incentive mentioned above.

All city buses in Ethiopia are owned by the government and they all require subsidy to cover losses. Such subsidies are not unique to Ethiopia. Many city buses in other parts of the world are also operating under similar conditions (World Bank, 1983). The government should encourage and provide incentives to people who would like to invest in bus operations. Elimination of the hitherto existing monopoly and the establishment of competitive private operations will undoubtedly result in financially viable public transport systems.

Some of the measures prescribed in relation to expanding the fleet size – increased economic activity, encouraging and strengthening mass transport, and adjustments in office hours and working days – are equally useful strategies for meeting fuel demand. Follow-up of the local consumption trends for specific oil products and adjustment of the local refinery capacity and product configuration would also be important. A recent study (Technip, 1988) has recommended a crude throughput increase of about 20 per cent in the existing refinery, with minor measures to ease bottlenecks, as a priority task. It has also recommended the introduction of a cracker unit to convert fuel oil to middle distillates at a subsequent stage. In view of the existing and envisaged demand for diesel oil, these projects must be considered for implementation in the immediate future.

Improvement in fuel efficiency

Policy objectives on this particular point should be directed at institutionalizing a market-driven and government-assisted mechanism of creating fuel consciousness among users.

Except for petrol and inland fuel oil, all other products are priced below their import values, in economic terms. Moreover, there is still a wide gap between the prices of these fuels in Ethiopia. For example, petrol now sells at almost twice the price of diesel oil (150 Ethiopian cents per litre for petrol, 78 cents per litre for diesel oil) in Addis Ababa. The economic costs are, however, equivalent to 80.3 and 82.7 Ethiopian cents for petrol and diesel oil, respectively (Table 3.9). Although there is a case for keeping the price of petrol above that of diesel oil (the former believed to be consumed mostly by small private cars), the present price gap has the danger of signalling the wrong message that diesel oil is a cheap fuel. Government may also be losing potential revenue on diesel oil sales.

Setting the prices of fuels above their importation costs serves the double purpose of curbing demand and retrieving public money spent on fuel imports. Even in the case of kerosene, a household fuel, the prime objective must lie in ensuring its availability at points of demand rather than selling it at subsidized prices. At the risk of digression, we should mention here that the trend towards the increased use of kerosene in the household sector is fuel substitution in the wrong direction from the point of view of meeting the transport sector fuel demand. As such, the trend should not be encouraged to continue into the longer term. Rather, alternative non-petroleum substitute fuels must be sought in the household sector.

The provision of spare parts is obviously important in keeping vehicles

Table 3.9 Economic cost and retail prices of petroleum products in Addis Ababa, 1990

Product	Economic Cost (ec/l.)**	Retail Price (ec/l.)	Difference (RP/EC-1) 100
1. Petrol	80.3	150.0	+87%
2. Diesel	82.7	78.0	−6%
3. Kerosene	83.1	65.4	−21%
4. LPG	88.2	68.0	−23%
5. Fuel oil	55.8	59.9	+7%

ec − Ethiopian cents
EC − economic cost
RP − retail price
** A factor of 1.33 used to obtain shadow value of foreign exchange.
Source: Based on UNDP/WB, 1984

roadworthy and fuel-efficient. The importation of spare parts can be supplemented by local factories replicating original designs, under licence if necessary. To date, the role of local factories in supplying spare parts has been minimal, but the situation can be improved by utilizing existing capacity or adding more facilities to existing establishments in spare parts production. Effort has to be directed towards training and handling drivers and mechanics with regard to improved upkeep of vehicles and fuel utilization. In parallel, the existing system of vehicle performance follow-up must be strengthened, especially in publicly run transport subsectors.

Monitoring the flow of petroleum energy is made difficult by the lack of a properly structured and adequately detailed database. Such data must essentially be able to indicate the user sector and activity for each type of fuel each year. Presently available data is more like guesswork than a systematically compiled report. For example, fuel sold at retail stations is reported under transport sector consumption, irrespective of its end use. Similarly, fuel purchased in bulk by a power company is reported under power generation, though part of it goes for transport activities. It may be impossible to trace the end-use activity and sector for each barrel of oil every year, but the existing database can be and must be improved to enable meaningful analysis and decision-making.

Evaluation of selected policy options

The growing demand for modern transport services will result in the steady rise of Ethiopia's imports of petroleum fuels. Fortunately, however, the presence of indigenous energy reserves allows some intervention by way of fuel substitution and modal shift to accommodate demand. Available technical options include:
1. Ethanol.
2. Natural gas.

3. Electrical grid energy.
4. Improved telecommunications services.

The above options are evaluated briefly in the following sections. The most promising technical options are then included in a comparative economic assessment that evaluates policy options.

Ethanol

Ethanol can be used as a petrol blend up to 20 per cent by volume. Ethanol can also be used as a diesel fuel blend but with greater problems. In both cases, the problems have to do with damage to the rubber parts, pipes, carburettors and injection equipment on the fuel supply line if the components are not specifically made for ethanol use.

At an annual consumption level of about 125,000 tons of petrol, Ethiopia presently has a demand potential for approximately 25,000 tons of ethanol per year. Current availability of molasses from local sugar plants is about 75,000 tons per year. This figure could double with the commissioning of a new sugar plant at Finchaa in western Ethiopia. Local liquor factories would consume about 20,000 tons of molasses per year, with the balance destined for export or disposed of as waste.

The export of molasses has not been a significant foreign exchange earner, with the highest revenue of about US$1.7 million being attained in 1982. Export prices have varied between US$36 and US$80 per ton. The quantity of export has remained below 25,000 tons in the years 1982–8 (ONCCP, 1982–8). Several studies carried out by various groups since the early 1980s have indicated the viability of ethanol production from surplus molasses in local sugar plants, albeit using different figures for the export price of molasses and import price of petrol.

A 1981 study (Filli, 1981) indicated that an ethanol plant of 19,200 tons per year capacity, requiring an investment of US$12.3 million, would result in a pay-back period of only 1.3 years on the basis of a petrol price of US$420 per ton and molasses feed stock price of US$5 per ton in Ethiopia.

A 1984 UNDP/World Bank study put the case for a typical ethanol plant in Ethiopia as follows:

> The mission reviewed the capital and operating costs for a 20-25 million litre per year ethanol plant at the Wonji–Shoa plantation complex and found the likely cost of production to be between 0.18–0.20 USD per litre compared with the present border price for petrol at Addis Ababa of about 0.30 USD per litre. The economic internal rate of return on the Wonji-Shoa investment is estimated to be about 39 per cent at the investment cost of USD 0.56 million per million litre per year of firm capacity. Doubling this cost will still yield over 20 per cent ERR. (UNDP/WB, 1984)

A 1986 CESEN study also supported the idea of utilizing surplus molasses for ethanol fuel production for petrol blends. That study actually went further and investigated the feasibility of sugar cane plantations solely aimed at providing ethanol fuel for the transport sector in Ethiopia.

While the concept of growing sugar cane for ethanol production is a potentially attractive alternative, the market price of petrol that was used in the economic calculations in the CESEN report looks too high.Unless the price cited above refers to black market transactions, the official retail price at Addis Ababa in 1986 was 1.20 birr per litre. The import price of petrol at port Assab was about US$0.25 per litre for the same year. The effect of considering too high a price for petrol has resulted in an extremely high set of figures for FIRR and ERR.

A more recent paper by J. Baguant *et al.* (1988) puts the production cost of high-grade fuel alcohol at US$0.28 per litre, for a plant capacity of 18 million litres per year requiring molasses feedstock of 75,000 tons/year, at an investment cost of US$8 million and at molasses costs of US$32 per ton. This production cost reduces to US$0.16 per litre, 90 per cent of cost in FC, at molasses costs of US$5 per ton. Even this lower production cost compares unfavourably with an import cost of US$0.14 per litre, FOB Assab port, for petrol in Ethiopia today.

The viability of ethanol projects is obviously highly susceptible to the price of molasses, capacity of plants and import price of petrol. For the price level of molasses (US$5 per ton) indicated above, ethanol plants of 20 million litres per year capacity range would be economically viable at a petrol price of over US$0.16 per litre in the case of Ethiopia.

Natural gas

Recent reports indicate the existence of 30–50 billion cubic metres of natural gas reserves in the south-east region of Ethiopia. Studies have been carried out on the possible utilization of this resource (GDC,1984 ; GDC, 1985). One of the alternative uses of natural gas in Ethiopia would be as vehicle fuel in the transport sector. Compressed natural gas (CNG) can be used as either a supplementary fuel in dual-fuelled spark-ignition and diesel engines or as the sole energy source in the so-called Dedicated Natural Gas Vehicles (Rodrigues, 1989). Several countries outside Africa, notably Italy, New Zealand, Canada, USA, Brazil, Argentina, USSR, People's Republic of China, Australia, Indonesia and Pakistan, have experimented with the use of CNG as vehicle fuel. The problems usually raised in the discussion of CNG vehicles are:

- Fire hazards in the event of accidents involving collisions;
- Loss of power;
- Limited driving range corresponding to the capacity of cylinders containing the compressed gas.

Past and present experience does not indicate that any of these problems would prohibit a wider application of CNG vehicles. Improvements in technology and performance can be expected in the future. Meanwhile, Ethiopia is taking the first steps in the experimental use of natural gas as a vehicle fuel. A feasibility study of small-scale utilization of natural gas in Ethiopia includes demonstration programmes on 125 vehicles. An earlier study has established that the conversion of 50 per cent of the entire fleet to natural gas operation by the year 2000 would result in a demand for natural gas of about 1.2 million cubic metres per day. This demand level could be accommodated comfortably from the point of view of reserves depletion.

The capital cost of vehicle conversion, operational costs and the technical feasibility of the larger scheme would have to be determined in the course of the small-scale demonstration programme. An alternative application foreseen for the Ogaden gas is condensate fuel extraction. Petrol, diesel and LPG are the main products which could be extracted if separator equipment is installed at the well site . At a gas off-take of 0.85 million cubic metres per day, such a plant would yield condensate fuel amounting to about 34,000 tons per year. At an investment level of US$25 million, the economics of the scheme appear positive . However, the quantity of petrol and diesel obtained in the process would amount to only 5 per cent of the national consumption of these fuels.

Another possible direction in the use of natural gas is conversion to liquid fuels. A Shell company report (Shell World,1989) imparts the promising experience of Malaysia. According to this report, Malaysia is investing US$660 million for a natural gas/middle distillate conversion plant, the first of its kind in the world. The plant would produce 500,000 tons of middle distillate fuels per year at a natural gas intake of 100 million cubic feet (about 2.8 million cubic metres) per day.

If the Malaysian experience proves a success, there would be several developing countries who would follow suit. In the Ethiopian case, the Ogaden gas reserves can provide the feedstock for the conversion plant for about three decades, which in any case would be within the range of the expected economic life of the plant. The amount of investment for the conversion plant does not appear prohibitively high, at least in comparison to the annual oil import bill which is around US$200 million. The prospect of reliance on an indigenous resource for the transport sector, with no major alterations or dislocations in the present infrastructure, is also appealing.

Electrical grid energy

Ethiopia has a sizable hydro-electric potential, estimated at 70,000–120,000 GWh per year. The generating capability of hydro plants commissioned to date amounts to about 1760 GWh per year. There is always the natural inclination to hypothesize that the indigenous hydro-electric energy can economically substitute imported oil energy in the transport sector in Ethiopia. However, the economics are sensitive to the production cost of electricity, the import price of petroleum and specific fuel consumption figures for the vehicles under consideration.

For the conditions prevailing in Ethiopia, the following rudimentary analysis shows the economics for the use of diesel fuels in buses and grid electricity in trolleys:

Specific fuel consumption (CESEN, 1986)
Bus (125 persons capacity): 0.51 l./km
Trolley bus (125 persons capacity): 2.0 KWh /km
Import price of diesel:24 Ethiopian cents /l. (1989 price)
Marginal production cost of electricity: 13 Ethiopian cents /KWh
(Coopers and Lybrand,1983)

Therefore, energy costs per km are : *bus* : 12.2 Ethiopian cents
trolley bus: 26.0 Ethiopian cents

On the above figures, one can assign 100 per cent and 70 per cent, respectively, to the foreign currency components of the import price of petroleum and the marginal cost of production of electricity. One can also assign a generous shadow-pricing factor of 2 (the officially adopted factor is 1.33) to the foreign currency component and recalculate the energy costs. The energy costs per km under these assumptions are :

bus: 34.4 Ethiopian cents
trolley bus: 44.2 Ethiopian cents

It appears that trolley buses would not be an economic proposition from the point of view of energy considerations before petroleum prices rise to about double the present level. Other factors like a higher rolling stock cost and extra costs incurred in electric supply infrastructure work against the case for trolley buses.

Hydro systems have surplus energy from time to time when new hydro plants are commissioned. One may argue that trolley buses could be used to take up this energy at virtually no cost. But the energy consumption of a fleet of 72 trolleys (a recommended figure for Ethiopia in CESEN studies) would not be significant:

No. of trolley buses : 72
Average km travelled by each trolley: 45000 / year
Average energy consumed by each trolley bus: 2 KWh/km
Energy consumed by all trolley buses: 7.1 GWh

A typical hydro plant with an annual energy capability of 500–1009 GWh would result in a temporary surplus energy of about 300 GWh per year and the trolley buses would consume only 2 per cent of this surplus. Thus the amount of electrical energy recovered or petroleum energy saved by switching to trolley systems would not be significant. In any case this energy saving has to be weighed against the annualized costs of the electric energy supply infrastructure required for the trolley bus system.

Comparison of buses with more sophisticated mass transit systems relying on grid energy is, however, more complex because the haulage capacity, infrastructure costs and energy consumption become significant parameters in calculations. In such instances, a case by case analysis is mandatory. Potential areas for electric rail feasibility studies would be such important corridors as the Addis Ababa/Assab route, transport systems in major urban centres, main inter-city links and other routes with particularly high levels of goods (industrial raw materials, agricultural/industrial products) and passenger transport. It is logical that Ethiopia should commission such studies as a priority task if decisions on matters of self-reliance are to be based on comprehensive analysis of issues.

Telecommunications

Telecommunications can supplement and actually reduce transport services demand. Table 3.10 below portrays Ethiopia's position *vis-à-vis* other African countries. Since telephone communication is an urban phenomenon, comparison is made on the basis of telephone availability to the urban population. Ethiopia's position is not particularly disadvantaged, but the need for improvement is clear enough.

Table 3.10 Telephone sets per 100 persons in urban areas of selected African countries

Country	Year		
	1980	1985	1986
1. Ivory Coast	2.9	2.5	2.3
2. Nigeria	1.0	1.0	1.0
3. Egypt	2.8	2.8	2.9
4. Ethiopia	2.2	2.3	2.3
5. Kenya	7.3	5.5	5.1
6. Uganda	4.1	3.8	3.6

Source: UN, statistics year books 1986, 1987.

Comparative assessment of selected policy options

A conceptual model depicting the influence of the various policy measures on savings in petroleum fuels is shown in Annexe 3.1. The selected policy options were:

1. Technical efficiency improvement.
2. Fuel substitutions.
3. Modal shift.
4. Pump price changes.

The net annual savings would be positive if the policy measures are sound, at least in financial terms. A tabular version, along with the various parameters obtained through the present research, is shown in Annexe 3.1. Table A, in particular, shows that annual savings in diesel and petrol amount to about 49,500 cubic metres for the first year alone. At mid-1990 oil prices this amounts to an annual saving of 12.8 million birr. The annual costs of effecting these four measures are discussed briefly below.

Technical efficiency improvement

Total annual costs of spare parts directly contributing to fuel efficiency improvement = 36.4 million birr. Assuming 40 per cent of the demand for fuel-related spare parts is actually being met presently, and also assuming that average fuel efficiency is presently in the range of 70 per cent of the practically achievable maximum, a 5 per cent increase in fuel efficiency would require [5 / (100–70)] x (100–40) per cent (i.e 10 per cent) increase in annual expenditure for the purchase of these parts. Thus, additional expenditure required for improving technical efficiency by 5 per cent = 0.1 x 36.4 million birr/ year =3.6 million birr per year.

Fuel substitution

Annualized cost of a 20 million litres/year ethanol plant (investment of 30 billion birr, 25 years plant life and discount rate of 10 per cent per year) = 3.3 million birr.

Modal shift

Cost of additional buses minus cost of taxis otherwise required (carrying capacity of one bus assumed equal to carrying capacity of ten taxis) = 0 birr.

Pump price changes

This option would involve no major expenses.

The total cost of the above options is 6.9 million birr/year. If import prices of fuel prevailing at mid-1990 (before the 1990 Gulf crisis) are taken, the net benefits amount to about 12.8 – 6.9 million birr/year = 5.9 million birr/year for the first year of demand management. The net benefit would increase for subsequent years of demand management and for higher prices of oil.

Utilization of the Ogaden gas reserves by way of condensate fuel extraction (a relatively easier option) is not included in the above analysis (Annex 3.1). Petrol and diesel extraction by this option amount to about 21,000 cubic metres and 15,000 cubic metres respectively per year. The annualized cost of such a scheme is about 5.5 million birr. The import value (at mid-1990 prices) of the extracted oil equivalent is about 9.5 million birr.

Under the assumptions made earlier, the greatest net saving is realizable from condensate fuel extraction followed by technical efficiency improvement, pump price change, modal shift and fuel substitution, in that order. Petrol substitution by ethanol will not result in any significant net benefit beyond the break-even point until the import price of petrol rises perceptibly.

Each of the above measures is complementary to the total package and can be taken up in any sequence deemed necessary for practical implementation.

Key recommendations

To recap, the key challenges facing the road transport sector in Ethiopia are :
1. Expanding fleet size to meet the growing passenger and freight transport services demand.
2. Meeting the demand for petroleum fuels generated by expanding fleet size.
3. Improving efficiencies of petroleum fuels utilization to curb the overall cost to the transport sector.

Key recommendations for addressing the above challenges are given below.

Fleet size

- Government must encourage financiers to invest and operate in the transport service sector, as the financial burden would be too heavy for the government alone to bear.
- Import regulations and duty tax schemes must encourage the influx of passenger vehicles both for public and private use, at least until such a time as the transport service demand is met satisfactorily.
- Bus transport must be expanded and quality of service must be improved to encourage mass transport in the urban centres. The alternative of relying on an expanded taxi service would require large growth in the size of the taxi fleet.
- In extreme cases of large unsatisfied demand for passenger transport in cities, rearrangement of working days and hours may be looked into.

Rising petroleum fuel demand

- Take up the issue of substitute automotive fuels like ethanol and natural gas more seriously. Prior to the actual implementation of the projects, however, working visits must be made to countries with long experience in the production and use of these fuels. In the case of natural gas, care must be taken in selecting between mutually exclusive development schemes. Condensate fuel extraction appears to be a good starting point in practice.
- Contrary to widely held expectations, trolley buses do not appear to be an economic alternative in Ethiopia. However, investigation must continue into other transport systems using hydro-electricity.
- Implement projects, like crude throughput capacity increase and addition of a cracker unit, to obtain optimal use of the refinery at Assab.

Efficiency in petroleum fuel utilization

- Measures must be taken to bring up pump prices of petroleum products close to their economic costs. This will minimize subsidies to unintended beneficiaries, enhance fuel use efficiency and curb demand to some extent.
- Opportunities for an upward tariff revision for city bus services must be looked into, along with possibilities for improving the quality of services.
- Effort must be made to alleviate the spare parts problem by way of increased imports or local manufacture of parts.
- Greater effort (by way of improved maintenance practices and spare parts provision, especially as regards fuel injection pumps and injectors) must be made to reduce truck fuel consumption to international standards. Greater effort must also be made to coordinate freight transport services with the aim of improving the load factors of trucks.
- A thorough review of Addis Ababa's bus routes must be undertaken to arrive at an optimal route system in the immediate future.
- Both positive and negative incentives must be offered to employees at all levels of responsibility so that better performance and productivity is obtained in return.
- Management should be vested with the necessary power and autonomy

to enforce the rules and regulations, as well as implement the policy of the organization.

- More effort must be put into the training and handling of drivers and mechanics with regard to improved upkeep of vehicles and fuel utilization.
- With regard to an improved understanding of the flow of petroleum energy in various sectors of the economy, a more reliable system of reporting on the end use of petroleum products must be introduced.

Thus a number of policy measures could be taken to minimize petroleum consumption without hampering the socio-economic goals of Ethiopia. The savings from some of the measures presented here in some detail amount to about 9.9 million birr per year, but these savings would become more significant as the demand for transport services grows, or as fuel prices rise.

Annexe 3.1

Table A on the next page contains the formulae for a spreadsheet model pertaining to fuel demand under various conditions. Table B is a numerical output corresponding to actual data fed into the spreadsheet model. The following points are noteworthy in Table A.

- The first column contains ten categories of transport services with further breakdowns by petrol and diesel vehicle types.
- Column groups 2–4 pertain to business-as-usual (no policy intervention) conditions. Column groups 6–10 pertain to some form of policy intervention in demand management.
- $r_1, r_2 \ldots r_{10}$ are the annual growth rates (in decimals) established in the present research for the relevant transport service categories. These growth rates are then taken as growth rates for fuel demand in the absence of any policy intervention. Thus, unimpeded demand for fuel for year n from base year (1990) = base year demand x $(1+r)n$.
- Vehicle technical efficiency improvement amounting to a 5 per cent saving in fuel consumption is envisaged. The new fuel demand then becomes 0.95 x unimpeded demand.
- It is assumed that ethanol will replace 10 per cent of petrol used in road vehicles.
- Modal shift is assumed away from taxi services and towards increased use of buses. Hence the relative changes in the growth rates in fuel consumption for these services.
- A 25 per cent increase in the pump price of diesel is assumed (b = 25 per cent).

The price elasticity of demand for diesel, k, is assumed as 10 per cent. A factor of bk = 1–(0.1 x 0.25) = 0.975 is thus introduced on the unimpeded demand to account for pump price rise.

- Overall savings are calculated in the model as the difference between the unimpeded demand and the demand expected when all measures are taken.
- With values of r, f, g, h, b and k fixed, output data is generated for each input value of n.

Table A Implications of some demand management policy measures

Type of transport	Key parameters without demand management				Annual fuel demand for year n with demand management				
	Service annual growth % 1990-2005	Type of fuel	Present demand for for fuel (m³/yr)	Unimpeded demand for fuel at year n	Technical improvement	Fuel substitution	Modal shift	Pump price rise	All measures taken
1. Taxi	100r1	Petrol	F1	F1(1+r1)Expn	0.95F1(1+r1)Expn	F1(1+r1)Expn -0.lF1	F1(16q)Expn	NA	0.95F1(1+g)Expn-0.1F1
2. Comm. petrol vehicle	100r2	Petrol	F2	F(1+r2) Expn	0.95F2(1+r1)Expn	F2(1+r2)Expn -,1F2	NA	NA	0.95F2(1+r2)Expn-0.1F2
3. Private auto	100r3	Petrol	F3	F3(1+r3)Expn	0.95F3(1+r3)Expn	F(1+r3)Expn -0,1F3	NA	NA	0.95r3(1+r3)Expn -0,1F3
4. Gov. petrol vehicle (non-comm.)	100r4	Petrol	F4	F4(1+r4)Expn	0.95F4(1+r4)Expn	F4(1+r4)Expn -0,1F4	NA	NA	0.95l4(1+r4)Expn -0,1F4
5. NGO petrol vehicle	100r5	Petrol	F5	F5(1+r5)Expn	0.95F5(1+r5)Expn	F5(1+r5)Expn -0,1F5	NA	NA	0.95r5(1+r5)Expn -0,1F5
Total petrol	xxxx		xxxx	xxxx	xxx	xxx	xxx	xxx	xxxx
6. Comm. rd. tr. trucks	100r6	Diesel	F6	F6(1+r6)Expn	0.95F6(1+6)Expn	NA	NA	F6w(1-bk) (1+r6)Exp	0.95F6w(1-bk) (1+r6)Exp
7. Non-comm. gov. trucks	100r7	Diesel	F7	F7(1+r7)Expn	0.95F7(1(1+r7)Expn	NA	NA	F7w(1-bk) (1+r7)Exp	0.95F7w(1-bk) (1+r7)Exp
8. Comm. city buses	100r8	Diesel	F8	F8(1+r8)Expn	0.95F8(1(1+r8)Expn	NA	F8(1+h)Expn	F8w(1-bk) (1+r8)Exp	0.95F8w(1-bk) (1+r8)Exp
9. Comm. intercity buses	100r9	Diesel	F9	F9(1+r9)Expn	0.95F9(1(1+r9)Expn	NA	NA	F9w(1-bk) (1+r9)Exp	0.95F9w(1-bk) (1+r9)Exp
10. NGO diesel	100r10	Diesel	F10	F10(1+r10)Expn	0.95F10(1(1+r10)Expn	NA	NA	F10w(1-bk) (1+r10)Expn	0.95F10w(1-bk) (1+r10)Exp
Total diesel	xxxx		xxxx	xxxx	xxx	xxx	xxx	xxx	xxxx
Grand total petrol & diesel	xxxx		xxxx	xxxx	xxx	xxx	xxx	xxx	xxxx

NA = Not applicable

g<<r1. (=0.06 when modal shift assumed for 50% of growth in taxi service)

h>>r0. (=0.096 when modal shift assumed for 50% of growth in taxi service)

k = long-term price elasticity of demand for diesel for price revisions effective day 1 of year 1.

b = % change in price

(k = and b = 25% for this exercise)

Savings
• Savings in petrol (qty) at year n from present =
• Savings in petrol (money) at year n from present =
• Savings in diesel (qty) at year n from present =

Table B: Implications of some demand management policy measures

Type of transport	Key parameters without demand management				Annual fuel demand for year n with demand management				
	Service annual growth % 1990–2005	Type of fuel	Present demand for fuel (m³/yr)	Unimpeded demand for fuel at year: n	Technical improvement	Fuel substitution	Model shift	Pump price rise	All measures taken
1. Taxi	12	Petrol	24200	27104.0	25748.8	24684.0	25652.0	27104.0	21969.4
2. Comm. petrol	2	Petrol	19100	19482.0	18507.9	17572.0	19482.0	19482.0	16597.9
3. Private auto	3	Petrol	51200	52736.0	50099.2	47616.0	52736.0	52736.0	44979.2
4. Gov. petrol vehicle (non-comm.)	2	Petrol	22000	22440.0	21318.0	20240.0	22440.0	22440.0	19118.0
5. NGO petrol	0	Petrol	2590	2590.0	2460.5	2331.0	2590.0	2590.0	2201.5
Total petrol			119090	124352.0	118134.4	112443.0	122900.0	124352.0	104946.0
6. Comm. rd. trucks	5.5	Diesel	263300	277781.5	263892.4	277781.5	277781.5	269448.1	255975.6
7. Non-comm. gov. trucks	1.5	Diesel	41400	42021.0	39919.9	42021.0	42021.0	40760.4	39722.4
8. Comm. city buses	6.5	Diesel	8000	(8520.0)	8094.0	8520.0	8768.0	8264.4	8079.7
9. Comm. intercity buses	3.2	Diesel	25500	(26316.0)	25000.2	26316.0	26316.0	25526.5	24250.2
10. NGO diesel veh.	0	Diesel	31000	(31000.0)	29450.0	31000.0	31000.0	30070.0	28546.5
Total diesel			369200	385638.5	366356.6	385638.5	385886.5	374069.3	355594.4
Grand total Petrol & diesel				xxxx	xxx	xxx	xxx	xxx	xxxx

NA = Not applicable

g<<r1. (=0.06 when modal shift assumed for 50% of growth in taxi service)

h>>r0. (=0.096 when modal shift assumed for 50% of growth in taxi service)

k = long-term price elasticity of demand for diesel for price revisions effective day 1 of year 1

Ck = 0.1 for this exercise

n = no of years from the present (1990)

b = % change in price (b = 25% for this exercise)

Bibliography

Baguant, J. *et al.* (1988). *Exploring the Possibility of Using Low-grade Ethanol as a Kerosene Substitute for Cooking*, University of Mauritius, December.

Central Statistical Authority. (1989). *Transport and Communications Statistics*, Statistical Bulletin No 69, Addis Ababa, January.

CESEN–Ansaldo. (1985). *Transport and Mobility in Addis Ababa 1982–2000*, January.

CESEN–Ansaldo. (1986). *Cooperation Agreement in the Energy Sector*, September.

Coopers and Lybrand Associates. (1983). *Electricity Tariff Study and Asset Evaluation* (for EELPA), June.

Ethiopian Petroleum Corporation. Unpublished reports.

Filli, C. I. (1981). *Evaluation of Feasibility for the Production of Power Alcohol*, Addis Ababa, November.

GDC Inc.(1984). *Prefeasibility Study of Natural Gas Utilization*, Vol. II, November.

GDC Inc. (1988). *Feasibility Study of Small-scale Gas Utilization in Ethiopia*, December.

Geltner, D. (1985). *Transportation and Energy in the Developing Countries*, ERG Review Paper No. 014, April.

Jorgenson,Roy. (1983). *Road Transport Study, Transport Demand General and Passenger*, Addis Ababa.

Louis Berger International. (1983/4). *Transport Sector Study*, Vol. 2.

Office of National Committee for Central Planning (ONCCP)/Road Transport Authority (RTA), 1970/80–1987/88 Reports Compilation.

Public Transport Corporation. (1989). Compilation of annual financial reports.

Public Transport Corporation. (1989). Planning Department report.

Public Transport Corporation. (1990). Compilation.

Rail India.Technical and Economic Service Limited (Technico). (1986). *Economic Feasibility Study of the Transportation System Addis Ababa– Assab Corridor*, Vol. 2.

Rodrigues, A. (1989). 'Natural gas as transport fuel', paper presented at SADCC Energy Conference, Maputu, December.

Sedin Consultants/Swedish Development Corporation. (1987). *The Future of Ethiopia's Relief Transport Fleets, Strategies and Policy Options*, October.

Shell World.(1989). No. 5, London, October.

Trindade, Sergio C. (1984). *Alternative Transport Fuel Supply, Consumption and Conservation*, ERG Review Paper No. 088, November.

UNDP/World Bank. (1984). *Ethiopia: Issues and Options in the Energy Sector*, July.

World Bank. (1983). *World Development Report*.

World Bank. (1984). *Kenya: Transport Sector Memorandum*, Report No. 4610, July.

World Bank. (1988). Staff Appraisal Report, Infrastructure Operations Division, Eastern Africa Department, 5 June.

Abbreviations

APMC	Agricultural Products Marketing Corporation
C&F	Cost and Freight
CESEN	Centro Studio Energia, Italia
CIF	Cost, Insurance, Freight
CNG	Compressed Natural Gas
CSA	Central Statistical Authority
EBCA	Ethiopian Building Construction Authority
EC	Economic Cost
ec	Ethiopian cents

EDDC	Ethiopian Domestic Distribution Corporation
EELPA	Ethiopian Electric Light and Power Authority
EPC	Ethiopian Petroleum Corporation
EPTC	Ethiopian Passenger Transport Corporation
ERR	Economic Rate of Return
ETCA	Ethiopian Transport Construction Authority
ETH	Ethiopia
FC	Foreign Currency
FIRR	Financial Rate of Return
FOB	Freight On Board
FTC	Freight Transport Corporation
GC	Gregorian Calendar
GDC	Gas Development Corporation, USA
GDP	Gross Domestic Product
GWh	Gigawatt hour
HV	High Voltage
IDA	International Development Association
IRR	Internal Rate of Return
KGOE	Kilogramme of Oil Equivalent
km	kilometre
l.	litre
LPG	Liquefied Petroleum Gas
NA	Not Available
NFTC	National Freight Transport Corporation
ONCCP	Office of National Committee for Central Planning
PTC	(National) Public Transport Corporation
Pkm	Passenger kilometre
Rites	Rail India Technical and Economic Services
RP	retail price
RTA	Road Transport Authority
RTS	Road Transport Study
Tcal	Teracalorie
TCD	Transport and Communications Department
Tkm	Ton kilometre
TSS	Transport Sector Study
TWh	Terawatt hour
UN	United Nations
UNDP	United Nations Development Programme
USSR	Union of Soviet Socialist Republics
WB	World Bank

1 Ethiopian Birr = 100 Ethiopian cents = US$0.48

PART II

Energy Management in Manufacturing Industry

4 The Case of Kenya

P. M. Nyoike and B. A. Okech

The economic background

Economic growth

Kenya's post-independence economic history can be traced through five distinct periods. The first period runs from 1964 to 1973. It witnessed an annual average real growth of approximately 7 per cent, the share of the agricultural sector in total output falling from 38 per cent in 1964 to 33 per cent in 1971. This drop was a result of the gradual diversification of the economy. The manufacturing sector recorded a growth rate of 8.2 per cent and its share of total GDP increased from 9 to 10 per cent over the same period. The record GDP growth rate of 8.2 per cent in 1977 reflects the coffee and tea booms of 1976 and 1977.

This period was characterized by economic stability, food self-sufficiency, balance of payments stability, high savings and interest rates, and credit worthiness.

The second phase, 1973/4, was deeply marked by the first oil crisis, the first of a number of external shocks that adversely affected the country's economy. There was a sharp drop in the annual GDP growth rate from 6.7 per cent in 1964–72 to only 3.1 per cent in 1975. This can be traced to a steep increase in the import price of crude oil and other goods. The free on board (FOB) price of crude oil paid by Kenya nearly doubled in 1973 and almost tripled between December 1973 and the end of the first quarter in 1974.

The third period was 1975–8, during which GDP growth more than doubled from about 3 per cent in 1975 to about 8 per cent in 1978. This period was characterized by high prices for coffee and tea, the two leading export earners. The price of coffee increased by an average annual rate of about 158 per cent between 1975 and 1977. Over the same period, tea prices realized an average annual growth of 67 per cent.

The next phase, 1978–84, is characterized by the steady fall of GDP growth rates to 0.8 per cent in 1984. This severe decline was the result of a combination of factors: the 1980 and 1984 droughts, the unstable petroleum energy situation, the collapse of the East African Community, unstable export prices for coffee and tea, low growth rates in gross investment, and budgetary deficits.

Economic recovery began yet again during the fifth period, 1984–90, helped by favourable weather conditions, government budgetary discipline and improved economic management policies, the decline of world oil prices and moderate increases in coffee prices. In 1986, the economy recorded a GDP growth rate of 5.5 per cent in real terms.

Structural change

Over the last 25 years, the economy has undergone a structural change visible in the relative shares of various sectors in the total GDP, including changes in finance and external trade. This change is attributable to the expansion and growth of monetization and to government participation in the economy. The transformation is characterized by a decline in the share of agriculture in total monetized output, and by the increasing shares of manufacturing, banking, insurance and real estate. Although agriculture continues to be the dominant sector in the economy, its share of the GDP has declined from 42 per cent in 1964 to 28 per cent in 1988. On the other hand, the manufacturing sector's share increased from 10.5 to 13.2 per cent within the same period.

Kenya's fiscal and monetary system, relatively sophisticated at the time of independence, has become even more so over the past 25 years. The high degree of monetization in the economy is indicated by the relatively high level of the money supply in relation to GDP. By the second half of the 1970s, money supply was growing at an average annual rate of about 20 per cent. The rising rate of growth was accounted for by expanded activities of both private and public sectors which resulted mainly from the coffee boom earnings of 1975–8. The end result was a dramatic surge in domestic demand which pushed the rate of inflation to over 22 per cent in 1982. On the institutional front, the changes occurred by way of increased numbers of both commercial banks and non-bank financial establishments. In 1964 there were only nine commercial banks. Currently they number 23, with over 430 branches nationwide. The number of other financial establishments has risen from a handful in the mid-1960s to over 55 by 1990.

The growth of the money sector has been accompanied by significant depreciation in the value of money. Inflation started its steep climb in the mid-1970s. The rate of inflation rose from a mere 2.6 per cent in 1972 to 15.6 per cent in 1975, peaking at 22.3 per cent in 1982 before falling to its current rate of 15 per cent.

Over the 1964–79 period, the share of expenditure going to economic services declined from 29 to 22 per cent of total government spending, whereas expenditure for social services rose from 17 to 29 per cent. In the domain of public finance, structural change has been characterized by a fluctuating budgetary deficit relative to GDP, and by increased domestic and external public indebtedness. The country's external debt reached crisis proportions in the mid-1980s; the debt crisis has continued to deepen since then. About 37 per cent of the total value of exports in 1987 went to service the external debt.

It is important to note that all along Kenya has remained an open economy with a high degree of dependence on external trade. Kenya's international trade dependency index, expressed as the ratio of the value of imports and exports to GDP, has averaged 60 per cent annually since independence. The notable structural change in Kenya's imports during the post-independence period has been the decline in the share of finished manufactured goods from about 39 per cent in the 1960s to about 16 per cent in 1986. An important feature of external trade is the large deficit which has persisted despite a steady increase in export earnings. A deterioration in the balance of payments was the natural consequence.

In exports, tea and coffee have continued to predominate. The contribution of coffee to export earnings has held firm at about 25 per cent for the last 25 years; tea has fluctuated slightly, between 13 and 11 per cent, over the same period. The joint contribution of these two commodities to foreign exchange earnings is about 70 per cent.

Economic planning

After independence, the Kenyan government saw an emphasis on planning as the key to rapid changes in the economy. In the mid-1970s, economic planning took on a new dimension as a way of meeting the very stiff conditionalities imposed by the IMF and the World Bank. The government has responded to the pressure in a series of Sessional Papers and Development Plans. The major themes of the First Development Plan, covering the period 1970–8, emphasize the development of the rural areas (where more than 80 per cent of the population continue to live), employment creation and improvement in income distribution.

The first Sessional Paper (No. 4 of 1975 on Economic Prospects and Policies), to which IMF and World Bank lending in that year was linked, put forward a strategy to deal with the already serious problems of imported inflation, balance of payments deficit and slowing growth. It proposed that domestic price increases should be held to no more than half of the increase in import prices, that wage increases should be less than domestic price increases, and that imports should be restrained and exports expanded.

The 1979–83 Development Plan took this further. Its principal theme was alleviation of poverty with particular reference to pastoralists, small farmers, landless rural workers, the urban poor and the handicapped. It talked also of reduction in inequalities, utilization of domestic resources and a more balanced type of economic growth. But the emphasis in its growth strategy was on stabilization and structural adjustment or, as the Plan put it, 'on achieving greater efficiency in resource use by restructuring the pattern and reforming the process of growth.'

In practice, this meant shifting the emphasis from manufacturing industry to export crop agriculture, from import-substituting to export-processing industry, and from infrastructure services to directly productive sectors; another broad priority was reducing biases in exchange rates, interest rates, prices, tariffs and protective systems.

The plan put a good deal of stress on a shift in manufacturing 'from producing goods for our domestic use to the more difficult challenge of increasing our exports in highly competitive world markets.' Specifically, the plan proposed the phasing out of all non-tariff protection to existing industries within five years; further concessions would be limited to new, genuinely 'infant' industries, and to a maximum period of five years. Tariff protection would be standardized and extended to all types of imports, including industrial equipment, raw materials and agricultural products, and rates would be reduced gradually to between 20 and 30 per cent, except in those cases where high tariffs are aimed at raising revenue.

The 1980 Sessional Paper No. 4 on Economic Prospects and Policies emphasizes changed external circumstances, scales down growth expectations (from 6.3 to 5.4 per cent) and proposes fiscal and monetary reform along with the removal of quantitative restrictions on imports. It also establishes three new measures to encourage manufactured exports and heralds government withdrawal from detailed control of industry. The first new measure would establish an export credit and guarantee scheme, under which exporters would be able to obtain insurance against the risk of non-payment from abroad and local commercial banks would be guaranteed against non-payment of credit by exporters. The second measure transfers the administration of the export compensation scheme, under which local manufacturers who export their products are entitled to claim a refund of import duty provided their exports have at least 30 per cent local content, to the Central Bank, operating through the commercial banks in accordance with Finance Ministry guidelines. Payments would be made automatically for approved categories of exports upon presentation of export documents and payment of foreign exchange. Thirdly, the scheme would be kept under review to ensure that the rate of compensation (raised to 20 per cent in the budget) was sufficient 'to make efficient exports at least as rewarding as local market scales.'

The Sessional Paper No. 4 of 1982 on Development Prospects and Policies, to which the World Bank's second structural adjustment loan and credit were linked, tightens the screw further. It looks for increased agricultural yields and energy savings, and introduces fiscal and monetary austerity measures. The paper underlined four aspects of structural adjustment already in place: the relaxation of price controls, which would be extended as competition from imports increased; further devaluations; tariff adjustments, mainly upwards but occasionally, as in the case of some important inputs for export industries, downwards; and the introduction of a new, potentially more liberal import licensing system.

The 1984–8 Development Plan, the theme of which is 'mobilizing domestic resources for equitable development', spells out the strategy on government finance, promotes exports and improves incentives. Its main preoccupation is with the high cost of servicing external debt, which has brought the Kenyan economy to a 'critical juncture'. Two of the obvious means of reducing dependence on external finance – raising taxes and increasing domestic borrowing – are regarded as 'not promising in present circumstances', so the Plan puts forward a programme to reduce the cost to the budget of government services. This involves, firstly, the supplementing of government provision of selected essential services and the sharp curtailment of non-essential government investments and services, both of which will in some cases be left to the private sector; secondly, a shift in the focus of planning to the level of the district, which becomes 'the management centre for rural development'; thirdly, improvement in the efficiency of planning and delivering government services and in the productivity and discipline of the civil service; and, fourthly, the shifting of more of the burden of the cost of government services to those who benefit from them, through fees and other charges.

These policies, the plan hopes, 'will bring the budget deficit under firm control while at the same time promoting greater independence in the development of the nation.' Strict controls are envisaged over new government and parastatal investment projects and over the terms and conditions on which government lends or guarantees loans. Direct government involvement in commercial activities is to be reduced. The Plan's aim is to cut the proportion of GDP that is 'diverted to government use' from nearly 30 per cent in recent years to approximately 25 per cent, 'thus leaving more resources for direct use by Kenyans'.

Sessional Paper No. 1 of 1986, on Economic Management for Renewed Growth, takes the structural adjustment process further. It looks towards the year 2000 and spells out a programme of slower growth in spending on social services, particularly health and education; an end to the practice of virtually guaranteeing public sector jobs for graduates of universities and government training institutions; the development of a secondary capital and money market to help finance budget deficits; improved incentives for agriculture and export-oriented industry; reforms in the system of price and monopoly control; a new development policy for the informal sector; and tax reforms aimed at pushing revenue towards 25 per cent of GDP.

The outcome of these policies and plans has been positive real interest rates (after adjusting for inflation), very substantial devaluations, controlled inflation, a fall in real wages, increased unemployment, reduced government borrowing, smaller budget deficits, a rise in agricultural production and manufactured exports, a better-managed response to drought and a reduction in the foreign exchange burden of oil imports. The cost of servicing the external debt, however, has been rising.

Kenya's energy profile

Like many developing countries, Kenya has a dualistic economy: one part very monetized and modern, the other non-monetized and traditional. This dualism is an important determinant of energy supply and demand, and of the country's energy structure. Woodfuel is the predominant energy source in the traditional sector. The modern sector – commerce, industry and the urbanized communities – depends largely on fossil fuels and electricity. This structure is not static, however, but is changing fast in line with structural changes in the rural economy and demographic changes such as mass migration from the countryside to urban areas; the demand for modern forms of energy is increasing rapidly.

There is a strong correlation between the growth rates of modern energy consumption and monetary GDP. Okech (1986) demonstrated a strong linear relationship between the two growth rates in Kenya. His statistical analysis shows an R-square of about 90 per cent and a significant coefficient of GDP at a 5 per cent level. For petroleum products, Senga and Manundu (1980) showed positive linear relationships between consumption and GDP, with a significant coefficient of elasticities and R-squares.

Energy supply

The Kenyan economy depends on seven different types of energy sources: woodfuel, petroleum fuels, electricity, ethanol, wind and solar radiation. The last two sources remain marginal, with limited markets in the irrigation, livestock, rural residential and social institutional sectors.

Table 4.1 presents different aspects of Kenya's energy supply, identifying the types of energy, their supply bases (indigenous or foreign), the amounts of energy imported or acquired from domestic sources, and the amounts lost within the supply system.

Table 4.1   Kenya energy sector: source, process and end user

Source	Resource base/ location	Extraction/transfer process	End use
Coal	Foreign	Importation, inland transport and distribution	Industrial and transport sector
Crude oil	Foreign	Importation, refining, inland transport and distribution	Industrial, transport, commercial agricultural, residential, secondary electric generation sectors; also export
Hydro-electric	492.5 MW/ Domestic	Conversion, transmission and distribution	Industrial, commercial and urban residential sectors
Geothermal	45MW/ domestic	Exportation, production, conversion and transmission	Secondary electric generation
Ethanol	Renewable/ domestic	Extracted from biomass, transported and distributed. Planting, harvesting, collection and transportation	Transport
Woodfuel	Renewable/ domestic	Planting, harvesting, collection and transportation	
Fuelwood	Domestic	Planting, harvesting, collection and transportation	Rural residential sector
Charcoal	Domestic	Conversion and transported	Urban residential sector
Wind energy	Renewable/ domestic	Conversion and transmission	Agricultural irrigation, livestock and rural residential
Solar energy	Renewable/ domestic	Conversion and transmission	Residential sector and rural social services institutions

Table 4.2 Energy supply by source 1984–9: absolute values (000 toe) and percentage share

Energy type	1984		1985		1986		1987		1988		1989	
	000 toe	%	000 toe	%	000 toe	%	000 toe	%	000 toe	%	000 toe	%
Fuelwood	3381	57.0	3550	58.0	3728	55.9	3914	56.2	4110	56.2	4316	55.7
Charcoal	586	10.0	645	10.5	710	10.7	781	11.2	859	11.8	945	12.2
Woodfuel sub-total:	3967	67.0	4195	68.5	4437	66.6	4695	67.4	4969	68.0	5260	67.9
Coal	83	1.4	60	1.0	68	1.0	82	1.2	79	1.1	92	1.2
LPG	24	0.4	24	0.4	27	0.4	28	0.4	29	0.4	29	0.4
Petrol	475	6.0	318	5.2	339	5.1	374	5.4	380	5.2	388	5.0
Kerosene (DPK)	359	6.0	369	6.0	404	6.1	414	5.9	439	6.0	481	6.2
Gas oil (auto)	483	8.0	513	8.4	565	8.5	629	9.0	598	8.2	611	7.9
Diesel (IDD)	25	0.4	25	0.4	32	0.5	31	0.4	23	0.3	27	0.3
Petrol (aviation)	7	0.1	7	0.1	7	0.1	8	0.1	8	0.1	8	0.1
Fuel oil	355	6.0	441	7.2	600	9.0	496	7.1	571	7.8	627	8.1
Sub-total:	1728	29.0	1697	28.0	1974	29.6	1980	28.4	2049	28.0	2171	28.0
Ethanol	5	0.1	4	0.1	4	0.1	6	0.1	6	0.1	6	0.1
Electricity	154	2.6	169	2.8	183	2.7	203	2.9	208	2.8	217	2.8
Totals	5935	100.0	6124	100.0	6666	100.0	6966	100.0	7310	100.0	7746	100.0

Sources: Ministry of Energy and Central Bureau of Statistics, Nairobi, and project-generated numbers

Woodfuel

Woodfuel is the major source of energy in Kenya, accounting for about 70 per cent of the net energy supply. It is consumed in two different forms: as fuelwood, which is the biomass that has not gone through any conversion, and as charcoal. As shown in Table 4.2, the percentage contribution of this energy source has not varied significantly over the 1984–90 period.

Petroleum

Petroleum is the second largest energy source in Kenya's economy and the largest source of energy for the modern sector. Its consumption grew from 17.28 million tons of oil equivalent (TOE) in 1984 to 21.771 million TOE in 1989. As can be seen from Table 4.2, the contribution of this source to total energy consumption averaged 28 per cent in the second half of the 1980s. The highest percentage share (30 per cent) was reached in 1986.

The bulk of petroleum fuel is imported into Kenya in the form of crude oil from the Middle East and is refined in the country's only refinery at Mombasa. The history of the Kenyan crude oil refining process dates back to 1959, four years before independence, when a decision to construct the oil refinery was made by foreign private investors. The design capacity of the oil refinery, which is 4 million tonnes per annum of heavy crude oil, was meant to serve Tanzania, Uganda, eastern Zaire and southern Sudan. But its highest recorded throughput since it was commissioned was about 3 million tonnes, in 1980. In 1971 the government bought 50 per cent of equity in the refinery company, but without the right to appoint the general manager, who influences major policy decisions. The government's vote in the refinery company at that time was only used to protect its share of the profits.

The output of the refinery consists of liquefied petroleum gas (LPG), petrol, kerosene (domestic), gas oil (automotive diesel oil), industrial diesel oil, aviation fuel, residual (or industrial) fuel, bitumen and lubricants. Occasionally, Kenya imports refined petroleum fuel products, but usually only to plug the gaps created by short-term supply and demand imbalances arising when processing additional crude oil volume is not financially viable.

Crude oil imports are undertaken by Shell, British Petroleum (BP), Esso, Caltex, Total, Agip, Kobil, Kenya Oil Company (KENOL) and the National Oil Corporation of Kenya (NOCK). All are privately owned foreign companies except NOCK, which is entirely state-owned, and KENOL, which is owned by Kenyans. Total also has a minority local equity participant. The private companies account for 70 per cent of the total crude oil imports, while the balance is imported by NOCK. The marketing is undertaken by the private companies only, since NOCK does not have its own retail outlets. NOCK sells petroleum crude; only rarely does it sell other products to the private companies.

In order to influence the type of crude oils imported into the country, all applications for petroleum crude and other products are first submitted to the Ministry of Energy for analysis of freight rate and FOB unit prices, together with other relevant factors such as the ship's length of stay in Mombasa (the port of discharge), the off-shore credit period and the attendant interest rates.

Insurance period underwriting is done in Kenya and only a fixed percentage, usually around 0.15 CF, is allowed for costs recovery in the marketplace.

After the Ministry of Energy is satisfied with the terms, it forwards applications to the Ministry of Commerce where they are further scrutinized. At this point, if the Ministry of Commerce is not satisfied with the supply terms, it returns the application to the Ministry of Energy for further review and re-submission to Commerce. In the event of inter-ministerial dispute, applications are forwarded with the observations of the two ministries to the Foreign Exchange Allocation Committee which is chaired by the Minister of Finance and includes representatives of the Ministry of Commerce, the Ministry of Industry, the Central Bank and the Office of the President. The Committee is the final authority on all imports into Kenya and meets weekly to consider all applications submitted by the Ministry of Commerce, which is the only official channel for processing import applications before they are sent to the Committee. After applications are approved by the Committee, the Central Bank is authorized to issue foreign exchange.

Any company that fails to adhere to the agreed crude shipment timetable (which is normally quarterly but firmed up monthly) is not allowed to bring in its cargo. Monthly meetings attended by all the oil companies are held to confirm the shipment timetable, with the oil refineries chairing the supply coordination committee. Government does not sit on this committee, but the Ministry of Energy is furnished with the updated quarterly oil import programmes on a monthly basis, to ensure a constant flow of oil into the domestic economy. Any supply disputes with regard to importation and processing which cannot be resolved by this committee are referred to the Ministry of Energy for adjudication, but this rarely happens.

The supply and distribution of petroleum products in Kenya is controlled by the government through an agreed pricing mechanism between the government and the distributors of the refined products who happen to be the same oil multinationals who also import the crude (KENOL and NOCK do not participate in this activity).

In order to ensure a reliable supply of petroleum products to Nairobi and up-country, the government in 1976 constructed the 440 km oil pipeline from Mombasa to Nairobi. The pipeline has an installed capacity of 5.2 million litres per annum. It has continued to earn the government good revenue and provided employment. Because of this positive performance, the government has decided to extend the pipeline to western Kenya, with a terminus at Kisumu on the shores of Lake Victoria and another at the town of Eldoret.

Electricity

Electricity is the third largest source of energy in Kenya. The internal generating capacity is about 705 MW, an almost ninefold increase from 79 MW at independence in 1963. Of this capacity, about 168 MW is from thermal generation and is not taken into account when considering primary energy sources. Accounting of indigenous primary capacity of electric power in Kenya therefore considers only hydropower and geothermal installed capacities. The Kenyan hydropower capacity currently stands at about 492 MW and geothermal capacity at 45 MW.

The 45 MW geothermal power capacity, the first of its kind in Africa, is located in the Olkaria. Exploration work was first undertaken between 1956 and 1959 when two wells were drilled in the area. They failed to produce steam and were abandoned. No more work took place until the mid-1960s, after independence, when the government undertook to continue exploration. By April 1976 six new wells had been drilled in the Olkaria, this time yielding promising results. They form the basis of the existing 45 MW plant.

Except for two small units, existing hydropower capacity is on the Tana river, distributed by stations as follows:

Station	Capacity (MW)
Small hydro units	6.2
Tana	14.4
Wanjii	7.4
Kamburu	91.5
Gitaru	145.0
Kindaruma	44.0
Masinga	40.0
Kiambere	144.0
Total	492.5

In addition, the Turkwell Gorge Multi-Purpose Project with a rated capacity of 106 MW is nearing completion.

Kenya imports some electricity from the Uganda Electricity Board (UEB) which generates its power at Owen Falls at Jinja on the River Nile. Supply from this source is provided under a 50-year agreement, ending in the year 2010, under which the UEB is to supply Kenya with 30 MW on a regular basis and up to 15 MW more whenever need arises. Due to the volatile political situation in Uganda throughout the 1970s and 1980s, the amount of power imported averaged less than 30 MW, at times dropping to below 10 MW.

Kenya has established an extensive grid network covering the major population centres, its expansion financed through heavy external borrowing by the power industry

The Rural Electrification Programme, commenced in 1974, has continued to depend on financial assistance from foreign donors in the form of grants and soft loans. The government's contribution is currently in the region of Ksh40 million per annum, while the Kenya Power and Lighting Company contributes 2 per cent of its gross sales revenue to the programme annually.

Coal

Coal accounts for only 1 per cent of Kenya's energy consumption. All of it is imported from Swaziland; it is railed from there to the port of Maputo in Mozambique, then shipped to Mombasa. The availability potential of current sources of coal and the potential for new sources have been discussed by Okech (1988). The political situation in the Southern African region is seen as the major potential constraint on the supply of coal from current sources.

The domestic demand for coal is also heavily influenced by fuel oil prices because the latter is a direct substitute in the firing of kilns at the cement factory in Mombasa. Fuel oil is likely to become coal's major competitor in new applications which might emerge.

Ethanol

Ethanol accounts for less than 1 per cent of Kenya's energy requirement. It is produced as a by-product of sugar refining at Muhoroni in western Kenya and is transported by road in tankers for blending with petrol in Nairobi. As a comparatively small quantity is blended, it is consumed only in Nairobi and the nearby areas around the towns of Thika, Kiambu and Machakos.

Renewable sources

Available data on the wind regime in Kenya still do not provide a basis for large-scale investment decisions. As for solar power, Kenya's average insolation of 5.5 KWh/square metre daily, with half of the country receiving over 5.8 KWh/square metre annually, is an indication of reasonable potential for this energy source. However, solar water heating at today's electricity tariffs and fuel oil prices is not financially viable.

Energy demand

Table 4.3 and Figure 4.1 display the amounts and percentage shares of energy used by the five main sectors of the Kenyan economy: households, transport, manufacturing, agriculture and commerce.

Household sector

Kenyan households depend on four sources of energy; in order of importance, these are woodfuel (fuelwood and charcoal), kerosene, electricity and LPG. For the 75 per cent of the population who live in the rural areas, woodfuel is the predominant source of energy, accounting for over 95 per cent of total consumption (Table 4.3, Figure 4.1). Although this proportion has not changed significantly within the 1984–9 period, the amount of energy consumption from this source has increased significantly from 3075 thousand TOE in 1984 to 4105 thousand TOE in 1989. This trend represents an average annual growth rate of about 6 per cent. It is important to note that whereas the rural area depends predominantly on fuelwood, the urban areas depend on charcoal. This explains why consumption of fuelwood predominates over charcoal: the former accounts for 80 per cent, the latter for 15 per cent.

Kerosene is the next largest supplier to the household sector, accounting for 4 per cent of consumption. The absolute quantity of kerosene consumed by the sector increased steadily throughout the 1980s.

Table 4.3 Energy demand by sector, 1989 (000 toe)

Sector / Energy source	Households 000 toe	%	Commercial 000 toe	%	Manufacturing 000 toe	%	Transport 000 toe	%	Agriculture 000 toe	%
Fuelwood	3237	74.6	43	15.1	432	43.6			604	88.5
Charcoal	868	20.0	18	6.3	59	6.0				
Woodfuel sub-total:	4105	94.6	61	21.4	491	49.6			604	88.5
Coal					92	9.2				
Cooking gas (LPG)	14	0.3	9	3.1	5	0.6				
Petrol			12	4.2	5	0.6	341	32.2	4	0.6
Kerosene (DPK)	166	3.8	16	5.6	3	0.3	283	26.7	1	0.1
Gasoil (AUTO)			78	27.4	26	2.6	416	39.3	29	4.2
IDO (Industrial)			13	4.5	8	0.8			2	0.3
Petrol (aviation)							7	0.7		
Fuel oil			60	21.1	246	24.9	3	0.3	29	4.2
Power ethanol							6	0.6		
Electricity	54	1.2	35	12.3	115	11.6			13	1.9
Total	4339	100.0	284	100	990	100.0	1056	100	682	100

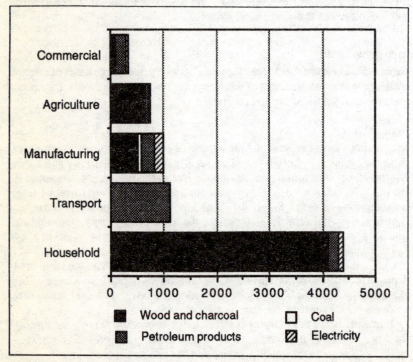

Figure 4.1 Energy demand by sector, 1989

Transport sector

The transport sector is the second largest energy user in the Kenyan economy, although in some years this sector's consumption has been overtaken by that of the manufacturing sector. Petroleum fuel products dominate the sector's energy supply base: gas oil (diesel) is in greatest demand, followed by petrol and kerosene. In the second half of 1980s, gas oil met over 35 per cent of the energy requirement within the sector. Petrol, at 30 per cent, was the second largest contributor, as Tables 4.2 and 4.3 show. Unlike the rising trend of gas oil consumption, the share of petrol consumption has been more or less constant throughout the second half of 1980s, while rising in volume from 250,000 TOE in 1984 to 341,000 TOE in 1989.

The share of kerosene varied between 28 and 32 per cent of the sectoral energy consumption over the later half of 1980s. The amount consumed from this source has changed moderately over the period, remaining below 268,000 TOE during most of the period, and increasing to 283,000 TOE in 1989.

Manufacturing sector

The manufacturing sector is the third largest energy end-user in the Kenyan economy. Over 60 per cent of the energy consumption in the manufacturing sector is accounted for by only two sources: woodfuel and residual fuel oil. On average, the proportion of energy consumption by this sector stood at about 14 per cent of the entire economy's energy consumption in the second half of the 1980s. With the exception of 1986/7, when consumption declined from 917,000 to 897,000 TOE, there is an increasing trend as consumption grew from 747,000 to 990,000 TOE over the 1984–9 period, a growth rate increase of about 3 to 5 per cent annually.

Agricultural sector

Although this sector is the mainstay of the Kenyan economy, it comes only fourth in the list of energy-consuming sectors, with woodfuel the predominant form of energy used. Agriculture accounts for only about 10 per cent of the country's energy consumption and this proportion has not changed significantly in the latter half of 1980s, although the actual consumption has changed considerably. In 1984 consumption was 529,000 TOE and in 1989 it was 682,000 TOE, an average annual growth rate of about 5.5 per cent, with all the intervening years witnessing over 5 per cent growth rate except for 1988/9, when growth rate was a moderate 2.6 per cent.

It is important to note that whereas cash crop agriculture provides the bulk of hard currency foreign exchange earnings, its use of petroleum fuel, whose import it finances, is negligible.

Commercial sector

The commercial sector is the smallest energy-consuming sector in the economy. It accounts for only about 5 per cent of the country's energy consumption.

Energy pricing

There is no uniform energy pricing policy and practice in Kenya. The position of government with respect to energy pricing and associated practices depends both on the nature of the energy sources and on the basic conditions and characteristics of markets for the individual energy types. One, therefore, finds considerable divergence in pricing for modern energy forms such as petroleum fuels, electricity and coal as well as traditional forms such as fuelwood and charcoal. Prices are rarely synchronized. In the case of petroleum fuel products, the upward adjustment of prices takes into account the need to keep the consumer prices of kerosene, fuel oil and diesel at low levels relative to motor petrols, normally used by the more affluent members of society. While this consideration is satisfied, however, the intention to ensure that consumers pay the full cost of petroleum supply is sidetracked.

Electricity pricing

Pricing of electricity is in accordance with the Electric Power Act, which empowers the Kenya Power and Lighting Company (KPLC) to formulate and propose the levels and structures of electricity prices through their by-laws. According to the Act, the company is supposed to inform the government through the Ministry of Energy of price changes, indicating the tariff rates as well as when the new rates will be introduced. In theory, the Ministry is supposed to give instructions on charging policy and no price changes can be made without the Minister's consent. However, past experiences tend to suggest that, more frequently than not, the price formulations and proposals are accepted by the Ministry in their original form.

The objectives of tariff changes are frequently imprecise and ambiguous. One source states that prices are based on supply and transmission costs, plus a factor for future harnessing of both hydro and geothermal sources. According to a recent study, a discussion with the KPLC revealed that the tariffs are based on long-run marginal costs calculated from five-year capital investment plans and demand projections. However, the study notes, recent tariff increases have had more to do with changes in the exchange rates relative to the currencies in which debts are denominated and the effect on their capital and interest payment. Furthermore, other studies have also observed that it has become difficult to say whether equilibria or levels of return have been the basis for pricing electric power in Kenya. The demand for electricity has been frequently used to rationalize power tariff increases. KPLC and the government have in the past justified tariff hikes on the basis of the need to meet some anticipated demand. It has been argued that the demand for power will grow faster than the GDP, thereby overtaking supply capacity in the future.

The current electricity structure and consumer categories are shown in Table 4.4. Whereas the classifications shown have been in existence for a number of years, the level of charges came into effect only in June 1990.

Table 4.4 Electricity tariffs from June 1990

Tariff category/ sub-category	Consumption monthly (Kwh)	Consumer type	Fixed charge (Ksh/ month)	Demand charge (Ksh/KVA/ month)	Energy charge (Ksh/Kwh)
A	0–7,000				
AO		Household	30		
	0–50				0.37
	50–100				1.00
	100–300				1.25
	Over 300				1.66
A1		Small commercial	45		1.46
B	7,000–100,000	Medium commercial/industrial	120		1.46
B0		Irrigation pumping	120		1.17
B1		Supply at 240kv or 415 volts	120	50	1.28
B2		Supply at 11kv or 33 kvolts	720	45	1.23
B3		Supply at 66kv or 132 kvolts	3280	40	1.19
C	Over 100,000	Large commercial/industrial			
C1		Supply at 415 volts	120	50	1.19
C2		Supply at 11kv or 33 kvolts	720	45	1.15
C3		Supply at 66kv or 132 kvolts	3250	40	1.10
D	Interruptable supply (off-peak)	Household water heating	50		1.16
E	Supply available at least 11 hrs per day	Street lighting	65		1.46
F	Company (KPLC) staff	Household			

Source: KPLC (1990)

Petroleum pricing

Oil pricing is based on some key parameters which are discussed below. A committee with membership drawn from government and the oil companies meets regularly in order to monitor the developments of those parameters that determine retail pump prices (FOB crude oil prices, freight rates from the Persian Gulf to Mombasa, the Kenya shilling/US dollar exchange rate, cost of working capital, return on fixed assets, and the level of operating losses including inter-country transhipment and related expenses). Monthly meetings are held to review and take stock of over- or under-recoveries with regard to FOB crude oil prices, freight rates and exchange rates, as these three parameters change on a daily basis.

The factors which determine the procurement and refining cost (PRC) and petroleum pricing formulae are as follows:

1. Crude cost per barrel in US dollars in the Persian Gulf.
2. Freight rate for a medium-sized vessel with a load not exceeding 84,000 long tonnes of crude oil, the rate converted to US dollars per barrel equivalent. Depending on the cargo size and the ship's rated capacity, per unit rate applicable could be either the normal Average Freight Rate Assessments (AFRA)/World Scale rates, as reported in the daily issues of the Plats Oilgram, or something higher than that, adjusted for any space not utilized. The charge for the unutilized space is known as dead freight which is a very common occurrence in oil trading. The freight rate could also be higher if the ship calls at two ports for loading different crude oils. The basic standard rates for shipment of oil from different parts of the world are published monthly in a World Scale book, with monthly variations over or above basic rates being shown in indices form as Average Freight Rate Assessments.
3. The Foreign Exchange Allocation Licence Fee (FEAL), which is imposed by the Central Bank of Kenya at 1.5 per cent CIF. The FEAL used to be 1 per cent CIF until early 1989.
4. Insurance on CIF value of the cargo, which is on the basis of payments made by the oil industry to insurance companies. Until 1988, the maximum allowance made for this in the pricing formula was 0.15 per cent CIF.
5. The processing fee, which is denominated in US dollars per barrel but is charged in Kenya shillings. The denomination of the processing fee in US dollars is meant to protect the Kenya Petroleum Refineries Company (KPRC) from any losses associated with the devaluation of the Kenya shilling, whose exchange rates against all major convertible currencies and other regional currencies are fixed daily.
6. Wharfage, which currently stands at 1.5 per cent CIF and is paid by all the oil importers to the Kenya Ports Authority for services rendered.
7. Ocean loss, which is internationally agreed as equivalent to 0.5 per cent of all costs incurred (CIF, Central Bank fee and Wharfage).
8. Exchange rate – a very important parameter since all the above costs are fixed in US dollars and then converted into the Kenya shilling equivalent on a monthly basis. This is because since 1980 the government has been pursuing a flexible exchange policy which is determined principally by Kenya's terms of trade and the resulting balance of payments. Between 1980 and 1990 the Kenya shilling had been devalued by more than 300 per cent relative to the US dollar.

Since PRC parameters can undergo frequent variations, consumer prices of various petroleum fuels are in most cases adjusted only in response to substantial changes in PRC. Each time consumer prices are reviewed, a new base PRC is established, which is a weighted average of all crude oil cargoes imported into the country in a base monthly period as agreed by the government and the oil industry. The base PRC is then used to generate either over- or under-recoveries

Table 4.5 Percentage growth in Nairobi retail petroleum product prices

	LPG		Premium petrol		Regular petrol		Kerosene		Gasoil (diesel)	
	Kshs per 1000 litres	Growth %	Kshs per 1000 litres	Growth %	Kshs per 1000 litres	Growth %	Kshs per 1000 litres	Growth %	Kshs per 1000 litres	Growth %
1984	4013		8407		7927		4213		5787	
1985	4219	5.1	8610	2.4	8130	2.6	4370	3.7	5940	2.6
1986	3858	-8.6	8170	-5.1	7760	-4.6	3920	-10.3	5500	-7.4
1987	4085	5.9	8663	6.0	8160	5.2	3770	-3.8	5540	0.7
1988	4219	3.3	9160	5.7	8530	4.5	3770	0.0	5670	2.3
1989	4435	5.1	9603	4.8	9018	5.7	3975	5.4	5981	5.5
Average		2.2		2.8		2.7		-1.0		0.8

	Industrial diesel oil		Fuel oil-125		Fuel oil-180		Fuel oil-280	
	Kshs per 1000 litres	Growth %	Kshs per 1000 litres	Growth %	Kshs per 1000 litres	Growth %	Kshs per 1000 litres	Growth %
1984	3633		2530		2439		2199	
1985	3767	3.7	2631	4.0	2557	4.8	2262	2.9
1986	3390	-10.0	2440	-7.3	2370	-7.3	2072	-8.4
1987	3580	5.6	2536	3.9	2462	3.9	2167	4.6
1988	3767	5.2	2631	3.7	2557	3.9	2262	4.4
1989	3928	4.3	2823	7.3	2734	6.9	2429	7.4
Average		1.8		2.3		2.4		2.2

in the subsequent months, until such time as the two parties agree on a future consumer price adjustment. The last adjustment based on this arrangement was made in February 1990 when the PRC differential was Ksh508.40 per cubic metre of crude oil imported and refined in Kenya for local consumption. This PRC differential was derived by subtracting the August 1989 base PRC from the PRC agreed for January 1990. The August 1989 PRC was used as the base for future comparisons in granting a price increase to oil companies in September 1989.

This petroleum pricing arrangement has served all the parties very well and the only complaints that have been raised against it by the oil companies are alleged delays in the implementation process. According to the oil companies, long delays cause serious cash flow problems to those big oil marketers who on average import monthly crude oil cargoes of over 600,000 barrels each for domestic consumption. This argument can only be valid if the exchange rates sharply deteriorate and/or both the exchange rate and crude oil prices rise steeply over short periods of time. In a price-controlled regime it is simply not easy to have monthly upward adjustments in consumer prices, as it would mean preparing monthly cabinet papers for consideration and subsequent endorsement. The preferred arrangement, unless the prevailing circumstances are rather dramatic, is to take monthly stock of over-/under-recoveries and then at an appropriate time in the near future make the necessary adjustments that include past under-/over-recoveries and a new PRC base. This arrangement has been followed by the government since 1985 when the petroleum pricing formula was officially adopted.

Table 4.5 and Figure 4.2 show changes and the associated rates of growth in prices in Nairobi for the 1984–9 period. The highest price growth rates were recorded by premium and regular brands of petrol, which grew at an average rate of about 2.8 and 2.7 per cent per annum, respectively. In contrast, kerosene prices were allowed to fall to about 1 per cent per annum.

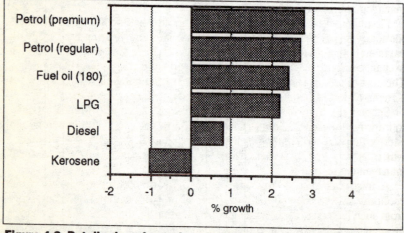

Figure 4.2 Retail price of petroleum in Nairobi, % growth (1984–9)

Coal pricing

Kenya's pricing structure for coal is probably simpler than that for any other modern form of energy. The price of a unit volume of weight simply consists of CIF price plus import duty and handling costs. As we have seen, coal is imported to Kenya from Swaziland. If coal were to come from a source outside the Preferential Trade Area (PTA) of Eastern and Southern Africa, a 20 per cent duty would be charged. However, coal from Swaziland benefits from the PTA concession and only 8 per cent of CIF price is imposed on coal from this source. The components of the price of coal in Kenya are as follows:

Parameters	Costs: (Ksh/ton)
CIF price	1,150.00
Duty 8% of CIF	92.00
Demurrage	32.00
Wharfage 1.5% CIF	17.25
Insurance, brokerage, interest	20.00
Import licence fee	16.00
Handling cost	18.00
Handling losses	19.00
Rail loading	25.00
Total Ksh/ton	1,389.25

Industrial energy demand management in Kenya

The purpose of energy demand management is to reduce energy consumption per unit GDP; to control growth so as to reduce its cost to the economy; and to substitute less costly, indigenous energy sources for more costly imported ones. In Kenya several factors justify the need for a sound energy demand management package.

First, there is the great dependence on imported petroleum, which accounts for nearly 85 per cent of modern energy consumption. The imported crude oil payment continues to impose a heavy burden on the country's limited foreign exchange resources, with attendant negative effects on the balance of payments. The cost of crude oil procurement has increased from about 7 per cent of net Kenyan export value in the early 1970s to about 40 per cent in the 1980s.

Second, the Kenyan industrial sector presently has a very limited capacity to improve the use of energy. The industrial sector is still dominated by old energy-inefficient technologies which were adopted when the cost of energy was relatively low. It is still characterized by a failure to invest in demand management measures.

A third factor is the potential demand for modern energy in the rural economy, which can suddenly translate into actual demand under pressure from such factors as structural change in the rural sector, demographic change through migration from the countryside to urban areas, or change in the supply base due to depletion of the traditional woodfuel-based energy.

The industrial sector has begun to diversify into the ten major sub-sectors listed in Table 4.6. Of these, the cement manufacturing sector is the largest energy user. This activity alone accounts for about 70 per cent of modern energy used in the industrial sector, mainly residual fuel oil and coal. In fact, cement production accounts for over 95 per cent of coal consumed in the country.

The next largest energy consumer in the industrial sector is pulp and paper manufacturing, which accounts for about 12 per cent (see Table 4.6 and Figure 4.3). It is followed closely by the food and beverage sector (10 per cent). Then comes textiles (4 per cent) and chemicals (3 per cent). Printing and publishing and non-metal manufacturing are the least energy-intensive at only 0.2 per cent.

Table 4.6 Modern energy use in industry (000 toe)

Year	Petroleum		Electricity		Coal		Total	
	000 TOE	growth %	000 TOE	growth %	000 TOE	Growth %	000 TOE	Growth %
1984	213		82		83		378	
1985	229	7.51	89	8.54	60	−27.71	378	0.00
1986	339	48.03	97	8.99	68	13.33	504	33.33
1987	273	−19.47	107	10.31	82	20.59	462	−8.33
1988	294	7.69	110	2.80	79	−3.66	483	4.55
1989	298	1.36	115	4.55				
Average growth		9.03		7.04		0.51		7.34

Table 4.7 Kenyan industrial energy consumption pattern

Industry	Consumption share %
1. Food and beverage	10
2. Textiles	4
3. Printing and publishing	
4. Pulp and paper	12
5. Chemicals and fertilizers	
6. Rubber and plastic	3
7. Cement	68
8. Glass, clay and pottery	
9. Metal and metal fabrication	3
10. Non-metal and miscellaneous	
Total	100

Source: Okech (1988)

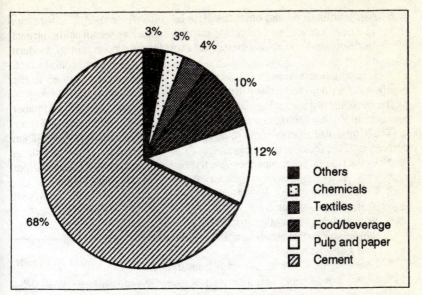

Figure 4.3 Industrial energy consumption, Kenya

Institutions

The interest in energy conservation in Kenya is of relatively recent origin. The importance attached to it is growing and so is the number of institutions involved. The Ministry of Energy and the Kenya Association of Manufacturers (KAM) are the leading institutions in this area.

Ministry of Energy

The Ministry of Energy was created at the end of 1979 after the Kenya government realized that the energy sector continued to present a growing challenge to the country's national development. Prior to its establishment, energy policies and issues were being handled by various sectoral institutions. For instance, petroleum management was entirely in the hands of private companies. The Ministry of Power and Communications was responsible for electric power development. Later on, a National Sub-Committee on Energy was established within the National Council for Science and Technology, the only central body which debated national energy issues. With time the Ministry of Energy has developed to embrace the following functions:

- Energy policy formulation and management of the entire energy sector.
- Electric power development by way of the following activities: national grid system expansion; rural electrification; hydropower development; exploration, development and exploitation of geothermal resources; development of thermal power.
- Registration of electricians and electrical contractors.

- Exploration of oil and other fossil fuels.
- The development of renewable energy, including woodfuel resources (agroforestry) and alternative sources such as solar power, wind, biogas, etc.
- Energy conservation.

The management and coordinating functions often entail direct involvement by the Ministry of Energy through provision of leads and guidelines. It is also involved indirectly through equity ownership and control over parastatals.

The Ministry of Energy seeks to achieve the objectives of energy conservation through the following strategies:

- Reduction of price subsidies given directly or indirectly to consumers.
- Provision of assistance to industry in the form of energy audits.
- Collaboration with relevant organisations such as KAM and the Kenya Transport Association.
- Provision of information to the public on the potential for energy conservation and the financial benefits that would accrue to the individual as well as to the country.
- Encouraging research on energy conservation.
- Developing energy efficiency standards and guidelines to assist consumers in choosing energy efficient appliances.
- Seeking ways to enable new buildings to incorporate energy conservation design features and existing buildings to retrofit.

The low capacity of the Kenyan industrial sector to conserve energy is one of the major justifications for a systematic energy demand management strategy. When the need to conserve energy was realized in Kenya, it was observed that Kenyan industrial plants were equipped with thermal systems which for the most part were designed during the era of low energy costs. Such outdated plants were operated at well below optimum levels and poorly equipped with control and monitoring equipment, compared with those countries that have taken up energy conservation more seriously. The other problems encountered include: (1) the lack of suitably trained manpower; (2) lack of appropriate measuring equipment, both in the public and private sectors; and (3) lack of information and knowledge on how to effect reduction in the energy bill.

The Ministry's first major initiative on energy demand management in the industrial sector was to conduct a comprehensive industrial energy use survey. Its main purpose was to acquire information on the fuels used by type, amounts and cost. The study determined the patterns of fuel use in the industrial sector, identified opportunities for conservation and fuel substitution (together with the major alternative fuels available) and also determined the intensity of energy use in different industrial sectors. The Ministry makes data and information relating to the above available to the industrial community. Its information and data base has also helped to mould the initiatives subsequently undertaken by other institutions.

Following these efforts, the Ministry has initiated two major programmes to facilitate industrial auditing. The Kenya Industrial Energy Management

Programme (KIEMP) and the Kenya Energy Auditing Programme (KEAP) both fall under the energy conservation section of the Ministry.

Kenya Industrial Energy Management Programme (KIEMP)

KIEMP was established jointly by the Kenya government and KAM in 1985, apparently in response to the need for nationally coordinated energy conservation programmes in those sectors where they would have immediate impact. Only in 1988, however, did KIEMP really take off. Effectively, the programme is administered by KAM. It provides industrialists with information on the potential savings that would accrue from energy conservation measures and the free audit services provided by the Ministry. This is done through publications, seminars and industrial visits.

Any industrialist who decides to take advantage of the audit services is asked to communicate directly with the Ministry. The free services are restricted, however, to those industrial establishments whose annual energy budget exceeds one million Kenya shillings. It is assumed that plants with energy bills of less than a million shillings are not financially capable of investing in the conservation measures that may be recommended. For those industrial establishments which do qualify, the Ministry presents the findings and recommendations of the audit in a report which it discusses with the client.

KIEMP has received a 5-year grant of Ksh1,751,000 from the Canadian International Development Authority (CIDA) through the Ministry of Energy. The grant is on a 20 per cent annual phase-out and is expected to expire in the 1992/3 financial year. It is also expected that the local industry will be ready to take over the running of the programme gradually during the grant period and in full after 1993. KAM meets all expenditures of KIEMP on a daily basis and at the end of every quarter claims reimbursement from the Ministry of Energy. This arrangement appears to be working reasonably well.

Kenya Energy Auditing Programme (KEAP)

KEAP was launched in February 1989. Although some energy auditing efforts had been made earlier, no formal auditing programme existed before that date. The programme analyses patterns of energy use and distribution, and identifies savings opportunities as a basis for:
- Increasing industrial and commercial competitiveness of good services.
- Reduction of energy bills through implementation of conservation measures.
- Increasing number of cost-effective energy investments.

The strategies for the programme include:
- Provision of technical assistance to industry, commerce and institutions established to promote better energy utilization.
- Conducting of free energy audits.
- Circulation, through KIEMP, of information on energy conservation.
- Provision of grants for energy conservation feasibility studies by local consultants.

KEAP is at present composed of ten engineers from the Ministry of Energy, the majority of them chemical engineers.

World Bank (IBRD)/UNDP.

Through the Energy Sector Management Assistance Programme (ESMAP), the World Bank and UNDP have funded two Kenyan projects in the area of energy management: Kenya Coal Conversion, Energy Conversion and Fuel Substitution, and Energy Efficiency in the Tea Industry

The first study considered substitution of fuel oil with coal, fuelwood and biomass residues. The energy audits covered 21 plants, accounting for approximately 50 per cent of the total industrial energy demand in 1984. In the second study, substitution of fuelwood for fuel oil in the Kenyan Tea Development Authority (KTDA) factories was considered but rejected because of problems associated with availability, transport infrastructure and limited access to modern fuelwood preparation and combustion technology. The study, which audited 19 KTDA factories, identified potential savings amounting to 282.2 terajoules per annum and an investment of Ksh 34.4 million, with a payback period of less than a year.

The findings of these studies indicated that considerable industrial energy savings can be achieved in Kenya in the short term by introducing energy management practices at minimal financial cost. The indication was that most of the industrial plants can achieve 10–30 per cent savings on their energy bills through good housekeeping measures. Most of the savings are on fuel oil through boiler efficiency improvement and steam distribution or through fuel substitution (e.g. use of biomass residues) as well as through better electrical power usage.

Other institutions

There are other institutions with an interest in and the potential to implement energy management activities. They include the Kenya Industrial Research and Development Institute (KIRDI), the National Council for Science and Technology (NCST), the Faculty of Engineering at the University of Nairobi and the Appropriate Technology Centre at Kenyatta University.

Technological choice

Technology of energy firing devices

As has been mentioned, most of the country's imported industrial machines were designed when energy efficiency was not a major factor to be taken into consideration. The type and size of machines to be bought were at that time mainly influenced by the initial capital costs. In today's terms, existing industrial production technology in Kenya is far from efficient in its use of energy.

The energy firing devices which are commonly in use in Kenya's industrial sector are boilers, kilns and furnaces. The basic structures of these installed devices have not been adapted to make them more energy-efficient. K. K. Engineering Services (a fabricator of boilers, kilns and furnaces) has indicated that improvement of energy efficiency has never been a consideration during the fabrication process – despite the presence of technicians from the company at a boiler efficiency improvement seminar in 1987 (although our survey indicates that the technicians in the company found the seminar useful).

Instrumentation

The following are the instruments which industrialists are commonly encouraged to use to ensure operation at peak efficiency:

Description of instrument	Type of measurement
Thermometer	Temperature
Orsat for measuring carbon dioxide and oxygen	Flue gas composition
Electronic oxygen and combustibles indicator	Flue gas composition
Smoke spot test for measuring unburned fuel	Flue gas composition
Carbon monoxide indicator	Flue gas composition
Ultrasonic detector	Steam leaks

Standardization and quality control

A number of countries have set standards and regulations towards rationalization of energy consumption. For example, in Japan, factories whose annual consumption of energy exceeds 3 million litres of oil equivalent or 12,000 megawatt hours of electricity are required to have qualified and certified energy managers for effective rationalization of energy use.

Although ten years have elapsed since the Kenyan government initiated steps towards energy conservation, there are still no official efficiency standards or regulations for industrial energy use. Thus, Kenyan industries are under no obligation to maintain certain energy efficiency standards. In other words, no matter what serious energy conservation campaign is undertaken, its effectiveness is dependent on the ability of industry to recover the higher energy costs from consumers. Those who are able to pass on higher production costs associated with inefficient systems have no incentive to enhance the efficiency of their equipment.

The Kenya Bureau of Standards (KBS), the legal authority for setting standards with the help of other relevant bodies, has never been involved in the formulation of standards relating to industrial energy-using devices. KBS has indicated that standards in this field have not been seen as a priority.

The position of the Ministry of Energy is that it must determine the effectiveness of an awareness campaign, currently in progress, before considering the introduction of regulatory, mandatory standards. The Ministry, therefore, has not yet approached KBS for collaboration to develop standards for energy-using equipment.

It must be recognized that the regulatory route brings with it the need for bureaucratic intervention. In addition, regulations are, of course, always open to abuses. It might be more realistic to provide intensive energy-efficiency training to key personnel in industry and then leave the market forces to operate in a climate of domestic and international competition by relaxation of import and price controls.

After sales services

Most industrial and major commercial energy firing devices being used in Kenya are not manufactured locally but imported by local agents, the major importers being K. K. Engineering Services and Wormald Kenya Limited (formerly Mather and Platt). These agents also keep spare parts. A number of firing devices are also imported as part of a package loan to the projects by external institutions. The principal equipment that is usually imported is the shell; the finishing, which includes welding, refractory cement lining and pipe fitting, is done locally. However, there are some industries that import fully assembled devices direct from manufacturers.

According to surveys on suppliers to members of KAM, the after sales services provided by the local agents have generally been adequate. This does not rule out incidents of spare parts being out of stock when they are needed. However, the view of the local fabricators is that such incidents are due to delays in approval of foreign exchange or even the total denial of import licences in some instances. Cases have also been observed where a company's management may decide to extend usage of a plant component in operation beyond the replacement time. In most cases such a decision may be due to financial constraints.

Technical and management training

As the major body dealing with industrial energy conservation, the Ministry of Energy has since 1983 instituted various training programmes, based locally as well as abroad, for specialized training. Training abroad has been supported through technical assistance from donor agencies. In most cases the resource persons for the courses mounted locally have come from abroad under various technical assistance programmes. Local training has been mounted jointly by the Ministry and KAM, and in cooperation with the Directorate of Industrial Training (DIT). Participants have often been drawn from major energy-intensive industries in the country.

The training courses have focused primarily on methods for improving technical efficiency, on fuel substitution and on the introduction of new technology. In the case of Energy Audit Training at Mohawk College, an evaluation follow-up was undertaken by an instructor from the college. Between February 1988 and July 1989 he visited the industries from which the participants were drawn. Results from the follow-up indicated that, except for one participant from the private sector and two from the Ministry, they were actively implementing energy conservation skills acquired on the course. As a result of energy conservation efforts by the participants (except those from the Ministry) since leaving Mohawk College, savings in energy bills are anticipated in many companies, while in two companies they have been confirmed and quantified. These confirmed savings, amounting to Ksh18.8

million, are an encouraging vindication of training staff in industrial energy conservation.

Public awareness campaigns

The Kenyan government believes that a voluntary approach to energy demand management is also an important strategy. Hence, public awareness campaigns have been adopted by the government using posters, stickers, booklets and public media.

Constraints and barriers

The perceptions of industrial management

Some industrial managers, usually those having little or no technical background, are unjustifiably cautious in responding to technological initiatives. There is a reluctance to adopt innovations.

Trained and competent engineering staff are wrongly perceived as having more value in areas other than implementing energy efficiency and are deployed almost exclusively in project design work, production, routine maintenance, etc. It is therefore not uncommon to find that in some factories there is no staff set aside for energy management.

Management, particularly in emerging and developing enterprises, usually favours increased production and sales over energy conservation activities. This implies that the decision-makers in a number of factories do not fully understand or appreciate the fact that energy conservation and efficiency will bring financial benefits.

Complexity of energy conservation

Energy conservation measures are often complex, requiring decentralization of responsibility within the enterprise. They are difficult to assign and their results difficult to measure.

Investment risk

The uncertainty about future tangible energy savings and the attendant payback period leads to a belief that energy conservation is a high-risk undertaking. For example, the Bamburi Portland Cement Factory switched to coal in 1979 in the hope that oil prices would continue to rise, but there was a dramatic downturn in 1986. The economics of coal, which carried a 20 per cent duty, became very unattractive relative to oil. This resistance to investment by the industrial sector is stiffened by the scarcity of capital and the strain on foreign exchange.

Differential energy pricing

As has been mentioned, differential energy pricing is widely practised in Kenya. The implication is that some market prices do not always reflect the true cost of energy resources. For example, the price of fuel oil in Kenya is relatively low compared to other refined products. This cross-subsidy between the products implies that the real cost of using some of them is not felt, a situation unlikely to encourage energy conservation.

Lack of sound financing arrangement

Since energy conservation activities began in the country no special arrangements for financing demand management programmes have been made. Knowledge on the subject of energy conservation in the lending institutions is lacking. Attempts have been made in the past, however, to encourage development financial institutions (DFCK, EADB, IDB and ICDC) to provide capital for the replacement of energy systems in those cases that prove viable. The first three institutions provided financial support denominated in freely convertible foreign currencies which became more and more expensive as the domestic currency was progressively devalued to reflect its true exchange rate. Currently, however, arrangements are being made for the IDB to loan funds at fixed exchange rates, with the government absorbing any devaluation risk.

Regulatory measures

Legislation and regulations on import duties, tariffs and prices, together with administrative practices, can end in irregularities and inconsistencies that discourage conservation measures. Typical examples are the government policy on price control, which makes it possible for energy costs to be passed on to the consumers, and the relatively high rates of duty and value added tax on some items (thermometers and pressure gauges, for example) which are required by industry for improving energy utilization. Some policies in support of import substitution have also tended to make industry less efficient since competitive imports were either not allowed into the country or punitively taxed.

Scarcity of foreign exchange

Foreign exchange scarcity sometimes necessitates rationing, which often results in delays or even cancellation of projected investments in energy conservation. This problem is aggravated by the current flexibility of exchange rate policy which makes debt servicing difficult for loans sourced externally, since the domestic cost rises with the falling value of the local currency.

Lack of energy training institutions

Training curricula at the tertiary level (universities and polytechnics) do not contain detailed courses on energy conservation. General courses in heat transfer are tailored to other objectives such as refrigeration without due regard to cost of energy.

Some demand management options

Short-term engineering measures

Short-term energy demand management measures are those which can be undertaken immediately with minimum engineering requirement and capital investment. Although there are variations from plant to plant, the Kenyan industrial energy audit results tend to suggest that the following are the most prevalent conditions which must be attended to in order to achieve any significant energy savings and realize reduction in production costs in the industrial sector:

- Oil fired burners, mainly in boilers and furnaces, are often inefficiently adjusted and so waste fuel oil owing to poor atomization and/or incorrect fuel/air ratios. Excess air levels are often far above the realistic minimum for good combustion. However, controls and instrumentation are frequently not available, are not fitted or lack calibrations fine enough to detect such inefficiencies.
- Fouling of heat transfer surfaces by fireside deposits due to poor atomization and dirty burners is a problem which adds to maintenance as well as fuel costs.
- Faulty automatic burner controls. They need to be converted from high–low–off control to smoothly operating, continuously modulating systems for current fuel/air ratio control over the full firing range. This may require the installation of new burner control equipment but the efficiency gain should pay for this.
- Inability to follow closely the manufacturer's specified operating conditions for combustion equipment. This is a requirement if good furnace/boiler efficiency is to be achieved.
- Variation from standard combustion conditions needs to be monitored by continuously logging both furnace suction pressure and flue gas outlet temperature and composition (oxygen and/or carbon dioxide). In most factories this requires the addition of instrumentation.
- Steam and condensate return systems are often improperly designed, poorly insulated and riddled with leaks. Condensate is often discharged to waste. Attention to steam systems shows immediate return for limited outlay.
- Lighting systems, particularly in the older factories, are far from energy-efficient, given the availability of modern low-energy lighting systems.
- Compressed air systems frequently leak, or are set at needlessly high pressures.
- Electrical maximum demand control and the potentially large cost penalties that can arise are not well understood.
- Power factor correction is also poorly understood, even though some corrective equipment is installed in most factories.

Tariff measures

Virtually all the equipment for energy use and conservation in the Kenyan industrial sector is imported. Only small boilers and heat exchangers are manufactured in Kenya. Most of this imported equipment is subject to both customs duty and Value Added Tax (VAT). The locally manufactured equipment is subject to VAT only.

Although a number of changes have occurred in the rates of the customs duties, the rates for VAT have remained the same. Nearly 21 items were exempted in 1985. This situation remains the same at present, as does the VAT rate (17 per cent).

The tax rates on hardware that is essential for energy savings range between 17 and 77 per cent. The lowest rate applies to equipment which is subject to VAT only. But the rates are high and their implications for conservation measures are negative. More importantly, they are high enough to render some conservation measures uneconomic. However, the granting of exemptions has been restrained by the fear that the government might defeat its major aim of collecting revenue. This fear is not necessarily well founded. It has been demonstrated that, in some instances, the savings accruing from energy conservation measures can significantly offset losses in revenue for the government. For instance, according to a Kenya coal conservation study report, if exemption from these taxes had been given in 1985 to the 21 plants audited under the study, the government would have lost about Ksh30 million in revenue. However, at the 1985 energy prices, this loss would have been only about 10 per cent of the potential savings from the plants.

Prices, fiscal measures and supply restriction

A number of pricing, fiscal and supply strategies have direct implications for energy demand management in Kenya. For electricity and coal, the fiscal policy objectives tend to be restricted to revenue generation. With effect from July 1972 every unit of electricity consumed has been subject to a government tax of one cent. In the case of coal, as we have seen, customs duty applies. The rate is 8 per cent for supplies from Eastern and Southern African PTA countries and 20 per cent for those from outside the PTA.

In the case of petroleum fuels, differential pricing has socio-economic intentions, but the energy demand management dimensions are inescapable. As was observed earlier, the differential pricing strategy for petroleum fuels has meant that the prices of kerosene, fuel oil and diesel are lower than those of motor gasoline (petrol) which is normally used by the more affluent members of society. Very frequently, the components of the differences in price of these fuels are based on differences in tax rates. Nevertheless, from the demand management perspective, the implication is that the more affluent consumers would be discouraged from using more energy than is essential. For the industrial sector, however, since low-priced fuel oil is one of the major energy sources in the sector, the demand management incentives associated with differential pricing may not apply.

The government has also used supply limitation as a demand management tool for the petroleum fuels. For instance, in 1982, because of the worsening balance of payments, it was found necessary to reduce oil imports and ration petrol consumption to less than 90 per cent of the normal demand.

Fuel substitution

Fuelwood. As a substitute for fuel oil, woodfuel is used either for generating steam in boilers or for internal combustion in kilns. Woodfuel is used in limited proportions in a number of factories for maintaining temperatures to facilitate boiler ignition. Overall, widespread industrial use of woodfuel has met with serious supply constraints since 1987 as a result of the Department of Forestry's policy. A look at Table 4.8 shows that the volume of woodfuel sales by the Department of Forestry has registered slow growth rates after 1987.

Table 4.8: Sale of woodfuel by Department of Forestry (thousands of stacked cubic metres)

	1985	1986	1987	1988	1989
Volume	165	185	201	210	215
Growth (%)		12.1	8.6	4.5	2.4

Source: Various government publications

The reason for the decline in the rate of growth in sales is the official commitment by the government of Kenya to enforce stricter regulations on soil and water conservation practices. Fast-growing and high-yielding tree species such as eucalyptus, which are suitable for woodfuel production, are no longer being planted in large quantities since they are considered to be copious consumers of scarce groundwater resources and have also been proved to be poor soil conditioners. In view of these factors, such tree species are now considered as a threat to the current official drive on conservation of soil and water catchment areas.

Coal. The issue of substituting fuel oil with coal, and the general expansion of the use of coal in the Kenyan industrial sector, has been a major policy consideration for some time. A major factor behind the policy position is the trend towards increased production of the lighter petroleum distillates such as petrol to meet the growing demand from the high income groups, which results in proportionately less production of the heavier distillates such as fuel oil.

Despite a positive policy stance, the use of coal in the Kenyan industrial sector hardly extends beyond a single cement plant at the port city of Mombasa. Three main reasons can be given for this. The first is the lack of adequate infrastructural capacity at the port of Mombasa for handling the quantity of coal which would be required for a large-scale inter-fuel substitution. The second is the government policy which imposes a tariff on coal imports. As has been mentioned, the government's policy is to impose a customs tariff of 20 per cent on coal imported from outside the PTA and 8 per cent on imports from within the PTA. This situation puts coal at a cost disadvantage compared to the petroleum fuels which it can substitute, as they are not subject to any import levies. There is some evidence to suggest that the level of coal imports is influenced by the price level of fuel oil which it substitutes.

The third reason is the lack of adequate local capital and foreign exchange. conversion from the current oil-fired production systems to coal would require substantial volumes of both.

Bagasse. Bagasse is a by-product of sugar production. Bagasse-fired steam generation of electricity can partly supplement the supply from other thermal sources. Progress on this front has been negligible, however. For a start, some of the companies are not connected to the national grid (South Nyanza and Nzoia). Secondly, KPLC, the sole distributor of electricity, has refused to pay more than its own saved operating costs for electricity deliveries from sugar mills. This is a sore point, since KPLC imports a substantial quantity of electricity from the Uganda Electricity Board (UEB) and also generates some of its electricity from expensive imported petroleum fuels.

Bagasse could also be pelletized and sold as a solid fuel, either for direct combustion in industrial kilns or converted into clean charcoal. This fuel option has not been explored because the sugar companies which are the only potential consumers of such solid fuels in the manufacturing sector, are located more than 250 km from Nairobi. Another constraint on consumption of bagasse as an industrial process energy is that the current firing systems will have to be modified at a cost which potential users are very reluctant to incur.

Technical efficiency improvement and pollution control

Study of cement plants and tea dryers in Nairobi, Mombasa and Western Kenya reveals that plants vary widely in energy efficiency, though the technology is of a comparable standard. This indicates that there is room for energy saving through improvements in the handling and operation of inefficient plants. The efficiency of boilers could be improved by installing heat recuperators to reduce the flue gas temperature. In other cases, the installation of monitoring and control equipment for thermal energy flow would yield much greater efficiency.

In plants burning coal and bagasse, greater energy efficiency would also reduce pollution and environmental damage. Up to the present, economic development has taken precedence over any consideration of adverse environmental effects. This trend must be checked and eventually reversed, not least through industrial energy demand management.

Policy issues and recommendations

Broadening the supply base

Security of supply should be ensured by diversifying supply sources and maintaining good bilateral relations with energy-exporting countries.

The search for indigenous hydrocarbon resources should be intensified. The necessary legal and institutional framework is already in place, following the enactment of production-sharing contracts as a legal instrument by Kenya's parliament in 1984 and the establishment of the National Oil Corporation of Kenya in the same year.

In order to minimize dependence on external sources of energy, geothermal and hydro-power resources should continue to be developed for the generation of electricity. The use of hydro-power for mechanical applications has not received the backing of official policy; neither has any attempt been made to tap low-temperature geothermal heat for either crop processing or industrial applications.

Petroleum

Petroleum fuel prices should be de-controlled to promote efficiency. This will discourage inefficient and high-cost petroleum use.

The Mombasa oil refinery should be made more responsive to changes in demand for various distillates.

Electricity

Unlike the petroleum industry, which is dominated by private enterprise, commercial generation and marketing of electricity is undertaken by the state through its parastatal organizations. The size of the electric power sector is such that only the government can mobilize the large resources (both domestic and foreign) required for expanded generation and marketing of electricity throughout Kenya.

In order to ensure that electricity is affordable by a wider cross-section of Kenyan society, tariffs are controlled by government. Under this rating arrangement, poor and rural consumers are subsidized by both government and large consumers. This is a good policy as it promotes equity, in addition to enhancing the quality of life of the rural population and the urban poor.

The current policy on generation, transmission and distribution is expected to remain unchanged. Generation is expected to remain in the hands of the parastatal bulk-supply organizations, while distribution and sale will continue to be undertaken by the state-owned KPLC. The electricity supply and sale arrangements have been reasonably efficient, which speaks for a continuation of present policy.

The KPLC has always resisted buying electricity generated by other producers such as the sugar production companies, despite a general feeling within official circles that small-scale generation using indigenous resources should be encouraged. As a consequence, the development of alternative ways of generating electricity, such as bagasse burning or mini-hydro, have been neglected. A policy limiting the powers enjoyed by the KPLC in this regard should be initiated.

Fuelwood

Industrial users of woodfuel are now experiencing supply shortages. Industrial and commercial consumption of woodfuel on a sustainable basis would not only save foreign exchange but also encourage private production. Labour-intensive wood plantations would contribute substantially to employment creation. They would also benefit the environment.

Coal

Coal consumption should be encouraged by (1) removal of import duty in order to make it competitive with fuel oil which it substitutes; (2) encouraging large-scale consumption through the development of bulk handling and storage facilities at Mombasa and up-country; and (3) assisting Kenya Railways to develop its coal-handling capacity and also to acquire additional locomotives and wagons for transportation to coal distribution centres along the line of rail.

Inter-fuel substitution

The government should harmonize its policy on water and soil conservation with the need for inter-fuel substitution and diversification. Woodfuel offers high potential as a substitute for petroleum fuel in the industrial sector.

To enhance inter-fuel substitution, the government should promote the pelletization of bagasse from the sugar industry to enhance its competitiveness as a substitute for petroleum fuel in the industrial sector.

Financial incentives

Investments in retrofits and conversion systems, and in solid-fuel firing systems such as boilers, kilns and furnaces, should be encouraged as and when it is appropriate to extend tax credit, including soft financing terms. These ideas are not new but they have been denied a place in Kenya's policy framework by severe budgetary and foreign exchange constraints throughout the 1980s. The IMF/World Bank Structural Adjustment Programme currently being implemented in Kenya makes it almost impossible to consider extending tax credit and/or soft financing arrangements to the potential investors in inter-fuel substitution equipment. This policy approach should be reviewed, nevertheless.

The Kenya Industrial Energy Conservation Programme, a joint undertaking of the Kenya government through its Ministry of Energy and the private sector through KAM, is an ideal forum for exchanging and learning new ideas in energy conservation, in both financial and technical terms. The programme currently lacks adequate financial support as well as experienced technical personnel. This should be remedied through joint financial contributions by its two sponsors.

The current import licensing regime should be phased out as part of the overall gradual elimination of quantitative restrictions. This will contribute to making industry and commerce more efficient operators. However, the current licensing arrangement, which provides scarce foreign exchange on a priority basis, could be a useful lever in encouraging energy-efficient enterprises.

Energy conversion factors

Tonne of	TOE
Coal	0.70
LPG (Liquefied Petroleum Gas)	1.08
Petrol (Gasoline)	1.05
Dual purpose kerosene (household and industrial)	1.03
Gas oil (diesel oil)	1.02
Industrial diesel oil	1.01
Residual oil	0.98
Bitumen	1.00
Lubricants	0.99
Wood (air-dried 15% moisture)	0.22
Charcoal	0.70

1 TOE   = 11630 kilowatt hours (KWh) of electricity
1 Gigajoule = 10^9 joules
1 Terajoule = 10^{12} joules
1 TOE   = 41.867 gigajoules
1 Terajoule = 23.885 TOE

Abbreviations

AFRA	Average Freight Rates Assessment
CIDA	Canadian International Development Agency
CIF	Cost, Insurance, Freight
DFCK	Development Finance Company of Kenya
DIT	Directorate of Industrial Training
EADB	East African Development Bank
ESMAP	Energy Sector Management Assistance Programme
FEAL	Foreign Exchange Allocation Licence Fee
FO	Fuel Oil
FOB	Free on Board
GDP	Gross Domestic Product
IBRD	International Bank for Reconstruction and Development (World Bank)
ICDC	Industrial and Commercial Development Corporation
IDB	Industrial Development Bank
IDO	Industrial Diesel Oil

IMF	International Monetary Fund
KAM	Kenya Association of Manufacturers
KBS	Kenya Bureau of Standards
KEAP	Kenya Energy Audit Programme
KENOL	Kenya Oil Company
KIEMP	Kenya Industrial Energy Management Programme
KIRDI	Kenya Industrial Research and Development Institute
KPLC	Kenya Power and Lighting Company
KPRC	Kenya Petroleum Refineries Company
Ksh	Kenya shillings
KTDA	Kenya Tea Development Authority
KWh	Kilowatt hours
LPG	Liquefied Petroleum Gas
MW	Megawatts
NCST	National Council for Science and Technology
NOCK	National Oil Corporation of Kenya
OPEC	Organization of Petroleum Exporting Countries
PRC	Procurement and Refining Cost
PTA	Preferential Trade Area (Eastern and Southern Africa)
TOE	Tonnes of Oil Equivalent
UEB	Uganda Electricity Board
UNDP	United Nations Development Programme
USAID	United States Agency for International Development

References

Armand, P. *et. al.* (1987). *Social-Economic Implications of Energy Price Increases*, Grower Publishing Company, Brook Field, USA.

Government of Kenya. (1975–86). Sessional Papers, No. 4 of 1975 ('Economic prospects and policies'), No. 4 of 1980 ('Economic prospects and policies'), No. 4 of 1982 ('Development prospects and policies') and No. 1 of 1986 ('Economic management and renewed growth'), Ministry of Economic Planning and National Development, Nairobi, Kenya.

Government of Kenya. (1983). *Practical Guidelines for Energy Savings in Industry*, Ministry of Energy, Nairobi, Kenya.

Government of Kenya. (1983). *Statistical Abstract, 1983*, Ministry of Economic Planning and National Development, Nairobi, Kenya.

Government of Kenya. (1986). *Economic Survey, 1986*, Ministry of Economic Planning and National Development, Nairobi, Kenya, Table 10.3.

Government of Kenya. (1987). *Kenya: Coal Conversion, Energy Conservation and Substitution*, Ministry of Energy/UNDP, Nairobi, Kenya.

Government of Kenya. (1988). *1988–1993 Development Plan*, Ministry of Economic Planning and National Development, Nairobi, Kenya.

Kenya Power and Lighting Company Ltd (1990). *Bye-Laws: Methods for Charge*, KPLC, Nairobi, Kenya.

Okech, Benjamin A. (1986). *Kenya National Energy Policy Review*, Public Law Institute, Nairobi, Kenya.

Okech, Benjamin A. (1988). 'Coal supply situation: availability for substitution in the Kenya economy', Institute for Development Studies, Discussion Paper No. 289, University of Nairobi, Nairobi, Kenya.

Senga, W. M. and Manundu, M. (1980). 'Assessment of commercial energy supply and demand in Kenya', Institute for Development Studies, Consultancy Report No. 3, University of Nairobi, Nairobi, Kenya.

PART III

Energy Management
in Electricity Generation

5 The Case of Mauritius

J. Baguant

Socio-economic perspectives

The State of Mauritius, consisting of the main island of Mauritius (57 ° 35'E; 20 ° 15'S) and various more or less tiny specks of land scattered in the south-west Indian Ocean, has a land area of just over 2000 square kilometres (see Figure 5.1); under the UN Law of the Sea Convention, the State of Mauritius would have jurisdiction over 1.6–1.7 million square kilometres of ocean territory. The population, multi-lingual and multi-cultural, drawn originally from Europe, Africa, the Indian subcontinent and China, presently numbers just over 1 million. Long regarded as a text-book example of a mono-crop economy based on sugar cane, Mauritius has, over the past two decades, diversified into an Export Processing Zone (based primarily on textiles) and tourism. Mauritius, since independence from the British in 1968 as a parliamentary democracy, has been operating along the pattern of Westminster but with marked differences. Thus, there is only one Chamber, namely the Legislative Assembly, and Mauritius has a written constitution. The Head of State is, to all intents and purposes, the Governor General appointed by the British monarch, whose representative he is in Mauritius. The Head of Government is the Prime Minister.

Following the end of the Second World War, and in part due to successful attempts to eradicate malaria, Mauritius was to experience high population growth rates – so much so that the population of 600,000 at the end of the 1950s was expected to reach 3 million by the year 2000 with the then prevailing fertility rates and reasonable declining trends in death rates. Considerable efforts were made, and continue to be made, to curb population growth and make Mauritius a veritable success story in voluntary family planning. The population, which is gradually becoming an ageing one, is expected to reach 1.1 to 1.2 million by the year 2000 and between 1.4 and 1.6 million by 2025. The labour force (including those unemployed but earnestly seeking work), estimated at 273,000 in 1975, at 325,000 in 1980 and at around 410,000 in 1988, is expected to reach around 450,000 in 1990, 475,000 by the turn of the century and between 600,000 and 640,000 by the year 2025 (Bheenick and Hanoomanjee, 1988). The number of unemployed, estimated at between 20,000 and 30,000 in the mid-1970s and at over 60,000 in the early 1980s, is officially around 5 per cent of the labour force at present.

Figure 5.1 Map of Mauritius showing the sugar factories and power-generating stations

Mauritius has no mineral resources in its land area, although its zone of economic sovereignty is not lacking in renewable and non-renewable resources. It has, in sugar cane, not only the most efficient converter of solar radiation energy into dry matter production that is available for commercial exploitation (with a highly uncertain future as a sweetener), but also the crop most adapted to its bioclimatic conditions, including cyclones which periodically sweep the country. Mauritius has always had a very open economy. Although it is no longer the one-crop economy it was even in the 1960s, the sugar industry is still the dominant one in Mauritius. And although Mauritius has a high population density, its population is nonetheless small, only providing relatively small internal markets; these are often insufficient for modern large-scale activities in commerce and industry. Moreover, the country is relatively far away from large mass markets; in most lines of industry and trade, Mauritius can be described aptly as a 'sea-locked' economy.

Despite such handicaps, strenuous efforts have been made, and continue to be made, in the setting up of manufacturing industries, especially within the Export Processing Zone, in the intensification and diversification of agriculture, in tourism, in the setting up of the Export Services Zone and in attempts to promote regional economic cooperation. The pace of socio-economic development slackened considerably in the second half of the 1970s and the early

Table 5.1 Mauritius: evolution of gross domestic product (Rs million)

Year	1968		1973		1978		1983		1988	
Agriculture, hunting, forestry and fishing	193	23%	494	30%	977	20%	1465	14%	2835	13%
Mining & quarrying	1	0%	4	0%	11	0%	18	0%	27	0%
Manufacturing	124	15%	277	17%	803	16%	1678	16%	5432	25%
Electricity, gas & water	30	4%	43	3%	118	2%	245	2%	510	2%
Construction	49	6%	114	7%	506	10%	655	6%	1170	5%
Whole, retail trade, restaurants & hotels	92	11%	172	10%	430	9%	1455	14%	3518	16%
Trans., storage & communications	102	12%	161	10%	635	13%	1230	12%	2308	11%
Financing, insurance, real-estate & business	82	10%	108	7%	361	7%	1890	18%	2640	12%
Government services	110	13%	203	12%	760	16%	1327	13%	2100	10%
Others (social & personal services)	44	5%	76	5%	291	6%	650	6%	940	4%
of which										
Sugar	–	–	–	–	1285	(26%)	1275	(12%)	2747	(13%)
EPZ	–	–	–	–	160	(3%)	548	(5%)	3100	(14%)
Tourist	–	–	–	–	65	(1%)	275	(3%)	640	(3%)
Total GDP (@ current factor cost)	827	(100%)	1652	(100%)	4892	(100%)	10613	(100%)	21480	(100%)

1980s, as compared with the first half of the 1970s. In part this was because of the downturn in the world economy with high energy prices and, hence, restricted and uncertain markets for the products of the Export Processing Zone; in part it was because of static, if not declining demands for sugar, and hence export prices not keeping up with the cost of inputs in the sugar industry; it was also because of the heavy cost of the welfare measures Mauritius has introduced, which are generous and comprehensive by any standards except those of the rich and heavily industrialized countries; and, finally, it was because the country experienced a rather sustained spell of adverse bioclimatic, pest and disease conditions in the second half of the 1970s and the early 1980s. Mauritius, in the late 1970s, had to adopt a series of austerity measures taken in conformity with guidelines from the International Monetary Fund and the World Bank, including currency devaluation and readjustments. By 1984–5, a period of relative national prosperity started anew, one rather unique in Mauritian history since it is not centrally based on the sugar industry (see Table 5.1).

Energy sector

Energy supply

Mauritius is not an oil-producing country, neither does it have proven fossil energy reserves. Amongst the locally available energy resources the most important are hydro, bagasse from the sugar cane industry and woody biomass. Solar energy also has some potential in Mauritius.

Domestic energy sources

Hydro: Development of hydro sites was initiated well before the 1950s and the most recent major hydro-power development of 30 MW capacity was undertaken during the late 1970s and completed in the early 1980s, bringing the total installed capacity of hydro-power to around 50 MW. The maximum output so far has been 140 million KWh for the year 1987, representing 35 per cent of the total electricity requirement of that year. Potential for further development of hydro sites still exists.

The proportion of hydro-electricity supplied to the national grid, as compared to the total electricity requirement, has declined constantly from around 85 per cent in 1955 to around 30 per cent in 1989. Hydro-electricity is fed to the national grid from seven different sites with installed capacities ranging from 1 MW to 30 MW.

Bagasse: This by-product of the sugar industry is utilized to produce all the energy required (in the form of process steam and electricity) for the manufacture of sugar. Bagasse power plants have also been developed to produce excess electricity during the sugar cane harvest period, which is then fed to the national grid. Development of such installations was initiated during the mid-1950s, and 16 out of the 19 sugar factories produce excess electricity for the national grid during the harvesting season (June–December). However, during the mid-1980s a major development was carried out at the largest sugar factory on the island – Flacq United Estate Limited (FUEL). A dual fuel furnace, able to run on bagasse during the harvesting season and on coal during the rest of the year, has been installed. The system has also been equipped with a high pressure boiler (42 Bars) and a condensing turbine. These modifications have brought the total capacity to 21.7 MW. This provides electricity all year round and contributes around 25 per cent of the total annual electricity requirement. Potential exists for development of such systems at other sugar factories.

Woody biomass: According to surveys carried out by the Forestry Service of the Ministry of Agriculture, around 56,000 hectares, representing around 25 per cent of the total area of Mauritius, are classified as forest area (Forestry Service). This area consists of productive and unproductive woodlands which are partly government-owned and partly privately owned. The wood produced is used as timber, wood poles for scaffolding in the construction industry, and directly as firewood or indirectly for making charcoal for cooking. Wood is also burnt for curing tobacco leaves and in limekilns for the production of lime from corals.

Out of all the above-mentioned uses of wood in Mauritius, its use as firewood for cooking in the residential sector is by far the most important. A national survey on household energy consumption carried out in 1988 revealed that the contribution of woody biomass is as much as 50 per cent of the household primary energy requirement which represents almost 20 per cent of the total primary consumption of the island (Beeharry and Baguant, 1990).

Imported energy sources: Locally available energy resources being limited, imported fossil fuel – petroleum products and coal – remain the major source of energy. The total liquid fuel consumption, currently being of the order of 300,000 TOE (Tonnes of Oil Equivalent) annually, has not quite justified the setting up of a local oil refinery.

As a consequence, the imported fossil fuels are in the final refined form.of petrol, diesel, kerosene, fuel oil and LPG (Liquefied Petroleum Gas). Since 1984, coal has also been imported for supplementing the bagasse-fired electricity generation plant, as well as for steam production in the industrial sector.

Petrol: Since 1984 only premium petrol has been imported to Mauritius to provide the energy requirements of the light transportation industry. Other miscellaneous uses of petrol include: motor-boats, motor-cycles, lawn-mowers and two-stroke engines for operating small water pumps.

Diesel: The major portion of imported diesel oil is supplied to the heavy transport industry which consists mostly of buses used in the mass transit system and trucks used for transportation of goods and sugar cane. Diesel is also used in the light transportation of goods, public cars (taxis) and small vans. Diesel is, in addition, supplied to the Central Electricity Board (CEB) where it is used for starting up generators.

Kerosene: The importation of kerosene is primarily to meet the demand for cooking fuel in the residential sector; however, a smaller quantity of kerosene is also supplied to miscellaneous users (for pumps, cleaning purposes, etc.). The government has a 'zero tax policy' on kerosene in order to alleviate the lot of poor families with living standards below the average and, in addition, to counter potential firewood shortage problems in Mauritius.

Kerosene (of jet fuel grade) imported for bunkering purposes is kept separate from the kerosene for local consumption.

Fuel oil: The main portion of fuel oil is supplied to the CEB for electricity generation and the remaining portion is supplied to industries such as the beverage industry and industries of the Economic Processing Zone (EPZ) where it is utilized for raising process steam.

Fuel oil and diesel imported for supplying ships stopping at the harbour of Port Louis are separately accounted for and are not included in the Mauritian energy balance.

LPG (Liquefied Petroleum Gas): LPG, distributed in pressurized gas cylinders (bottled gas) is used mostly for cooking in the residential sector and the commercial sector (at restaurants and hotels). But the residential sector is by far the major user of LPG.

A smaller quantity of LPG is used in mini-industry, mostly for welding purposes.

Coal: Since 1984, coal has been imported and utilized primarily by the FUEL Sugar Estate to generate electricity during the inter-crop seasons. The FUEL Sugar Estate furnace is capable of burning coal and bagasse or various mixtures of these two fuels.

Energy flow in the Mauritian economy

Figure 5.2 illustrates the steps involved in the methodology used for the computation of energy demand by economic sectors for Mauritius for 1970 to 1989. This methodology was developed within the 'Energy Use and Policy Planning in Mauritius' programme, funded by IDRC (Manrakhan, 1990). The notes below provide in brief the computation and assumptions associated with the methodology. Data for woody biomass consumed for cooking purposes in the residential sector is obtained from the national survey on household energy consumption for 1988 and extrapolated for 1989.

- All petrol and the balance of diesel after meeting the requirement of the CEB are consumed by all the categories of transport devices within the transportation sector.
- Balance of fuel oil after being supplied to CEB for electricity generation purposes goes to the industrial sector.

Figure 5.2 Energy flow in the Mauritian economy (10^3 GJ)

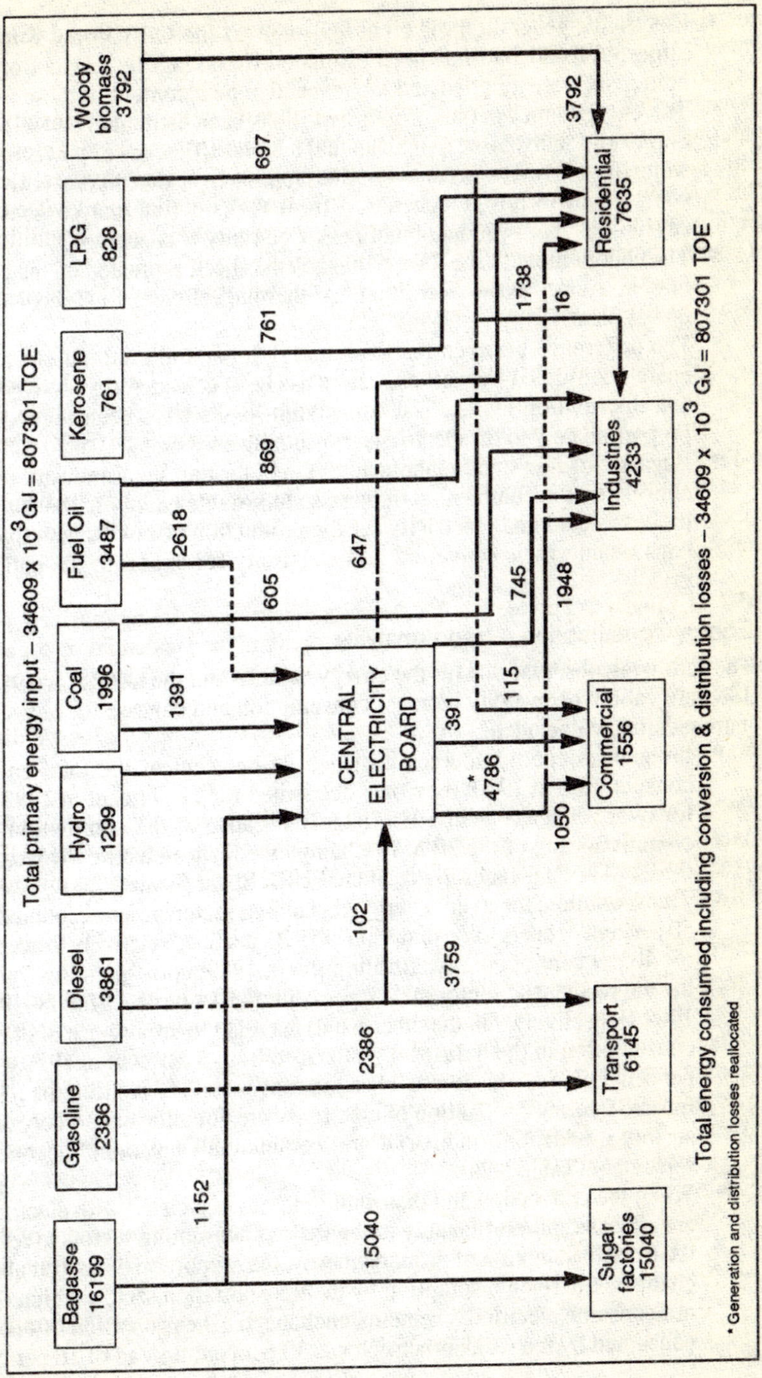

Total primary energy input – 34609 x 10^3 GJ = 807301 TOE

Total energy consumed including conversion & distribution losses – 34609 x 10^3 GJ = 807301 TOE

* Generation and distribution losses reallocated

- Electricity generation: The energy input to the CEB in the form of imported fossil fuel has been estimated by taking the product of the volume of fuel supplied and the respective heat content of these fuels. The energy input in the form of hydro has been estimated on the basis of fuel oil saving, at the overall annual thermal efficiency of power plants using fuel oil. The reason for this approach is that hydro-power is comparable to power generation from fuel oil (internal combustion engines) as far as production of peak electricity is concerned.
- The energy input in the form of bagasse has been estimated on the basis of coal saving, at the overall annual thermal efficiency of a coal-fired power plant.
- The difference between the total energy input and the total electrical energy consumed by various sectors has been considered as conversion and distribution losses. The conversion losses have been reallocated proportionately to the electricity-consuming sectors.
- Bagasse for raw sugar manufacture: the Mauritian sugar industry relies entirely on the combustion of bagasse to provide energy in the form of process steam and electricity for the production of raw sugar. Excess bagasse energy is converted into electricity for export to the national grid.

Energy consumption – trend analysis

The following observations for the energy balance and the trends for 1970 to 1989 are valid when woody biomass consumption and bagasse for raw sugar manufacture are excluded.

- Indigenous energy sources provided 21 per cent of the total energy consumption in 1970; they only accounted for 11 per cent in 1983 but for over 20 per cent in 1985, largely because of the completion and commissioning of the 30 MW Champagne Hydro-electric Project and the 22 MW dual-fuel furnace at the FUEL Sugar Estate.
- Transportation, the major energy-consuming sector which accounted for 50 per cent of energy consumption in 1970, declined relatively to account for 40 per cent of energy consumption in 1989; corresponding figures for the residential sector are 17 per cent and 14 per cent for 1970 and 1989 respectively. On the other hand, the relative importance of energy consumption in the industrial sector rose from 5 per cent in 1970 to 13 per cent in 1989. This is true when the conversion and distribution losses incurred during production of electricity are not allocated to economic sectors (residential, industrial and commercial) but rather accounted separately (Table 5.2a).
- When the conversion and distribution losses associated with electricity are allocated proportionately to the various consuming sectors to reflect the true consumption of primary energy, the proportion described above changes. Energy consumption by the transportation sector, which does not consume electricity, remains unchanged. The proportion of energy consumed by the residential sector is 30 per cent instead of 16 per cent

Table 5.2a Summary of sectoral energy consumption (generation and distribution losses accounted separately) (%)

Year	Trans.	Resid.	Indus.	Comm.	Gen & Dis. losses	Total
1970	49.1	16.0	5.5	1.7	27.6	100.0
1971	48.3	15.5	5.8	1.8	28.6	100.0
1972	50.2	15.5	5.9	1.9	26.5	100.0
1973	49.2	16.1	5.9	2.0	26.8	100.0
1974	50.3	15.0	6.4	2.0	26.3	100.0
1975	52.6	14.4	6.4	1.9	24.8	100.0
1976	48.9	15.0	8.2	2.2	25.7	100.0
1977	49.5	15.2	8.2	2.0	25.1	100.0
1978	48.5	15.9	8.1	2.1	25.4	100.0
1979	46.8	16.7	8.5	2.4	25.7	100.0
1980	46.4	15.4	9.0	2.5	26.7	100.0
1981	45.8	14.2	9.8	2.8	27.5	100.0
1982	44.4	14.2	8.9	3.0	29.5	100.0
1983	43.9	14.7	9.5	3.0	28.8	100.0
1984	43.9	14.1	10.1	2.9	29.0	100.0
1985	40.2	13.3	10.3	2.7	33.4	100.0
1986	39.5	13.5	9.9	2.7	34.3	100.0
1987	39.2	13.8	13.0	2.8	31.2	100.0
1988	39.6	13.5	12.0	3.2	31.8	100.0
1989	39.3	13.3	13.9	3.2	30.4	100.0

Table 5.2b Summary of sectoral energy consumption (including generation and distribution losses) (%)

Year	Trans.	Resid.	Indus.	Comm.	Total
1970	49.1	29.4	13.1	8.4	100.0
1971	48.3	28.9	14.0	8.8	100.0
1972	50.2	27.5	13.4	9.0	100.0
1973	49.2	28.1	13.7	9.0	100.0
1974	50.3	26.6	14.5	8.6	100.0
1975	52.6	25.0	14.7	7.6	100.0
1976	48.9	25.8	17.0	8.3	100.0
1977	49.5	25.9	17.0	7.5	100.0
1978	48.5	27.6	16.1	7.8	100.0
1979	46.8	28.5	16.4	8.4	100.0
1980	46.4	27.7	17.2	8.6	100.0
1981	45.8	26.7	18.3	9.3	100.0
1982	44.4	27.9	17.3	10.4	100.0
1983	43.9	27.7	18.3	10.0	100.0
1984	43.9	27.1	19.3	9.7	100.0
1985	40.2	28.0	21.3	10.5	100.0
1986	39.5	27.5	22.2	10.7	100.0
1987	39.2	26.0	24.8	10.0	100.0
1988	39.6	25.5	24.5	10.5	100.0
1989	39.3	24.5	26.2	10.0	100.0

in 1970 and 25 per cent in 1989. Corresponding figures for the industrial sector are 13 per cent in 1970 compared to 5 per cent, and 25 per cent in 1989. For the commercial sector, consumption goes to 8 per cent compared to 2 per cent in 1970, and to 10 per cent in 1989 (Table 5.2b).

- Generation of electricity rose from 136 GWh in 1970 to 584 GWh in 1989, an average annual increase of 7.5 per cent. Local energy sources (hydro and bagasse) accounted for more than 50 per cent of electricity production in 1970, for 20 per cent in 1983 and, with the coming into operation of the Champagne and the FUEL projects, for 40 per cent in 1986 and 35 per cent in 1989.

- The average annual rates of increase of electricity consumption from 1970 to 1989 were 7 per cent, 8 per cent and 11 per cent for the residential, commercial and industrial sectors respectively. While the share of the first two sectors has remained almost unchanged at around 30 per cent and 17 per cent respectively from 1970 to 1989, that for the industrial sector rose from 20 per cent in 1970 to 32 per cent in 1989.

Since the data for the contribution of woody biomass as an energy source is available only for 1988, it has been ignored in the above trend analysis. However, its importance is well illustrated in the energy balance presented in Figure 5.2 and in the energy matrix of Table 5.3, from which it can be observed that woody biomass provided 11 per cent of total primary energy requirement for 1989.

Similarly, it can be seen that bagasse provided 43 per cent of the total primary energy requirement when energy required for raw sugar manufacture is considered in the overall energy balance for Mauritius. When bagasse energy used for raw sugar manufacture is excluded from the overall energy balance, it can be seen that the percentages change drastically. For example, the contribution of woody biomass in terms of primary energy almost doubles from 11 per cent to around 19 per cent. These changes are illustrated in Table 5.3. The percentage of energy consumed in the form of electricity also increases from 19 per cent to almost 34 per cent.

Power sector

Historical background

The Central Electricity Board (CEB) is the sole distributor of electricity in Mauritius. Currently, it falls under the Ministry of Energy, Water Resources and Postal Services. The Board is composed of the Chairman, the members, representatives of the Ministry of Energy, the Ministry of Finance, the Ministry of Economic Planning and Development, the Central Water Authority, the Institution of Engineers and other members with experience in agricultural, industrial, commercial, financial, scientific and administrative matters (CEB, 1972).

The CEB was set up in December 1952 with the objective of developing, controlling and coordinating the electricity supply services throughout the

Table 5.3 Energy balance – Mauritius 1989 (10³ GJ)

	Sugar factory	Transport	Commercial	Industrial	Residential	Total	% (1)	% (2)
Bagasse	15040	–	–	–	–	15040	43.4	–
Petrol	–	2386	–	–	–	2386	6.9	12.2
Diesel	–	3759	–	–	–	3759	10.9	19.2
Coal	–	–	–	605	–	605	1.8	3.1
Fuel oil	–	–	–	869	–	869	2.5	4.4
Kerosene	–	–	–	–	761	761	2.2	3.9
LPG	–	–	115	16	697	828	2.4	4.2
Electricity	–	–	1441	2743	2385	6569	19.0	33.6
Woody biomass	–	–	–	–	3792	3792	11.0	19.4
Total (1)	15040	6145	1556	4233	7635	34609	–	–
Total (2)	–	6145	1556	4233	7635	19569	–	–
% (1)	43.4	17.8	4.5	12.2	22.1	–	100.0	–
% (2)	–	31.4	8.0	21.6	39.0	–	–	100.0

1. Percentage computed includes bagasse energy consumed by sugar factories for raw sugar manufacture.
2. Percentage computed does not include bagasse energy consumed by sugar factories for raw sugar manufacture.

island. The total electricity-generating capacity of the island in 1955 amounted to some 11 MW out of which 7.6 MW was hydro-based and the balance accounted for by diesel engines. At that time, it was mainly the cities that were electrified, with some 30,000 customers. The total length of overhead line erected up till then was around 607 km. Underground cables were introduced only in 1958.

To supplement the CEB's own generation resources, negotiations were undertaken with the St Antoine Sugar Estate in 1956 for the supply of power during the sugar cane harvest season (June to December) using excess high pressure steam produced from bagasse. It was a form of mutual aid agreement under which the factory would export electricity to the Board when they had a surplus, and import from the Board when they were short, during the inter-crop period. The above arrangement was to eliminate all danger of power shortages.

In 1957, some 278,000 units were purchased from St Antoine at the rate of 4 cents per unit (based on fuel cost substitution). Gradually, negotiations were concluded with the other estates.

From the early 1960s, several development programmes were undertaken, namely:

- Rural electrification programme
- Hydro-power development
- Installation of bagasse-powered plants at sugar factories
- Installation of more oil-based power plants

The work during the decade progressed satisfactorily, and for all practical purposes Mauritius in 1970 was considered to have a complete network, though there were some small villages in the remote areas which did not have access to electricity. In absolute terms it was only in 1981 that the last village in the south – Chamarel – was able to have access to the grid.

With the increasing dependence on oil for power generation and the economic downturn which Mauritius was encountering in the late 1970s and early 1980s, further development of locally available resources (bagasse from the sugar industry and hydro-power development) were given serious attention. Table 5.4 below indicates the progress made from 1955 to 1989; it also illustrates the dependence on imported energy resources, especially oil for power generation purposes. In what follows, the development of the network, of installed capacity, and of electrical energy requirements are summarized. The discussion also covers the price structure, resource development policies and the consequences of increasing dependence on petroleum products.

Table 5.4 Development of power generation, 1955–89

		1955		1989	
Population	(000)	563		1018	
GDP/CAP	(1980 USD)	300		1865	
No. of customers		33500		211,274	
Network	(km)	607		5000	estimated
Electrical energy consumed					
kWh/cap.		65.4		568.0	
Total (GWh/y)		36.4		583.4	
Total electrical energy produced					
Local sources–GWh	(%)	31.7	(86.1)	205.4	(35.2)
Imported products					
Petroleum–GWh	(%)	5.1	(13.9)	310.0	(53.3)
Coal–GWh	(%)	0.0	(0.0)	68.0	(11.7)
Total installed capacity	MW (%)	11.08	(100)	276.97	(100)
CEB-Oil	(%)	3.48	(31)	169.18	(61)
Coal/bagasse	(%)	0.00	(0)	21.70	(8)
Bagasse	(%)	0.00	(0)	26.75	(10)
Hydro	(%)	7.60	(69)	59.34	(21)
Peak power demand	(MW)	15.30*		120.80	

* Peak power of 1960

Growth of the network

At the beginning of the 1960s, development of the network was virtually at a standstill. However, the year 1963 saw the resumption of major development schemes, mainly in the rural areas. Thirty-five additional villages were supplied with electricity during this year. The extension of supply to rural areas continued until 1968 when, owing to shortage of funds, the electrification programme had to be stopped. In fact, since 1966 the return on investment had declined unacceptably. Since industrial power requirements in the villages were virtually non-existent at that time, their load factor was extremely low and practically the whole demand occurred at system peak.

Rural electrification was resumed in 1970 and the extension of supply to these areas continued favourably until 1975 when the country was struck by cyclone Gervaise, which caused severe and extensive damage to the network. The rural electrification programme, scheduled to be near completion in early 1976, had been considerably delayed. In December 1979, the country was again hit by a violent cyclone, Claudette, which caused considerable damage to the network. To make matters worse, work on the network was greatly hampered by no less than four other cyclones, especially Hyacinthe in January 1980. The rural electrification programme was finally completed when the village of Chamarel was electrified in 1981. Figure 5.3 illustrates the evolution of the network from 1955 to 1989.

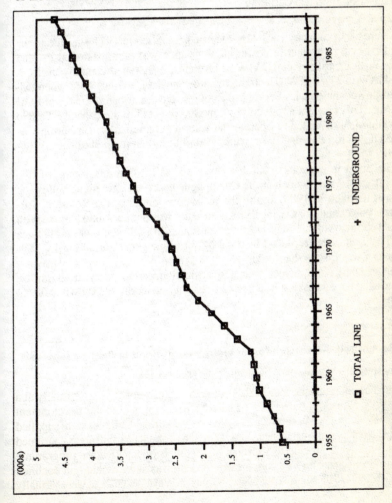

Figure 5.3 Growth of electrification network (km)

Apart from rural electrification, supply was also available for industrial development as from 1966. During the year 1971, several new industries started operations in the industrial zone of Plaine Lauzun and the network was extended to meet this industrial demand. With industrial development progressing steadily, the network had to be strengthened again in 1985. In that year, however, the construction of several industrial sectors and the impetus this gave to small-scale industries created a further escalation in demand. In 1988, not only was the distribution network extended, but new substations were erected in many regions to supply new industries, commercial complexes and hotels.

Thus the CEB network has increased from 607 km in 1955 to almost 5000 km, an almost eight-fold increase. The total number of customers has increased almost seven-fold, from around 30,000 to 211,274.

Evolution of installed capacity

Hydro

The increase in capacity for hydro-electric generation in 1971 was due to the new Ferney hydro-electric power station which was commissioned in June 1971. With a capacity of 10 MW, it brought the installed capacity up from 15.74 MW to 25.74 MW. The trend remained unchanged until 1978 when two hydro-power stations, La Ferme and Reduit, were out of operation for most of the time. This brought a reduction of about 8 per cent in the capacity. Due to unavailability of water to operate the station economically, La Ferme was closed down in February 1978, while Reduit Station remained idle until July 1978.

The boost in capacity from 1984 was due to the commissioning of two generators of 15 MW each at the Champagne hydro-electric plant, following a decision taken in 1980, and to the recommissioning of the Reduit hydro-electric power station. During 1988, La Ferme was put back into service with a plant capacity of 1.2 MW, while at the Tamarin Falls station two obsolete 500 KW units were replaced by a 4.3 MW turbine generator, and a 1.2 MW alternator was installed at Reduit.

Mean energy output per year and utilization period per year, based on historical data, and taking into account climatic variation, are shown in Table 5.5 below.

Table 5.5 Hydro-electric plants: energy output and utilization periods

Power station	Ratings (MW)	Mean energy (GWh/y)	Utilization (hours/y)
Champagne	28	46.69	1668
Ferney	10	29.16	2916
Other hydro stations	13	32.53	2502
Total	51	108.38	

CEB-thermal

The term CEB-thermal refers to oil-based power stations equipped with internal combustion engines. From 1955 to 1960 the total CEB-thermal capacity gradually increased from around 3 MW to almost 7 MW. In the early 1960s the thermal capacity increased four-fold to 28 MW with the completion of what was known as the Phase I development programme at St. Louis power station and partial completion of the Phase II programme. Almost no further development took place until 1974. From 1974 to 1979 further development programmes were undertaken at Saint Louis and Fort Victoria power stations, and the CEB-thermal generating capacity increased to 146 MW. Meanwhile, the generation efficiencies of power plants based on fuel oil increased from an average of 33 per cent in the 1970s to reach about 40 per cent during the 1980s.

The capacity remained at 146 MW until in 1988 the CEB had to opt for a 23 MW gas turbine (using kerosene). This programme of development had to be undertaken as a matter of urgency, because the Board was running the risk of not being able to meet the peak demand due to rapid industrialization and the development of the tourist industry of the middle and late 1980s. This installation was made at a new site, the Nicolay power station. Currently, the total installed CEB-thermal system is 169 MW.

The present installed and effective production capacities of the CEB thermal plants are summarized in Table 5.6.

Table 5.6 Production capacities of the CEB thermal plants

Power station	Production plant	Nominal rating (MW)	Effective O/P (MW)
St. Louis I	Pielstick	6x11.9 = 71.4	6x10 = 60
Fort Victoria	FIAT	2x5.5 = 11.0	2x5 = 10
	KV16 Major	4x5.9 = 23.6	4x5 = 20
	KV16 Major	4x6.6 = 26.4	4x5 = 20
FUEL	Bagasse/coal	16.0/18.0	12.0/15.0
Nicolay Road	Alsthom GE	23	23
Total		171.4/173.4	145/148

Coal/Bagasse

In 1980 the CEB, in collaboration with Medine Sugar Estate, decided to try a pilot-scale 10 MW coal/bagasse-fired power plant (University of Mauritius, 1980). After completion of this pilot project, it was decided to go for a coal/bagasse power plant of 21.7 MW capacity at FUEL Sugar Estate – one of the largest sugar estates on the island. This power plant is operational all year round, from June to December mostly on bagasse, and from January to June almost entirely on coal, with the exception of one month's stoppage for maintenance. This project was completed in 1984 and has been fully operational since January 1985. Meanwhile, the Medine station has started to operate only on bagasse.

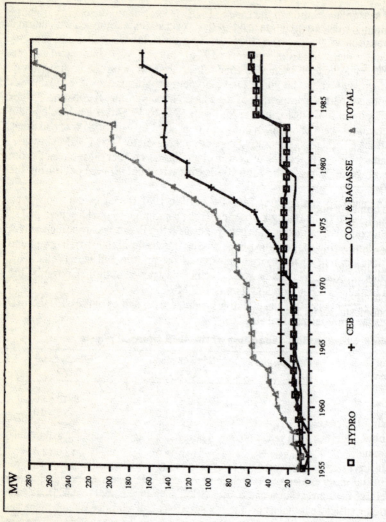

Figure 5.4 Installed capacity for electricity generation

☐ HYDRO   + CEB   —— COAL & BAGASSE   ▲ TOTAL

Bagasse

Bagasse power plants, which make use of excess high-quality steam for excess electricity generation for the national grid, were first initiated in 1957 as we have seen. From that time to 1971, more sugar factories installed such facilities and the total power increased from 2.07 MW to 19.65 MW before declining to around 15 MW for reasons that will be discussed below.

The evolution of installed capacity is graphically illustrated in Figure 5.4.

Total electricity output

Taking the factors such as maintenance and breakdown probability of each set and seasonal variation in the case of FUEL power plant, the energy output is computed to be as shown in Table 5.7.

Table 5.7 Total electricity output

		(GWh/year)	
		Normal year	Dry season
CEB	– Diesel/fuel oil	350.00	350.00
FUEL	– Coal/bagasse	72.51	63.02
CEB	– Gas turbine (Nicolay Road)	23.00	23.00
		445.51	436.02

The output of energy from the coal/bagasse station is affected by the dry season because drought affects sugar cane output and thus bagasse output.

Price structure and its evolution

Traditionally, the price structure of the sale of electricity has been such that it has encouraged end users, especially in the domestic sector, to consume more electricity. For example, during the period 1967 to 1972 (CEB, Annual Reports), the domestic sector price structure was as follows:

> Based on Monthly Consumption
> Initial 7 units : 78 cents per unit
> Next 15 units : 29 cents per unit
> Next 40 units : 19 cents per unit
> Additional units : 11 cents per unit

During the period 1973 to 1978, although the prices as well as the relative number of units within each price bracket changed, the basic structure remained the same.

In 1978, for example, the cost of the 61st unit was 55 per cent less than the 60 initial units (36 cents compared to 80 cents) which did not provide any incentive for conservation of electricity. The major argument that justifies such a pricing structure is that it encourages electricity consumption, which increases the load factor of the overall system, which in turn renders the system economically viable. According to various reports reviewed, this was necessary in the Mauritian context, especially when the price of fuel oil was considered to be cheap.

However, from the point of view of energy conservation, during the early 1980s when the Mauritian economy was being adversely affected by the foreign exchange required for energy imports, the above pricing policy could not be justified. For example, in 1982, though only a two-price bracket was adopted (initial 25 units were sold at 148 cents per unit and additional units at 112 cents) the fact that the 26th unit cost 25 per cent less than the 25th unit kept on encouraging end users to consume more electricity. However, this price difference gap was gradually closed to reach 2.5 per cent in 1990, when the 25th unit cost 163 cents and the 26th unit 159 cents. In November 1990 the price structure underwent a considerable change whereby units consumed beyond a certain initial limit cost more. This will be discussed below.

So far, the discussion has been confined to electricity consumption in the domestic sector, the major consumer of electricity (approximately 40 per cent of total electricity sold excluding CEB uses and line losses). Furthermore, for the other two sectors, commercial and industrial, such a price structure does not exist. The electricity sold to these two sectors is almost at a flat rate. Thus, the efficient use of electricity within these sectors is governed directly by the economic situation.

When the average trends of the price of electricity for all three sectors are

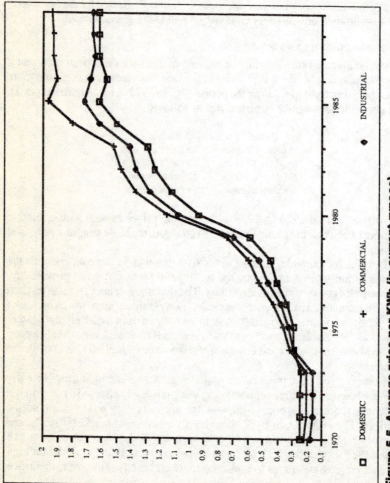

Figure 5.5 Average price per KWh (in current rupees)

analysed, it can be seen that though in current terms the cost of electricity increased ten-fold from 1970 to 1990, in real terms (measured in 1980 constant rupees) it remained the same. However, there was in fact a decline of almost 30 per cent during the 1970–5 period. The price then gradually rose to reach the 1970 figure and increased by 30 per cent to reach its peak in 1985, before declining again. These trends are illustrated in Figures 5.5 and 5.6.

Analysis of some existing policies and their implications

As the above discussion illustrates, the demand for electricity gradually increased at around 8 to 10 per cent per annum, from 36×10^6 KWh in 1955 to reach 584×10^6 KWh in 1989. Since the development of local resources for electricity production did not keep up with the electricity demand, the percent-

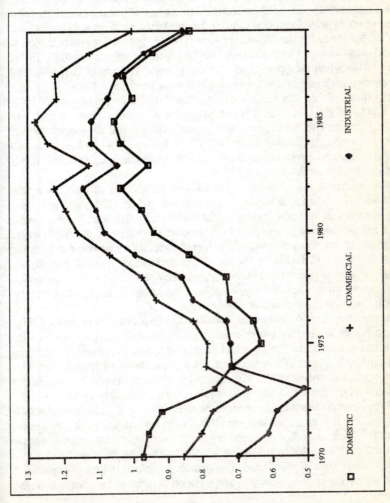

Figure 5.6 Average price per KWh (in constant 1980 rupees)

age contribution of electricity from local resources, which was 86 per cent in 1955, gradually declined to reach a minimum of 18 per cent in 1983, giving way to petroleum-based electricity.

This increasing dependence on petroleum products for electricity production is well illustrated in Figure 5.7, which shows the five-year moving averages of the percentage contribution of electricity from local resources and electricity from imported petroleum products for the period 1955 to 1989.

When the data for the late 1950s and early 1960s are closely analysed, it can be observed that due to the development of bagasse-based power stations at the sugar factories, electricity from local resources supplied up to 75 per cent of the total electricity demand, which was still increasing. This is easily explained by the fact that the CEB had adopted the policy of encouraging the sugar factories to develop excess power and produce electricity for the national grid. Consequently, the CEB had adopted the policy of pricing electricity from bagasse on an oil substitution (and/or saving) basis, at about 4 to 8 cents per KWh. This led to the development of small power generation plants at almost all the sugar factories on the island. This arrangement was successful until the early 1970s when the price of oil was still low and the cost of fuel oil/diesel to generate each unit of electricity was still no higher than 8 cents.

However, in the early 1970s the cost of fuel oil/diesel went beyond 20 cents per KWh, but the CEB was still purchasing bagasse electricity at 8 cents per KWh. Furthermore, during the same period, the demand for electricity had also increased considerably, from 54 GWh in 1960 to 204 GWh in 1973, and the percentage contribution of bagasse electricity had declined to below 10 per cent in 1973 (Manrakhan *et al.*, 1982).

The argument put forward by the CEB to justify this disparity was that electricity from the sugar factories was seasonal and unreliable and could not be considered as firm power comparable to electricity from oil; in other words, the CEB was no longer prepared to continue its policy of pricing bagasse electricity on an oil-saving basis. The fact that electricity production from the sugar factories had declined to below 10 per cent did not leave them with any strong counter-argument. Had this pricing policy been revised, the production of electricity from bagasse could have been increased; certainly, the technical possibilities and know-how were not lacking.

Several negotiations and technical studies were undertaken during the 1970s, but no policy for encouraging further development of energy from bagasse could be formulated. In 1980, even when the cost of fuel oil per unit of electricity had reached as high as 80 cents, the CEB was purchasing bagasse electricity at 16 cents. Nevertheless, the sugar factories continued to produce electricity during the crop season almost at the same level as in the late 1970s.

After several studies had been undertaken during the early 1980s the situation was revised. It was agreed that the CEB would find means to encourage the sugar factories to further develop electricity generation from bagasse for the national grid in order to minimize its dependence on imported petroleum products, the price of which had considerably increased in the early 1980s. A price for excess bagasse was also agreed upon in order to encourage factories

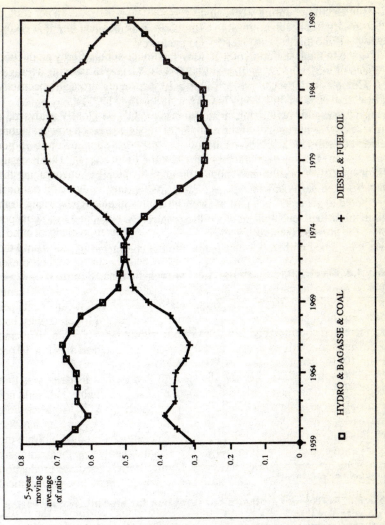

Figure 5.7 Evolution of resources used for power generation

□ HYDRO & BAGASSE & COAL   + DIESEL & FUEL OIL

to save bagasse and export any excess to other factories with new and more efficient generating facilities (high pressure boiler, condensing turbines and larger turbo alternators).

The supply of electricity from bagasse could be categorized as follows:

1. Firm power – all-year-round operation, using bagasse during crop season and coal during inter-crop.
2. Continuous and reliable supply during crop season (June to December), including production during weekends when the sugar factory is not operational.
3. Electricity *a bien plaire*, or only when the sugar factory is operational

(no electricity during weekends).

Electricity from each of the above categories was priced at different rates, category (1) the highest and category (3) the lowest.

This led to the installation of a 10 MW facility at Medine sugar factory in 1980 and of the 21.7 MW facility at FUEL sugar factory in 1984, as we have seen. Completion of these projects increased the supply of electricity from bagasse from 30 GWh in 1984 to 72 GWh in 1986. The FUEL facility uses coal during the inter-crop period (January to June) to produce an additional 40 GWh.

These new agreements and the completion of the bagasse projects can be considered a substantial achievement; however, the pricing policy for electricity from bagasse is still not satisfactory. In 1989, the CEB was paying the sugar factories (with firm or continuous power) around 40 cents per KWh of electricity generated from bagasse, while it was costing CEB around 80 cents for the fuel oil required to generate each unit of electricity at its thermal power plants. As a result no further development of similar projects has taken place since 1985, despite the proven potential.

As mentioned earlier, another major project completed during the early

Table 5.8 Electricity generation percentage contribution for selected years

Year	Petroleum products	Hydro, coal, bagasse
1955	13.9	86.1
1960	38.8	61.8
1965	24.0	76.0
1970	46.3	53.7
1975	67.4	32.8
1980	69.0	31.0
1983	81.9	18.1
1985	44.4	55.6*
1989	53.3	46.7

* Includes coal imported as from 1984

Table 5.9 Petroleum products consumption for electricity generation for selected years

Year	Total imported toe (10^3)	Consumed for electricity generation		
		toe (10^3)	Litres (10^6)	Percentage of total imports
1955	NA	1.6	1.7	NA
1970	86.1	15.6	17.0	18.1
1975	151.7	36.8	40.1	24.3
1980	190.6	52.9	57.6	27.8
1983	187.4	63.3	69.0	33.8
1985	198.3	36.4	39.7	21.3
1989	310.7	63.4	69.1	24.0

1980s was the Champagne hydro-electric station. The combination of the bagasse project and this hydro-electric project pushed up the percentage contribution of electricity from local resources from 31 per cent in 1980 to 45 per cent in 1985 and the percentage contribution of coal to nearly 12 per cent. Table 5.8 summarizes the evolution of the percentage contributions to power generation during 1955–89.

As illustrated in Table 5.9, the power generation sector consumed 17 million litres of fuel oil and diesel, representing 18 per cent (in terms of energy content) of the total petroleum products imported in 1970; this gradually grew to 60 million litres, representing 28 per cent in 1980. However, with the completion of the bagasse project at Medine, the bagasse/coal project at FUEL and the hydro-electric project at Champagne, the consumption of fuel oil for electricity generation dropped to 40 million litres, representing 21 per cent (in energy terms) of the total petroleum products imported in 1985. In 1989, the total stood at 70 million litres, representing 26 per cent of petroleum products imports. Had the above projects for tapping local energy resources not been developed, electricity generation would have required around 100 million litres in that year.

Electrical energy and power supply and demand

Energy demand trends and models

At the creation of the CEB in 1955, the total installed capacity was around 11 MW. Only cities and some surrounding villages had access to electricity, with a total network of around 607 km and a total electricity demand of 36.8 GWh. Due to the expansion of the network and the development of fuel oil, hydro-electric and bagasse power stations as described above, the total electricity demand grew at around 10 per cent annually to reach 136 GWh in 1970.

It is very difficult to carry out any trend analysis for electricity demand projections from 1955 to 1970 as the CEB was still expanding. However, beyond 1970, when most of the electrification programmes were reaching completion, analyses show certain explicable trends of electricity demand.

From 1970 to 1989, the total electricity demand increased from 136 GWh to 584 GWh, representing an annual growth of about 8 per cent. The per capita electricity demand increased at 6.7 per cent annually from 168 KWh in 1970 to 568 KWh in 1989. The peak power, which was 32 MW in 1970, grew to 78 MW in 1980 and reached 131 MW in 1990. For the same period the population grew at around 1.2 per cent annually from 806,000 to reach 1,028,000. The GDP per capita (constant 1980 US$) grew from US$800 in 1970 to US$1865 in 1989, representing an annual average growth of 4.6 per cent in real terms (see Figure 5.8).

Using this type of analysis, several national and international bodies such as the Ministry of Economic Planning and Development (MEPD), the Ministry of Energy, the CEB, the University of Mauritius, the World Bank and UNDP have been involved in model development for electricity demand projections

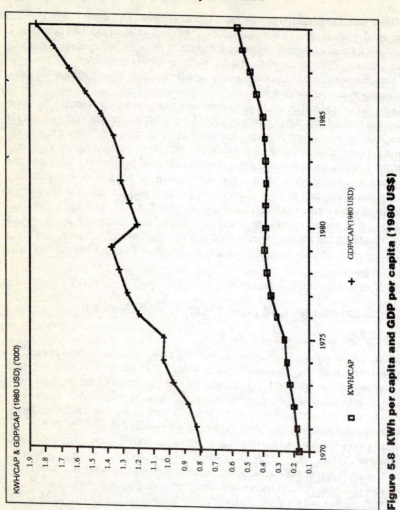

Figure 5.8 KWh per capita and GDP per capita (1980 US$)

for Mauritius (UNDP/World Bank, 1981; Nowbuth, 1986). Thus, more than a dozen models have been developed from the late 1970s to the present. These models have been studied and, for the purposes of this project, two of them have been retained. The Sectoral Energy Demand Model (SEDM) developed between 1987 and 1989 at the University of Mauritius within the Energy Use and Policy Planning Project, funded by IDRC, and the Harel model developed during 1987–8, as part of the author's PhD work (Harel, 1989). These two models have been reasonably well validated with historical data for the period 1970 to 1989 and are the most recent ones available. The models and their outcome are summarized below.

The Sectoral Energy Demand Model and Harel's model

Both models take into account population growth, economic development measured in terms of GDP and GDP per capita, total and per capita electrical energy demand, and energy–GDP elasticities.

The SEDM (Baguant *et al.*, 1990), as the term suggests, takes into account sectoral demand (commercial, residential and industrial) and the energy–GDP elasticities prevailing for 1970 to 1989 within each of the sectors. CEB electricity requirements and line losses are also allowed for within this model. The possibility of fuel substitution, expecially in the residential sector, from firewood/charcoal to kerosene, and kerosene to LPG or electricity, have also been considered. The time frame chosen is 1970 to 2010 (1970 to 1989 representing the historical trend and 1990 to 2010 representing the future trend).

Harel's model, unlike SEDM, does not consider sectoral electricity consumption, but looks instead at electricity consumption in an aggregated way which naturally includes CEB uses and line losses. Harel makes use of the good correlation of GDP (in 1980 US$) and electricity demand for the period 1968 to 1987 to extrapolate for the period 1988 to 2025. In order to avoid any arbitrariness caused by the extrapolation of GDP, he makes use of the assumption that Mauritius will follow an economic development path similar to Singapore and/or Hong Kong and argues that these two countries are around 25 to 30 years ahead of Mauritius (IMF, 1977; UN, 1976). In order to avoid any arbitrariness caused by assuming constant energy–GDP elasticity for the period 1987 to 2025, he makes use of the concept of time dependence for the elasticity and introduces the concept of the tunnelling effect (Thomas, 1987).

The assumptions and output of both models are quantified and summarized in the tables, figures and discussion that follow.

The sectoral energy demand model (SEDM)

The SEDM is based on the following parameters and assumptions:
- The population growth for 1990 to 2010 will be approximately 0.6 per cent annually (almost half the growth of 1970 to 1989).
- The medium-level GDP per capita in constant 1980 US$ will grow at approximately 3.81 per cent, about 10 per cent less than the growth rate registered from 1970 to 1989.
- The functional relationship (see Figure 5.9)

$$y = k\, x^E$$

where y = sectoral electricity demand per capita (KWh per capita)

x = GDP per capita (in 1980 US$)

k = Constant

E = Energy – GDP elasticity

E prevailing during 1970 to 1989 will persist for the next two decades for all three sectors (residential, commercial and industrial).

The values registered during 1970–89 are as follows:

	E	k	r^2 (corr. coef.)
Residential	1.21	–5.30	0.903

| Commercial | 1.36 | –6.58 | 0.961 |
| Industrial | 1.92 | –9.89 | 0.972 |

- Taking all the sectors together, the per capita electricity demand will increase from 568 KWh in 1989 to 1639 KWh in 2010, an average growth rate of 5.04 per cent as compared to 5.91 per cent registered during 1970 to 1989. This will mean that total electricity demand increases 3.5 times, from 584 GWh in 1989 to 2045 GWh in 2010 (see Table 5.10).

Harel's model

Harel's model is based on the following parameters and assumptions:
- The population growth would be similar to the one assumed for the SEDM.

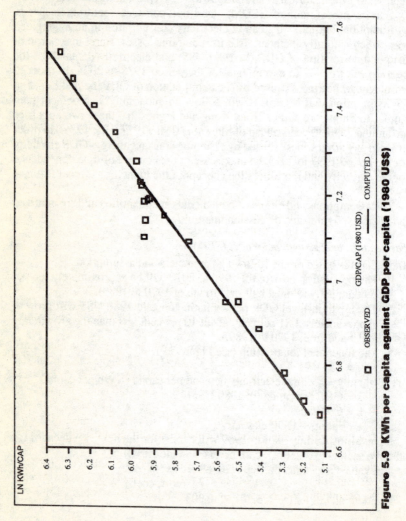

Figure 5.9 KWh per capita against GDP per capita (1980 US$)

Table 5.10 Sectoral energy demand model

Historical	Pop. (000)	GDP/cap. (1980 US$m)	GDP (1980 US$m)	Electricity demand GWh/y	KWh/cap.
1970	806	800	645	136	169
1975	867	1028	891	224	254
1980	937	1196	1121	355	367
1985	985	1444	1422	392	374
1989	1028	1865	1917	584	568
AGR (%) (1970–89)	(1.22)	(4.32)	(5.60)	(7.5)	(5.91)
Projections					
1990	1107	1950	2159	645	583
1995	1159	2372	2749	876	755
2000	1199	2886	3460	1145	955
2005	1227	3512	4309	1526	1244
2010	1248	4273	5333	2045	1639
AGR (%) (1990–2010)	(0.60)	(3.81)	(4.40)	(5.65)	(5.04)

- The Mauritian economy will follow the path of Hong Kong or Singapore which are 25 to 30 years ahead of Mauritius respectively, in terms of GDP per capita.
- The functional relationship (see Figure 5.9)

  $$y = k \, x^E$$

  where   y = electricity demand per capita (KWh per capita) all sectors taken together

              x = GDP per capita (in 1980 US$)

              k = constant

              E = energy–GDP elasticity

  (E registered 1968 to 1987 was 1.416)

However, Harel assumes that as from 2010 when the economy grows to beyond a certain limit E would gradually decline from 1.416 to around 1.0 by the year 2025. Thus, Harel introduces a concept of energy–GDP decoupling leading to a 'tunnelling' effect.

- The high-growth Singapore scenario results in a per capita electricity demand increase of 5.88 per cent for the period 1990 to 2025, from 568 KWh in 1989 to 2361 KWh in 2010 and reaching 5482KWh in 2025. The total electricity demand shows almost a four-fold increase from 1990 to 2010 and a two-fold increase from 2010 to 2025 (showing that the decoupling will occur beyond the year 2010).
- The low-growth Hong Kong scenario results in a per capita electricity demand increase of 5.61 per cent for the period 1990 to 2025. The total electricity demand increases slightly more than 3.5 times from 1990 to 2010 and there is a two-fold increase from 2010 to 2025 (showing that the decoupling will occur beyond the year 2010) (see Table 5.11).

Table 5.11 Harel's model – electricity demand

Year	Pop. (10³)	Hong Kong GDP/cap.	Hong Kong KWh/cap.	Hong Kong GWh/y	Singapore GDP/cap.	Singapore KWh/cap.	Singapore GWh/y
		Scenarios					
1968	782	792	161	126	792	161	126
1970	806	800	169	136	800	169	136
1980	937	1196	367	355	1196	367	355
1987	1020	1652	477	487	1652	477	487
AGR(%) [1968–87]	(1.34)	(3.74)	(5.58)	(7.00)	(3.74)	(5.58)	(7.00)
1990	1042	2283	636	663	2556	741	778
2000	1127	3694	1212	1366	4354	1476	1663
2010	1171	5977	2105	2465	7416	2631	3082
2020	1198	9672	3432	4110	12631	4386	5253
2025	1210	12303	4293	5193	16484	5482	6630
AGR(%) [1990–2025]	(0.43)	(4.93)	(5.61)	(6.06)	(5.47)	(5.88)	(6.31)

To check the validity of both models, the predicted values are compared to the measured values for the historical period 1970 to 1989 for the SEDM and 1968 to 1987 for Harel's model. As can be seen from Figure 5.10, for both models the measured values fluctuate around the predicted values with a basic period of the order of 12 years. The amplitude of the oscillations may result from conjunctural effects associated with world events.

Comparing the results of the models, it can be concluded that there is considerable divergence in the projected electrical energy demand trends, especially beyond the year 2000. However, from 1990 to the year 2000, the electricity demand predicted by the Hong Kong scenario of Harel's model and the prediction of SEDM show a difference of only 20 per cent, though this difference increases to 30 per cent by the year 2010. Comparing the Singapore scenario to the SEDM, the difference is almost 50 per cent for the year 2010.

For the purpose of this study, it has been assumed that the electricity demand is most likely to follow the trend projected by the SEDM.

Electricity demand characteristics – peak and base power

Assuming the trend projected by the SEDM holds, the total electrical energy demand would increase from 584 GWh in 1990 to 2045 GWh for the year 2010. For the CEB to meet this energy requirement, it has to develop an investment programme to increase its installed generating capacity. In order to enable the CEB to formulate a development programme, a knowledge of the demand characteristics is essential. That is, such aspects as the evolution of the peak power requirement, the base load, the mean load factor and the load duration characteristics must be studied.

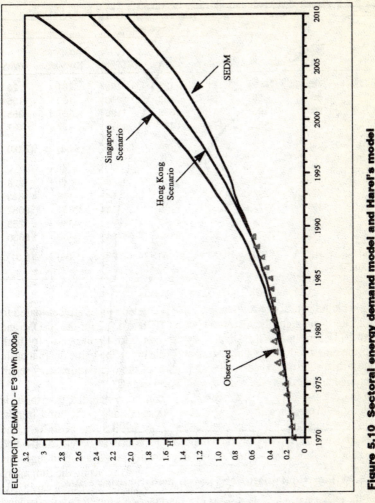

Figure 5.10 Sectoral energy demand model and Harel's model

Based on work already carried out at the University of Mauritius using historical data for the period 1960 to 1987 and updated to 1990 for the purpose of this current task (see Figure 5.11), the following observations are relevant:

1. The functional relationship between the peak power demand P(MW) and the total electrical energy demand E(GWH) is

    P = k + a E

    where k and a are constants.

    For the period 1960 to 1990 (for the range 55GWh < E < 585 GWh), the value of $r^2 = 0.99$ and k = 4.495 and a = 0.221

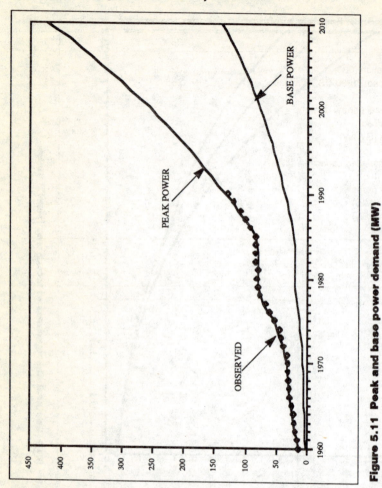

Figure 5.11 Peak and base power demand (MW)

Table 5.12 Electrical energy and power demand using SEDM

Year	Electricity (GWh/y)	Peak power (MW)	Mean load factor	Base power (MW)
Historical				
1960	55	15	0.417	3
1970	136	32	0.485	8
1980	355	83	0.487	20
1989	584	121	0.551	33
Projected				
1990	645	134	0.551	37
1995	876	173	0.578	50
2000	1145	215	0.605	65
2005	1526	275	0.634	87
2010	2045	352	0.664	117

Table 5.13 Possible evolution of the power sector

	1989	2010
Population (000)	1028	1248
GDP/cap. (1980 USD)	1865	4273*
Electrical energy demand		
KWh/cap.	568	1639*
Total (GWh/y)	584	2045*
Total installed capacity – MW	277**	352
Power demand		
Peak (MW)	121	352
Base (MW)	33	117
Mean load factor	0.551	0.667

* Using Sectoral Energy Demand Model

** According to the CEB actual capacity available to meet peak is 134 MW

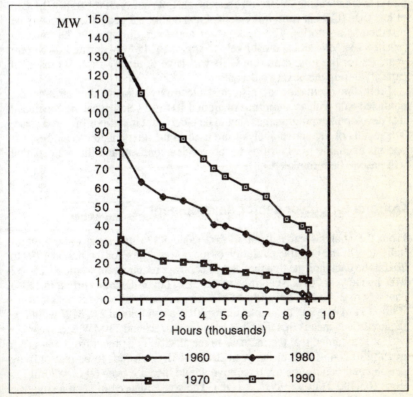

Figure 5.12 Load duration curve

2. The mean load factor (ℓ) defined as

$$\ell = \frac{E * 1000}{P * d * 24} \qquad \text{where } d = 365 \text{ or } 366 \text{ days per year}$$

increased from 0.412 in 1960 to 0.516 in 1975. Following a slight decline during the early 1980s, it increased to reach a maximum of 0.563 in 1989, representing an annual growth of 0.93 per cent. This is also reflected when the annual load duration curve is plotted (see Figure 5.12). It has been assumed that ℓ will continue to increase during the next two decades to reach 0.663 by the year 2010.

From the analysis, it can be concluded that if the current policies are maintained, it is very likely that the total electricity requirement will increase almost four-fold by the year 2010 and the peak power requirement will increase three-fold from 121 MW in 1989 to 352 MW in the year 2010. Similarly, the base power would also increase from around 33 MW to 117 MW for the same period. The trends are illustrated in Figure 5.11 and tabulated in Tables 5.12 and 5.13

For the CEB to provide the peak load beyond 135 MW (the current peak power available at the CEB) with a reasonable Loss of Load Probability (LOLP) of less than 0.15 per cent, it is essential that additional generation capacity be installed as a priority. The peak power registered during 1990 has already reached 131 MW and is most likely to approach 145 MW during this current year. As for the long term, the CEB will have to almost triple its installed capacity during the next two decades.

From the oscillation of historical electricity demand data around the predicted data with an amplitude of around 10 to 12 years, it can be concluded that development programmes should be phased out in periods of 5 to 6 years. The results of the above analysis are used in the next chapter to analyse the options available in Mauritius for power development and the policies that will have to be formulated.

Options for power sector development

From the analysis carried out so far, Table 5.13 summarizes some major indicators of the possible evolution of the power sector for the period 1989 to 2010. The data indicate that the total peak power requirement would reach 352 MW by the year 2010. According to the CEB, out of the total current installed capacity of 277 MW, only 134 MW can be relied upon to meet peak power. If this 134 MW is still available during 2010, an additional 218 MW would be required. This means that the CEB has to install around 11 MW each year.

If it is assumed that the increase in the electricity demand from 584 GWh in 1989 to 2045 GWh in the year 2010 (1461 GWh) has to be met only by petroleum products, the total required would increase from 69 to 487 million litres (63,400 TOE to 389,727 TOE). The consequences of such a situation need no elaboration.

However, Mauritius still has sufficient energy resource potential to ensure that the CEB does not become completely dependent on imported petroleum products. This will require proper planning and effective energy policy formulation on the basis of in-depth analysis of all the possible options for future development of the power sector.

Option 1 – Business as usual

The first option is to have no change in current policy – no incentive for electricity conservation, no effort to further exploit locally available bagasse or hydro-power, no further substitution by coal-powered stations. Any additional electricity demand is met by installation of new power stations equipped with internal combustion engines fed by additional importation of petroleum products.

Option 2 – Energy/GDP decoupling

Under this option, policy would be formulated to encourage electricity conservation in all sectors in order to bring the energy–GDP elasticity from 1.27 to below 1.0 – in other words, to trigger decoupling of electrical energy demand and economic development and enhance the tunnelling effect. This is best achieved by adopting a price structure which would discourage additional electricity consumption beyond a certain minimum limit.

Through the National Household Energy Consumption survey carried out at the University of Mauritius within the IDRC's Energy Use and Policy Planning project, it was shown that 75 KWh per month per household was enough to provide all the essential necessities for the family, as far as electrical energy is concerned. It was thus recommended that the rate charged for the first 75 KWh consumed per household per month be kept to a minimum, and any additional unit be made expensive so as to discourage customers from exceeding 75 KWh per month.

It is encouraging to report that as from December 1990 the CEB has introduced a new price structure, the major aim of which is to encourage electricity conservation. This new structure for the household sector is compared with the old structure in Table 5.14. Similar changes have been introduced for the other sectors.

Table 5.14 Electricity price structure for the household sector

Old	
Initial 25 units of the month	163 cents
Additional units	159 cents
New	
Initial 25 units of the month	163 cents
Next 75 units	180 cents
Next 150 units	200 cents
Additional units	250 cents

It is estimated that if the conservation policy is successful and the energy–GDP elasticity drops below 1.0, the total electricity demand for 2010 would be 1528 GWh, compared to a forecast 2045 GWh.

Option 3 – Use of solar water heaters

During the above-mentioned survey it was shown that 8.92 per cent of the electricity consumed in the household was used solely for water heating for the daily shower. In order to substitute electricity used for water heating with solar energy, it was recommended that the use of solar water heaters, which has already been tried and proven to be technically feasible, be encouraged. However, the relatively high capital investment required for solar water heaters compared to electric heaters has not encouraged their wider use. It was thus recommended that all taxes on material used for solar water heaters be removed, and that a loan on preferential terms be provided to purchasers. It is again encouraging to report that this scheme was adopted in December 1990. It is assumed that, in time, all hot water for the bathroom, as well as for the kitchen, will be provided by solar water heaters, so that some 10 per cent of electricity consumption could be substituted by solar water heaters by the year 2010.

Option 4 – Bagasse and coal for power generation

Sugar cane is the major crop which occupies some 80 per cent of the cultivable land (80,000 hectares) or 40 per cent of the total land of the island. Depending mainly on the climatic conditions, around 5 to 6 million tonnes of fresh cane, representing 500,000 to 650,000 tonnes of raw sugar, are produced annually.

The fibre content of fresh cane varies between 12 and 15 per cent by weight (Mauritius Chamber of Agriculture, Annual Reports; Mauritius Sugar Research Institute, Annual Reports). After the milling process, which separates the cane juice from the fibre, the latter ends up as bagasse which on an average contains 50 per cent moisture and 50 per cent fibre. The production of bagasse is around 270 to 300 kg per tonne of cane, or 27 to 30 per cent. Fresh bagasse is easily combustible and has an average heat content of 9.9 GJ/tonne at 50 per cent moisture. In all the sugar factories in Mauritius, as in many sugar cane growing countries, the bagasse is combusted in a specially designed furnace which enables production of process steam required for the raw sugar manufacture and production of electricity for the sugar factory. Sugar factories with a good steam balance end up with excess high quality steam and/or excess bagasse production. It is this excess steam and/or bagasse that is utilized for production of exportable electricity fed to the national grid. The yield of exportable electricity measured (Paturau, 1982; Hugot, 1986) in terms of KWh per tonne cane depends on numerous factors, a few of which are mentioned below:

* Fibre percentage of the cane, which in turn affects bagasse percentage.
* Variety of the cane and the climatic conditions.
* Overall steam balance of the factory, measured in terms of the steam to bagasse ratio (r_{sb}) and specific steam consumption (SSC).

- Power house efficiencies (furnace, boiler and turbo alternators).
- The technology used for steam and electricity production, as well as the type of equipment used for manufacturing raw sugar.
- Most important of all are incentives for the production of exportable electricity.

For the benefit of those not familiar with the sugar industry, it is important to explain the terms r_{sb} and SSC. The r_{sb} is measured in terms of tonne of steam produced per tonne of bagasse. This parameter can vary between 1.8 and 3.1 and is directly related to the type of boiler and furnace, indicating their overall efficiency. Currently, the average r_{sb} in Mauritius is 2.2. However, it has been demonstrated that this can be improved to reach 3.0.

The SSC is a measure of process steam consumption represented in terms of tonnes of steam required per tonne of cane processed. It is an indicator of the efficiency of process steam use and can be anywhere between 0.3 and 0.6. In Mauritius, the average SSC stands at 0.55 but it has been demonstrated that an SSC of 0.3 is achievable.

Based on experience acquired in this field, it can be concluded that the yield of exportable electricity, per tonne of fresh cane processed, can vary between 0 and 90 KWh, depending on the equipment used. In turn, the choice of equipment depends entirely on incentives presented to the sugar companies for producing excess bagasse and/or electricity.

As discussed earlier, had there not been any incentive in 1957, St Antoine sugar factory would not have developed the potential to produce excess electricity. A similar argument is applicable in the cases of other sugar factories which gradually adopted systems for producing exportable electricity during the 1960s.

Without going into too much technical detail, the potential for electricity production of the Mauritian sugar industry, as a function of the technology adopted, is described below. Four levels of technology are considered and classified as four sub-options (4a to 4d).

4a. Production of electricity a bien plaire

In the Mauritian context, electricity *a bien plaire* is defined as electricity produced by the sugar factories and exported to the national grid whenever excess power is available (Transenerg, 1982). It also follows that this electricity is available only during the harvest season (June to December) and only on weekdays (Monday to Saturday) when the factories are in operation.

On the basis of our experience of the local sugar factories, we conclude that factories with the following characteristics and equipped as presented below can produce almost 10 KWh of exportable electricity per tonne of cane.

- Crushing rate of above 80 tonnes of cane per hour.
- Total boiler capacity of above 40 tonnes and producing steam at 10 to 15 bar pressure (150 to 200 psig).
- Steam to bagasse ratio of 1.8 to 2.2.
- Reasonably good steam balance (SSC of 0.5 to 0.6 tonne per tonne cane crushed).

- Self-consumption of electricity not exceeding 20 KWh per tonne cane.
- Equipped with an *additional* turbo alternator of around 0.5 to 1.5 MW.

With the exception of some which do not have an additional turbo alternator to produce excess power, almost all the Mauritian sugar factories already have the above features.

Assuming an average annual sugar cane production of 5.5 million tonnes, the total electricity *a bien plaire* can reach up to 55 GWh. However, the historical data show that the total production of electricity from sugar factories (with the exception of FUEL) for the last 15 years has remained steady at approximately 25 GWh per year. This is so because the CEB's purchasing rate of 16 cents (1 US cent) per KWh is too low and offers no encouragement to the sugar factories to increase their electrical energy output. The major argument used by the CEB to justify this low rate is that electricity *a bien plaire* is not guaranteed and cannot be used to meet peak power, and thus cannot be compared to electricity from its own oil-based thermal power plant nor priced on the basis of fuel oil savings.

Though there is some truth in the above argument, a new pricing formula has to be devised and implemented if option 4a is to be adopted and the production of 10 KWh per tonne of cane (55 GWh) is to be attained. Based on previous work and updating during the current analysis, it is suggested that electricity from bagasse be compared to electricity from coal because both bagasse and coal are solid fuels. Thus the pricing formula should be devised on the basis of coal savings. Using current figures, this means a tripling of the price of electricity *a bien plaire* from 16 cents (1 US cent) to around 50 cents (3.3 US cents).

4b. Continuous supply of electricity during harvest

Continuous supply of electricity during harvest implies production for around 3000 hours per year, during weekends as well as during temporary factory breakdowns or stopovers. It has already been demonstrated in Mauritius that up to 60 KWh of exportable electricity per tonne can be attained through proper selection of equipment, modification of sugar manufacture and proper planning. Some of the major features of the sugar factory and equipment are summarized below:

- The minimum size of the power plant should be 15 MW, allowing a total production of around 40 GWh at 90 per cent load factor (10 GWh for self consumption and 30 GWh for exportation).
- To enable such a system to operate for 3000 hours on bagasse, the total supply of cane per year needs to be above 400,000 tonnes and the crushing rate to be above 150 tonnes of cane per hour.
- The steam to bagasse ratio needs to be at least 2.5.
- The SSC needs to be brought down to at least 0.4 through modification of juice heating, evaporation and sugar boiling systems.
- The total boiler capacity needs to be 120 tonnes per hour with pressure of 30 to 45 bar.
- A condensing turbine which is more efficient than back pressure turbine is required.

From the above, we can compute the output of a 15 MW power plant attached to a sugar factory crushing at 200 tonnes of cane per hour, operating for approximately 120 days and having a total of 500,000 tonnes of cane available per harvest. The output of such a system would be 40 GWh, out of which 30 GWh can be exported, representing 60 KWh per tonne of cane. It is estimated that such an installation would require an investment of approximately 150 million rupees (US$10 million) or about 10 million rupees per MW (US$0.67 million per MW).

If this option is adopted, total electricity production can reach 330 GWh per year for cane production of 5.5 million tonnes. For successful implementation of such a programme, major policies to facilitate availability of capital for investment and pricing of the electricity need to be formulated. Capital can easily be made available at low interest rates through the local development bank or from the international banking system. Since the electricity supply is not going to be available all year round, it cannot be priced at the same level as electricity from a coal-powered station, which is estimated to cost 120 cents per KWh (8 US cents) – 50 cents (3.3 US cents), being the cost of imported coal, and the balance of 70 cents (4.7 US cents) interest on capital operation and maintenance. Nor can it be priced as electricity *a bien plaire*, as discussed above.

Thus it is suggested that over and above the coal saving figure of 50 cents (3.3 US cents), a running cost including 5 per cent return on investment (ROI) be added. According to our calculation this would bring the electricity price to 90 cents (6 US cents), 50 cents (3.3 US cents) for coal substitution and 40 cents (2.7 US cents) for running costs.

4c. Firm power supply

Firm power means production of electricity all year round, which means 300 days (7200 hours) with 65 or 66 days allowed for maintenance. It has been demonstrated that this is only possible by making use of a dual-fuel furnace (coal and bagasse), which will allow combustion of bagasse during the harvest season (3000 hours) and combustion of coal during the inter-crop season (4200 hours). The technical details are similar to those described for option 2b above.

For a 15 MW plant producing 30 GWh of exportable electricity during the harvest, an additional 60 GWh can be produced by burning around 30,000 to 35,000 tonnes of imported coal during the inter-crop. Though the coal would have to be imported, the advantage is that coal is available from neighbouring countries and thus allows diversification of energy resource use.

For such an option to be successful, the price of 120 cents (8 US cents) per unit would have to be applied to all units of electricity.

4d. Electricity supply using enhanced technology

With the exception of the condensing turbine, which is generally not required in a sugar factory, the systems described in Options 4a to 4c are based on traditional equipment found in sugar factories. Through computer simulation, it has been demonstrated that through the use of boilers of pressure higher than

45 bars, the yield of exportable electricity can be considerably increased (from 60 KWh to 90 KWh per tonne of cane). This also necessitates drying the bagasse from 50 per cent moisture to below 30 per cent in order to enable combustion to occur at 1500°C, which is required for running high-pressure boilers. A boiler feed water treatment plant would also be required because the water must be free from any chemicals which would damage the water tubes and the boiler (National Energy Seminar, 1981; Harel and Baguant, 1991). Air to fuel ratio has to be monitored very closely in order to enable almost complete combustion, and the flue gas temperature must be brought down to a minimum of 125°C. All these above steps could increase the ratio of steam to bagasse to almost 3.0. In order to improve the balance and lower SSC to 0.35, new items of equipment, such as deep-vacuum crystallizers, are required.

Analysis also reveals that in the Mauritian context the size of such systems must be greater than 30 MW. The capital investment requirement is about 30 per cent higher than in the system described in 4b and 4c, at approximately 13 million rupees (US$0.87 million) per MW compared to 10 million rupees (US$0.67 million) per MW. Nevertheless, an improvement of almost 33 per cent in overall efficiency, from 60 to 90 KWh per tonne of cane, makes this system economically viable.

Implementation of such a system would require a policy of sugar factory centralization, closing small factories to further increase the size of others. That would obviously entail socio-political problems which cannot be ignored. As for the pricing structure, the one suggested for Option 4c would seem to be acceptable.

If the 30 MW size is adopted, only five or six power stations, totalling 150 to 175 MW of installed capacity, would be enough to burn all the bagasse. It is computed that these power stations, using bagasse during harvest, could produce up to 450 GWh during 3000 hours of operation per year at 90 per cent load factor. During the inter-crop, 625 GWh could be produced from these stations (at 90 per cent load factor) necessitating the import of about 300,000 tonnes of coal annually. Thus the total electricity output of these stations could reach 1075 GWh per year.

Option 5 – Use of a pump hydro scheme

We have seen that by the year 2010 the SEDM scenario would lead to:

Total electrical energy demand of	2045 GWh
Peak power demand of	352 MW
Base power demand of	117 MW
Mean load factor of	0.664

These figures indicate that for 33 per cent of the time(8 hours per day) there would be a surplus of 152 MW (see Figure 5.13). The possibility of using this excess power to run a pump hydro scheme has been studied by Harel.

Tamarin Falls, which has the highest drop (293 metres) for the minimum length of flow, has been proposed as the best site for the installation of a 150 MW pump hydro scheme. It is also proposed that the project be implemented in three phases of 50 MW each.

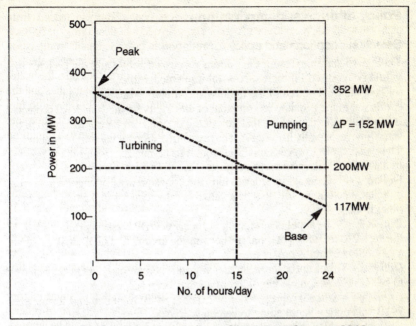

Figure 5.13 Peak and base power requirement at the year 2010

In simple terms, the use of a pump hydro system allows the conversion of excess base power into more valuable peak power. Though the system entails loss of energy during pumping and turbining and due to friction losses, the study shows that in the local context the scheme will not only be economically viable but also have several side benefits.

In the Mauritian context only two types of power station can provide peak power, one being a hydro-electric power station and the other a thermal power plant equipped with internal combustion engines running on fuel oil and/or diesel. So far the total installed capacity of hydro-electric power has reached 51 MW and it is believed that this can be increased to 75 MW by improving the already existing hydro-electric stations and tapping a few more small hydro-power sites. Once this maximum is reached, any additional peak power would have to be met by thermal power plant. It is also important to take into account that hydro-power plants are dependent on climatic conditions.

The development of a pump hydro scheme would extend the hydro-electric capacity of Mauritius. Another important aspect of the scheme is that once the water required for operating the system is procured, it will be independent of the climatic conditions, because the system can be operated as a closed circuit.

For this option to be successful it will be essential to study the overall development plan for power generation carefully and adopt an integrated strategy.

Policy options and implications

Selection of options and policy formulation

Table 5.15 summarizes all the options discussed above and the policies that would be required for their successful implementation.

The potential output of the options at completion are also summarized and compared to the possible requirement of electricity by the year 2010 projected using SEDM. It is obvious that not all the options can be implemented at the same time, especially in the case of bagasse utilization for electricity generation. Thus a screening process has been found to be necessary and the following remarks justify the screening exercise:

Option 1 – To be kept in order to indicate consequences of change in current policies. The output will also be a valuable reference for indicating how good other options are.

Option 2 – To be kept because, with the energy–GDP elasticity running at 1.27 during 1970 to 1989, potential for decoupling energy and GDP does exist and a tunnelling effect is possible.

Option 3 – To be kept because, technically and economically, it has been proven to be feasible and, most important of all, has been accepted socially.

Option 4a – Since it represents only 2.6 per cent of total demand for the year 2010, this option is not going to be considered.

Option 4b – Not to be considered because it is wasteful to operate power generating facilities for only 3000 hours per year.

Option 4c – To be kept, and appears to be the most promising option available in Mauritius.

Option 4d – Though theoretically this option has been demonstrated to be technically viable, in practice it has been used only to a limited extent in countries like Hawaii and Australia. The successful operation of the system in Mauritius is still questionable. This will not be considered at this stage.

Option 5 – To be kept because this is the only option which will allow production of peak power from local resources.

Thus the options selected are 1, 2, 3, 4c and 5.

Policy testing

The policies associated with the above selected options have been classified as Policy 1 to Policy 5 (P1 to P5). Since it would be very time-consuming to quantify the impact of these policies individually or in various combinations on the overall energy balance in the period 1989 to 2010, a system dynamics model using Dynamo has been developed.

The outputs of the model are summarized in Tables 5.16 to 5.21 and in Figures 5.14 to 5.15.

Policy 1 – Business as usual

This would result in a total electricity requirement of 2045 GWh/year compared to 584 GWh for 1989, representing a growth rate of around 6.2 per cent (see Table 5.16).

Policy 2 – Energy: GDP decoupling

If the decoupling of energy and GDP is successful, elasticity will decline from 1.27 to 0.8 and average out at 1.1 during the time frame 1989 to 2010. This would result in an energy saving of 41 GWh in 1992 which would increase to 517 GWh by the year 2010, representing a saving of 5.5 per cent in 1992 and 25.3 per cent in 2010.

Policy 3 – Use of solar water heaters

If solar water heaters are used to provide hot water in the household sector, some 7 GWh of electricity in 1992 and 157 GWh in 2010 could be substituted, representing a saving of 0.9 per cent to 7.5 per cent in 1992 and 2010 respectively.

Policy 4 – Firm power using bagasse and coal

The most promising policy, this would allow production of up to 1300 GWh of electricity per year, 540 GWh from bagasse and 760 GWh from coal, representing more than 60 per cent of the total electricity requirement of 2045 GWh for the year 2010 resulting from Policy 1.

This would, however, necessitate importation of around 350,000 tonnes of coal, the implication of which is discussed below.

Policy 5 – Pump hydro

This policy involves the installation of a pump hydro system, which as discussed earlier will not add any electricity to the national energy balance, but rather draw out 25 to 75 GWh per year from the network to convert base power into peak power.

Policies 2 and 3 combined

The impact of policies 2 and 3 combined is summarized in Table 5.17. A saving of 9 to 36.5 per cent of the petroleum products could be achieved, 10,284 TOE (11.53 x10^6 litres) in 1992 and 142,295 TOE (159.51 x 10^6 litres) in 2010, if these policies are successful.

Policies 4 and 5 combined

The impact of policies 4 and 5 combined is summarized in Table 5.18. The saving in petroleum products will rise from 1.2 per cent in 1992 to reach a maximum of 71.1 per cent in the year 2002. This saving would gradually decline to 61.9 per cent by the year 2010 because further development of the bagasse potential will not be possible, and the demand for electricity will continue to rise.

This policy will necessitate importation of around 380,000 tonnes of coal by the year 2010.

Policies 2 to 5 combined

The outcome of this combination is illustrated in Table 5.19. By the year 2008, the power sector can become almost entirely independent of petroleum

Table 5.15 Summary of options available and policies required

Options	Description	Policy required	Potential output by 2010
1. Business as usual	–	Current policies maintained.	Total electricity required 2045 GWh
2. Energy–GDP decoupling	Electrical energy–GDP elasticity to go down from 1.27 to 0.8 and average 1.1 for period 1990–2010.	Conservation policy – with price structure to encourage efficient end use.	Total electricity required by 2010 – 1528 GWh representing a saving of 517 GWh.
3. Use of solar water heaters	For substituting electricity required for water heating at households.	Loan at low interest and exemption of government tax on material for solar water heaters construction.	Total electricity saving around 10 % of 2010 requirement i.e. 205 GWh.
4. Utilization of bagasse			
4a. Electricity a bien plaire	Simple modifications at sugar factory and addition of small turbo alternator 0.5–3.0 MW for exportable electricity production when excess available.	Pricing on coal saving basis i.e. around 50 cents (3.3 US cents) per KWh.	Electricity products can reach 10 KWh/tonne cane i.e. 55 GWh/year representing 2.7 % of 2010 requirement. Basis of 5.5 million tonne cane per year.
4b. Continuous supply during harvest only (3000 hours/year)	Use of high-pressure boilers i.e. above 31 bar, condensing turbine, improvement of r_{sb} to 2.5 and SSC down to 0.4.	Facilitate availability of capital and price of electricity in between coal saving and firm power price i.e. 90 cents (6 US cents) per KWh.	Total electricity production can reach 60 KWh/tonne cane i.e. 330 GWh/year representing 16% of the year 2010 electricity requirement.
4c. Firm power supply i.e. 300 days = 7200 hours	Use of system as from 4b plus dual fuel furnace to enable burning of coal during inter-crop i.e. 3000 hours bagasse-based and 4200 hours coal-based.	Facilitate availability of capital and price of electricity based on assumption that system is running on coal only i.e. 120 cents (8 US cents).	Total production – 990 GWh i.e., 330 GWh from bagasse, 660 GWh from coal. On the basis of 2000 kWh/tonne coal, around 330,000 tonnes imported coal required.

Table 5.14 cont.

Options	Description	Policy required	Potential output by 2010
4d. Using enhanced technology	As in 4c but using higher pressure boilers, i.e. beyond 48 bars, high-temperature furnace, water treatment plant and bagasse driers to improve r_{sb} to almost 3.0.	Same as for 4c.	Almost 90 KWh/tonne cane resulting in total production of 450 GWh/year from bagasse at 90% recovery and 625 GWh/year from coal representing 300,000 tonnes coal at improved yield of 2200 KWh per tonne coal.
5. Use of Pump hydro scheme	Pumping turbining system of 50 MW per phase, to convert excess base power into peak power. System of 150 MW to be completed in 3 phases at Tamarin Falls.	Development of integrated strategy and facilitate availability of capital to CEB.	Total peak power attainable 150 MW. The system will not add any energy to the energy balance of Mauritius, instead for every 100 units of low-grade electricity consumed will produce 75 units of high-grade electricity.

Basis:

1. Total elasticity required by 2010	2045 GWh
Peak power required	352 MW
Base power	117 MW
2. Total cane yield/year	5.5×10^6 Tonne
Bagasse per cent cane	28 per cent

products. It is interesting to note that the 344,216 TOE (385.67 x 10^6 litres) of petroleum products required for the year 2008 could be entirely replaced by locally available bagasse and hydro, and 379,167 tonnes of imported coal.

Policy implications

Figure 5.14 and Table 5.20 illustrate the gradual increase in the installed capacity for 1992 to 2010, and the capacity required. It can be observed that if policies 2 to 5 are implemented, the installed capacity would be in excess of what would be required by 71.8 per cent in 1992, 61.3 per cent in 2000 and 67.0 per cent in 2010. It can be argued that such excess capacity leads to an increase in the cost of production. Nevertheless, it provides a safety net for the future.

Figure 5.15 illustrates future electricity demand and supply for 1990 to 2010. It is interesting to observe the gradual decrease in dependence on petroleum products, which declines to nil by the year 2008. (Note that to facilitate the illustration in Figure 5.14, electricity saving due to conservation measures has been treated as a source of supply.)

Table 5.21 summarizes the economic implication of the combined policies 2 to 5. The cost of importing coal at current prices would represent less than the cost of importing oil. For example, beyond the year 2000, if the power sector is to depend on petroleum products, its importation would represent around 2 per cent of GDP (measured in constant 1980 currencies). However, successful implementation of policies 2 to 5 would necessitate importation of coal which would represent around 8 per cent of the GDP.

It is important to add that other implications, such as capital investment for the development of pump hydro, bagasse and coal systems might necessitate international funding, which would have negative implications for the balance of payments in terms of a drain on foreign exchange and losses through fluctuations in exchange rates. It would also involve the use of foreign exchange for the importation of equipment such as high-pressure boilers and condensing turbines, and this drawback should be studied further. Nevertheless, policies 2 to 5 make an attractive combination and would lead the Mauritian power sector away from its increasing dependence on petroleum products (see Figure 5.16).

Development strategy

Based on the output of the model, an integrated development strategy of the power sector of Mauritius is proposed. The major aim of this strategy is to enable Mauritius to maintain a sustainable economic growth warranted by the future development needs with minimum petroleum resources.

The following notes characterize the integrated strategy proposed:
1. Time frame chosen is 1989 to 2010, with 1989 as the base year.
2 Energy–GDP elasticity to decline from 1.27 to 0.8 during the time frame, through conservation measures and pricing structure to be adopted for the end users, discussed above.
3. All water heating required for the household to be provided by solar

water heaters (the 10 per cent electricity for this purpose to be substituted at the rate of 0.5 annually).

4. In addition to the FUEL power station of 21.7 MW already being run on coal and bagasse, 6 additional 30 MW (each) power plants running on bagasse and coal to be installed during the time frame at the rate of one station every three years. It is suggested that two be installed in the south, one in the west, one in the east and two in the north. Excess bagasse from neighbouring factories needs to be fed to the power plant during the harvest to ensure 3000 hours of continuous operation. During the inter-crop period, 4200 hours of operation need to be guaranteed using imported coal.

5. Pump hydro power system to be installed in three phases, each phase consisting of a 50 MW pumping and turbining facility. The site proposed is the Tamarin Falls in the west of the island (see Figure 5.1).

Table 5.16 Individual policies. Possible saving and/or supply of electricity (GWh/y)

Time	Policy 1	Policy 2		Policy 3		Policy 4		Policy 5
1992	748	41	5.5%	7	0.9%	130	17.4%	0
1994	832	39	4.7%	16	1.9%	325	39.0%	0
1996	929	49	5.3%	26	2.8%	520	56.0%	0
1998	1036	64	6.2%	39	3.8%	520	50.2%	0
2000	1145	82	7.2%	53	4.6%	715	62.5%	−25
2002	1294	138	10.7%	69	5.4%	910	70.3%	−50
2004	1448	198	13.6%	88	6.0%	910	62.9%	−50
2006	1625	284	17.5%	107	6.6%	1105	68.0%	−75
2008	1831	394	21.5%	129	7.1%	1300	71.0%	−75
2010	2045	517	25.3%	153	7.5%	1300	63.6%	−75

Table 5.17 Combined policy – 2 and 3

Time	Demand GWh/y Policy 1	Electricity Supply GWH/Y			Petroleum Products Required toe		
		Current HYD+BAG	Policy 2 & 3	From oil	P1	P2 & P3	% saving
1992	748	210	48	489	114195	103911	9.0%
1994	832	210	55	568	132174	120549	8.8%
1996	929	210	76	643	152644	136579	10.5%
1998	1036	210	103	724	175500	153674	12.4%
2000	1145	210	135	799	198508	169763	14.5%
2002	1294	210	207	877	230193	186183	19.1%
2004	1448	210	285	953	262852	202303	23.0%
2006	1625	210	391	1024	300572	217478	27.6%
2008	1831	210	523	1097	344216	233039	32.3%
2010	2045	210	670	1165	389727	247432	36.5%

Table 5.18 Combined policy – 4 & 5

Time	Demand GWh/y Policy 1	Electricity Supply GWH/Y Improved Policy Hydro	4 & 5	From oil	Petroleum products required TOE P1	P4 & P5	% saving	Coal required (tonnes)
1992	748	87	130	531	114195	112772	1.2%	37917
1994	832	94	325	414	132174	87891	33.5%	94792
1996	929	100	520	308	152644	65502	57.1%	151667
1998	1036	107	520	409	175500	86914	50.5%	151667
2000	1145	114	690	341	198508	72372	63.5%	208542
2002	1294	121	860	313	230193	66507	71.1%	265417
2004	1448	121	860	467	262852	99166	62.3%	265417
2006	1625	121	1030	475	300572	100781	66.5%	322292
2008	1831	121	1225	485	344216	103010	70.1%	379167
2010	2045	121	1225	699	389727	148521	61.9%	379167

Table 5.19 Combined policy – 2 to 5

Time	Demand GWh/y Policy 1	Electricity supply GWH/y Improved Policy Hydro	2 to 5	From oil	Petroleum Products Required toe P1	P2 to P5	% saving	Coal required (tonnes)
1992	748	87	178	483	114195	102488	10.3%	37917
1994	832	94	380	359	132174	76267	42.3%	94792
1996	929	100	596	233	152644	49437	67.6%	151667
1998	1036	107	623	306	175500	65088	62.9%	151667
2000	1145	114	825	205	198508	43627	78.0%	208542
2002	1294	121	1067	106	230193	22497	90.2%	265417
2004	1448	121	1145	182	262852	38618	85.3%	265417
2006	1625	121	1421	83	300572	17687	94.1%	322292
2008	1831	121	1748	0	344216	0	100.0%	379167
2010	2045	121	1895	29	389727	6226	98.4%	379167

Table 5.20 Installed capacity in MW

Time	Hydro CEB		Petroleum CEB		Coal & Bagasse		Pump Hydro		Total power		SEDM-peak power required MW % of total	
1992	51	24.2%	140	66.4%	20	9.5%	0	0.0%	211	100.0%	151	71.8%
1994	55	22.8%	136	56.4%	50	20.7%	0	0.0%	241	100.0%	166	68.9%
1996	59	21.8%	132	48.7%	80	29.5%	0	0.0%	271	100.0%	181	66.9%
1998	63	23.2%	128	47.2%	80	29.5%	0	0.0%	271	100.0%	199	73.5%
2000	67	19.1%	124	35.3%	110	31.3%	50	14.2%	351	100.0%	215	61.3%
2002	71	16.5%	120	27.8%	140	32.5%	100	23.2%	431	100.0%	240	55.6%
2004	71	16.6%	116	27.2%	140	32.8%	100	23.4%	427	100.0%	262	61.4%
2006	71	14.1%	112	22.3%	170	33.8%	150	29.8%	503	100.0%	290	57.6%
2008	71	13.4%	108	20.4%	200	37.8%	150	28.4%	529	100.0%	320	60.4%
2010	71	13.5%	104	19.8%	200	38.1%	150	28.6%	525	100.0%	352	67.0%

Table 5.21 Some economic implications

	Policy 1				Policy 2–5			
Time	GDP (1980 US$m)	Petroleum (toe)	Cost (1980 US$m)	% of GDP	Petroleum (toe)	Coal tonnes	Total cost (1980 US$m)	% of GDP
1992	2392	114195	23	1.0%	102488	37917	23	1.0%
1994	2629	132174	26	1.0%	76267	94792	22	0.8%
1996	2891	152644	31	1.1%	49437	151667	20	0.7%
1998	3175	175500	35	1.1%	65088	151667	23	0.7%
2000	3460	198508	40	1.1%	43627	208542	23	0.7%
2002	3798	230193	46	1.2%	22497	265417	22	0.6%
2004	4139	262852	53	1.3%	38618	265417	25	0.6%
2006	4512	300572	60	1.3%	17687	322292	25	0.6%
2008	4922	344216	69	1.4%	0	379167	25	0.5%
2010	5333	389727	78	1.5%	6226	379167	27	0.5%

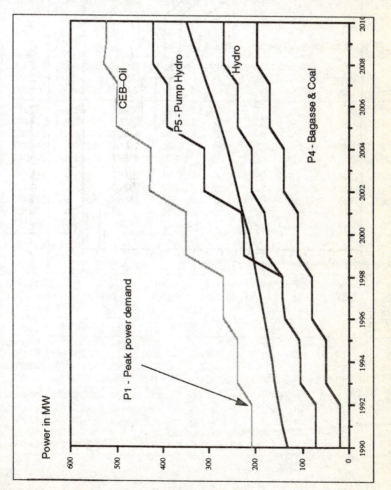

Figure 5.14 Future installed capacity (MW)

Electricity
(GWh/y)
(000)

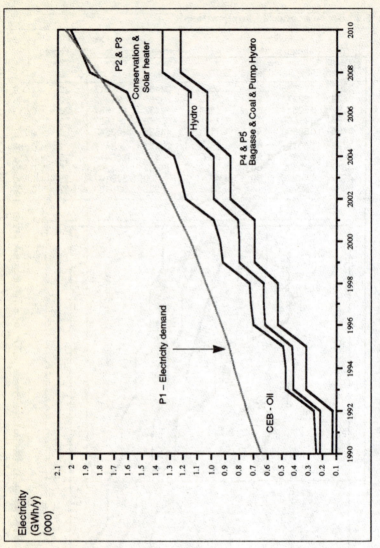

Figure 5.15 Electricity demand and supply

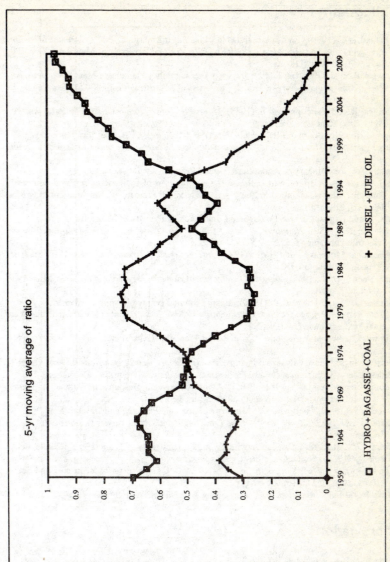

Figure 5.16 Evolution of resource used for power generation, 1955–2010

5-yr moving average of ratio

□ HYDRO+BAGASSE+COAL   + DIESEL+FUEL OIL

Bibliography

Baguant, J. *et al.* (1990). 'Energy Use and Policy Planning in Mauritius', *Energy Demand Modelling Aggregate and Sectoral Approach 1970–2010*, Vol. 3, University of Mauritius, Year 2000 Studies (funded by IDRC).

Beeharry, P. R. and Baguant, J. (1990). 'Energy Use and Policy Planning in Mauritius'. *Household Energy Consumption Survey*, Vol. 2, University of Mauritius, Year 2000 Studies (funded by IDRC).

Bheenick, R. and Hanoomanjee, E. (1988). *Mauritius: Towards an Industrial Training Strategy*, Port Louis, Mauritius, December.

Central Electricity Board (CEB). *Annual Report and Accounts*, CEB, Mauritius (several years).

Central Electricity Board (CEB). (1972). *Chronological Events – 8 December 1952 to 8 December 1972*, CEB, Mauritius.

Forestry Service, Ministry of Agriculture. *Annual Reports* (several years).

Harel, P. (1989). 'A strategy to optimize the contribution of indigenous energy resources in Mauritius', thesis submitted for the degree of Doctor of Philosophy, University of Mauritius, School of Engineering.

Harel, P. and Baguant, J. (1991). *Bagasse Combustion*, University of Mauritius.

Hugot, Emile. (1986). *Handbook of Sugar Cane Engineering*, third revised edition, Elsevier Scientific Publishing Co., New York.

International Monetary Fund (IMF). (1977). *International Financial Statistics*, IMF, Statistics Division, Washington, DC.

Manrakhan, J. *et al.* (1982). *Report of the Technical Committee on Sale of Bagasse*, Ministry of Agriculture, March.

Manrakhan, J. and Baguant, J. (1990). 'Energy use and policy planning in Mauritius', *Energy Data Book, Energy Supply and Consumption 1980–9*, Vol. 1, University of Mauritius, Year 2000 Studies (funded by IDRC).

Mauritius Chamber of Agriculture. *Annual Report*, Plantation House, Port Louis, Mauritius (several years).

Mauritius Sugar Industry Research Institute. *Annual Report*, Reduit, Mauritius (several years).

National Energy Conference. (1980). Proceedings, University of Mauritius, December.

National Energy Seminar. (1981). Plan of Action, organized jointly by the Ministry of Power, Fuel and Energy and the University of Mauritius, February.

Nowbuth, P. (1986). 'Energy paper', Ministry of Economic Planning and Development.

Paturau, J. M. (1982). *By-products of the Cane Sugar Industry*, Elsevier Scientific Publishing Co., New York.

Thomas, Dr Carl. (1987). Discussion with the author, University of Tennessee, Knoxville, USA.

Transenerg. (1982). *Production d'Electricite a Partir de la Bagasse*, Transenerg, Paris, January.

United Nations. (1976). *Statistical Yearbook 1975*, UN, Department of Economic and Social Affairs, Statistical Office, New York.

UNDP/World Bank. Report of the Energy Sector Assessment Programme.

Abbreviations

AGR	Annual Growth Rate	MEPD	Ministry of Economic Planning and Development
CEB	Central Electricity Board		
EPZ	Export Processing Zone	MW	Megawatt
FUEL	Flacq United Estate Ltd	psig	pounds per square inch gauge
GJ	Gigajoule	ROI	Return on Investment
GWh	Gigawatt hour	SEDM	Sectoral Energy Demand Model
IDRC	International Development Research Centre	SSC	Specific Steam Consumption
		TOE	Tonnes of Oil Equivalent
IMF	International Monetary Fund	UN	United Nations
KWh	Kilowatt hour	UNDP	United Nations Development Programme
LOLP	Loss of Load Possibility		
LPG	Liquefied Petroleum Gas		

Index

Abidjan, 43
Accra, 43
Addis Ababa, 42, 43, 45, 46, 47, 48, 49, 50, 51,
54, 55, 58, 61, 62, 71, 73, 74, 76, 79
AFREPREN, *vi, xi, xii,* 4
Africa, 127; East, *xi,* 2, 87, 105, 116; Southern,
xi, 2, 4, 9, 97, 105, 116; sub-Saharan, *viii,
ix,* 1, 2, 3, 4, 5
agencies, donor and international, 4, 23, 53, 69,
112
Agip, 94
agriculture, ix, 10, 42, 87, 88, 89, 90, 91, 97,
98, 99, 129, 131, 136
agro-processing industry, 119, 160
Akaki, 56, 61
alcohol, 19, 74
Angola, *xi*
animal (draught) power, 42
Argentina, 74
Asia, East, 1
Asmara, 43
Assab, 48, 49, 54, 55, 74, 76, 79
Australia, 74, 166
Awash Town, 54

bagasse, 4, 118, 119, 120, 130-1, 132, 133, 134,
136, 137, 138, 141, 142, 146, 147, 148, 149,
159, 160, 161, 162, 163, 164, 167, 168, 169,
170, 171, 172, 175
balance of payments, 10, 11, 16, 87, 89, 102,
105, 170
Batu Construction Agency, 61
bio-energy, *x, see also* biogas, biomass, etc.
biogas, 108
biomass, 9, 16, 42, 110, 130, 132, 133, 134,
136, 137
Botswana, *x,* 3, 9, 28, 29, 67; Air Botswana, 23
BP, 18, 21, 94
Brazil, 74
Britain, *x,* 9
bureaucracy, 48, 51, 111
Burundi, *x*

buses, 43, 44, 45, 47, 50, 53, 55, 63, 65, 67, 68,
69, 70, 71, 76, 78, 79, 80, 82, 131

Caltex, 18, 21, 24, 94
Canada, *x,* 74
centralization, 59, 164
Chamarel, 138, 139
charcoal, 92, 93, 97, 98, 100, 118, 131, 151
China, *x,* 74, 127
CNG, 74
coal, *x,* 3, 4, 16, 17, 42, 92, 93, 96-7, 98, 100,
105, 106, 110, 113, 116, 117, 118, 120, 131,
132, 133, 134, 137, 138, 141, 147, 148, 149,
159, 160, 162, 163, 167, 168, 169, 170, 171,
172, 175
coffee, 87, 88, 89
commerce, 21, 97, 99, 120, 129, 133, 136, 137,
144, 145, 152
communications, 51, 73, 77
cooking, 16, 131, 132
Cyclone Claudette, 139
Cyclone Gervaise, 139

debt, 88, 90, 91
decentralization, 48, 52, 59, 113
deforestation, 17
demand, *ix,* 16, 19, 36, 58, 59, 63, 68, 71, 79,
80, 91, 97, 100, 132, 141, 146, 149-58;
demand management, 5, 35, 36, 78, 105-
18
desertification, *viii*
diesel, 2, 3, 20, 24, 25, 35, 37, 38, 44, 57, 62,
64, 65, 66, 67, 71, 73, 75, 78, 80, 81, 82,
93, 94, 98, 99, 100, 103, 104, 116, 131, 132,
133, 137, 146, 147, 165, 175
Djibouti, 42
domestic, *see* households
drought, 11, 49, 87, 91
drying processes, 169
dung, *see* residues, animal
economic growth, 10, 11, 13, 16, 87-8, 89, 90,
91, 99, 129-30, 151, 153, 159, 170